# British Poets and Secret Societies

A surprisingly large number of English poets have either belonged to a secret society, or been strongly influenced by its tenets. One of the best known examples is Christopher Smart's membership of the Freemasons, and the resulting influence of Masonic doctrines on *A Song to David*. However, many other poets have belonged to, or been influenced by not only the Freemasons, but the Rosicrucians, Gormogons and Hell-Fire Clubs. First published in 1986, this study concentrates on five major examples: Smart, Burns, William Blake, William Butler Yeats and Rudyard Kipling, as well as a number of other poets. Marie Roberts questions why so many poets have been powerfully attracted to the secret societies, and considers the effectiveness of poetry as a medium for conveying secret emblems and ritual. She shows how some poets believed that poetry would prove a hidden symbolic language in which to reveal great truths.

The beliefs of these poets are as diverse as their practice, and this book sheds fascinating light on several major writers.

T0243563

# British Poets and
# Secret Societies

## Marie Roberts

Routledge
Taylor & Francis Group

First published in 1986
by Croom Helm Ltd

This edition first published in 2014 by Routledge
2 Park Square, Milton Park, Abingdon, Oxon, OX14 4RN
and by Routledge
711 Third Avenue, New York, NY 10017

*Routledge is an imprint of the Taylor & Francis Group, an informa business*

© 1986 Marie Roberts

**Publisher's Note**
The publisher has gone to great lengths to ensure the quality of this reprint but
points out that some imperfections in the original copies may be apparent.

**Disclaimer**
The publisher has made every effort to trace copyright holders and welcomes
correspondence from those they have been unable to contact.

A Library of Congress record exists under LC control number: 89201236

ISBN 13: 978-1-138-79620-1 (hbk)
ISBN 13: 978-1-315-75801-5 (ebk)
ISBN 13: 978-1-138-79621-8 (pbk)

# BRITISH POETS AND SECRET SOCIETIES:
## FREEMASONS AND CLANDESTINE BROTHERHOODS

**Frontispiece:**  Stewart Watson, *The Inauguration of Robert Burns as Poet Laureate of the Canongate Kilwinning Lodge* (By courtesy of the Grand Lodge of Scotland)

# BRITISH
# POETS
## AND
# SECRET
## SOCIETIES
## MARIE ROBERTS

**CROOM HELM**
London & Sydney

© 1986 Marie Roberts
Croom Helm Ltd, Provident House, Burrell Row,
Beckenham, Kent BR3 1AT
Croom Helm Australia Pty Ltd, Suite 4, 6th Floor,
64-76 Kippax Street, Surry Hills, NSW 2010, Australia

British Library Cataloguing in Publication Data

Roberts, Marie
    British poets and secret societies; Freemasons
    and clandestine brotherhoods.
    1. English poetry – History and criticism
    2. Secret societies – Great Britain – History
    I. Title
    821'.009    PR508.S4/
    ISBN 0-7099-2255-8

Printed and bound in Great Britain by
Biddles Ltd, Guildford and King's Lynn

# CONTENTS

*Plates*

*Preface*

*Acknowledgements*

*Frontispiece*

| | | |
|---|---|---|
| *Chapter 1:* | Introduction: Creative Underworlds | 1 |
| *Chapter 2:* | **Christopher Smart** | 10 |
| | Masonry and Madness | 10 |
| | *Jubilate Agno: A Song from Bedlam* | 18 |
| | "The Lord's builder": *A Song to David* | 27 |
| | Degrees of Initiation | 30 |
| | The Glory of God and Freemasonry | 43 |
| *Chapter 3:* | **Robert Burns** | 52 |
| | The Freemason's Poet-Laureate | 52 |
| | The Patronage of the Lodge | 60 |
| | The Mason's Apron | 64 |
| | "Tis Wine ye masons makes you free" | 67 |
| | "Brothers of the Mystic Tie" | 73 |

Chapter 4:    Percy Bysshe Shelley                        88

              The Bavarian Illuminati                     88

              *Nightmare Abbey*                            92

              The Rosicrucian                             95

Chapter 5:    Rudyard Kipling                            102

              An Empire of Freemasons                    102

              "A King and a Mason"                        109

              The Labour of Lodges                        113

              "In the Interests of the Brethren"          117

Chapter 6:    William Butler Yeats                        126

              Poet and Magician                           126

              The Hermetic Order of the Golden Dawn       131

              Father Rosycross                             141

              The End of all Mythologies                   149

*Bibliography*                                            159

*Index*                                                   170

# PLATES

Frontispiece:     Stewart Watson, *The Inauguration of Robert Burns as Poet Laureate of the Canongate Kilwinning Lodge* (By courtesy of the Grand Lodge of Scotland)

Plate 1:     A. Slade, *A Freemason Formed out of the Materials of his Lodge* (By courtesy of the United Grand Lodge of England)

Plate 2:     William Blake, *The Ancient of Days* (By courtesy of the Whitworth Art Gallery, Manchester)

Plate 3:     *A Masonic Engraving of 1769* (By courtesy of the United Grand Lodge of England)

Plate 4:     William Hogarth, *The Mystery of Masonry Brought to Light by the Gormogons* (By courtesy of the British Museum)

Plate 5:     *Robert Burns: Deputy Master, St James Tarbolton Kilwinning* (By courtesy of George Draffen)

Plate 6:     Burns's Masonic Mark in Highland Mary's Bible (By courtesy of George Draffen)

Plate 7:     William Hogarth, *Night,* from the series *The Four Times of Day* (By courtesy of the British Museum)

Plate 8:     Kipling's membership certificate (By courtesy of the Board of General Purposes of the United Grand Lodge of England)

Plate 9:     Views of the Rosicrucian Vault (Reproduced from Israel Regardie's *The Golden Dawn* (Minnesota, 1971) by courtesy of Llewellyn Publications, P.O. Box 43383, St Paul, MN 55164-0383)

Masons are ours, *Freemasons* - but, alas!
To their own Bards I leave the mystic Class;
In vain shall one, and not a gifted Man,
Attempt to sing of this enlighten'd Clan:
I know no Word, boast no directing Sign,
And not one Token of the Race is mine....
If, as Crusaders, they combin'd to wrest
From heathen Lords the Land they long possess'd;
Or were at first some harmless Club, who made
Their idle Meetings solemn by Parade;
Is but conjecture - for the Task unfit,
Awe-struck and mute, the puzzling Theme I quit:
Yet, if such Blessings from their Order flow,
We should be glad their Moral Code to know;
Trowels of Silver are but simple things,
And Aprons worthless as their Apron-Strings;
But if indeed you have the Skill to teach
A social Spirit, now beyond our reach;
If Man's warm Passions you can guide and bind,
And plant the Virtues in the wayward Mind;
If you can wake to Christian-Love the Heart,-
In mercy, something of your Powers impart.
    But, as it seems we Masons must become
To know the Secret, and must then be dumb;
And as we venture for uncertain Gains,
Perhaps the Profit is not worth the Pains....
    *Griggs* and *Gregorians* here their Meetings hold,
Convivial Sects and *Bucks* alert and bold;
A kind of Masons, but without their Sign;
The bonds of Union - Pleasure, Song, and Wine.
Man, a gregarious Creature, loves to fly
Where he the Trackings of the Herd can spy;
Still to be one with many he desires,
Although it leads him through the Thorns and Briers.
                                        Crabbe[1]

# PREFACE

This book investigates a hidden creative underworld; the relationship between poets and secret societies. Five major poets will be discussed: Christopher Smart, Robert Burns, Percy Bysshe Shelley, Rudyard Kipling and William Butler Yeats. Through the work of these poets the influence of the ritual and symbolism of secret societies will be explored. This will involve an investigation into the Freemasons, who recruited Smart, Burns and Kipling; the Rosicrucians and the *Illuminati* which appealed to Shelley, and the Hermetic Order of the Golden Dawn, which attracted Yeats. It will be argued that affiliation with these organisations was conducive to the poetic imagination since they influenced and provided inspiration for works of art. These societies should not just be regarded as external forces acting on literature but as living art-forms which re-enact myth and symbolism. Consequently an examination of secret societies and their influence on several poets will indicate the extent of the interaction between the arts and the esoteric movements.

The involvement of these five poets with the secret societies will also be viewed in terms of shifting literary genres and the history of ideas. The connection between Masonry and Christianity will be analysed in relation to Smart. His poetry, which reflects a watershed between Christianity and Masonic myth, throws into relief the antithesis between madness and reason: the madman who was also a poet of the Age of Reason. The contradictions inherent in Burns's roles as the people's poet on the one hand and the bard of the Freemasons on the other, mirror the Enlightenment antagonism between egalitarianism and elitism. During an age of political revolution and reform, Shelley was drawn towards subversive political sects such as the Rosicrucians, Illuminati and the Assassins in search of a persona for his Romantic aspirations. By identifying with the secret societies which were being condemned by public opinion and persecuted by witch-hunters, Shelley managed to enhance his own self-consciousness through a sense of alienation from main-stream society. In contrast, the communality and social acceptability of the Masons attracted Kipling. Through his poetry he conveyed the political impact of Freemasonry on the colonies as a tool of imperialism. On a less pragmatic note, Yeats recaptured through the magical Hermetic Order of the Golden Dawn the occult mysteries submerged by the scepticism of early twentieth-century thought. The Golden Dawn served to remind modern mankind of the importance of myth since it was a syncretic Order excavated out of the bed-rock of world mythologies. This survey of poets and secret societies will conclude with the example of Yeats who, after belonging to the Order of the Golden Dawn for most of his life, eventually resigned his membership. Evidently he was determined to invent his own mythologies and to achieve independence from the limitations imposed upon him by a group mentality. For Yeats, dissatisfaction with his status as an initiate of a secret society led him to "serve as his own group"[2] in the knowledge that ultimately the poet must find his own creative voice for the expression of his art.


Marie Roberts,
Manchester,
1985

# ACKNOWLEDGEMENTS

The author would like to acknowledge invaluable assistance from J.W. Hamill, Librarian and Curator of the United Grand Lodge of England, the Grand Secretary of the Grand Lodge of Scotland, Tom Crawford and Martin Ray from Aberdeen University, the Assistant Librarian of Pembroke College, Cambridge, Miss S.A. Milford of Oxford University Press, Professor Dodwell, Director of the Whitworth Art Gallery, George Draffen, the staff of the British Library and John Rylands Library in Manchester. I am also grateful to Professor C.B. Cox and members of the English department at Manchester University who have shown an interest in my work. Thanks are due to Deborah Carlisle, Dominique Murphy and Jane Sambrook for their secretarial assistance. Much appreciation goes to Michael George, Paul Dawson, Karina Williamson and David Lamb for their advice and encouragement. But most of all I would like to thank my family for all the help and understanding they have given me.

TO MY FAMILY

# 1 INTRODUCTION: CREATIVE UNDERWORLDS

> They have taken the Oath of the Brother-in-Blood
> on leavened bread and salt:
> They have taken the Oath of the Brother-in-Blood
> on fire and fresh-cut sod,
> On the hilt and the haft of the Khyber knife,
> and the Wondrous Names of God.
>
> Kipling[3]

It may be surprising to realise that many well-known poets have been members of various secret societies. A survey of the relationship between poets and clandestine brotherhoods will open up this neglected area of literary history and criticism. The difficulties in mapping out this unexplored region are compounded by the false trails and bogus claims which have always shrouded the study of clandestine organisations. Until recently the investigation of esoteric societies was believed to have little scholarly value. It has been suggested that the subject was shunned "because the historian passed by, the charlatan, the axe-grinder and the paranoiac long had the field to themselves".[4] The character of the researcher into secret societies had been blighted since, according to John Saltmarsh, this was

> a department of history which is not only obscure
> and highly controversial, but by ill-luck the
> happiest of all hunting-grounds for the light-headed,
> the fanciful, the altogether unscholarly and the
> lunatic fringe of the British Museum Reading Room.[5]

Such unflattering remarks made up the credentials of the investigator of secret societies until scholars such as Frances Yates gained credibility for the subject. While historians begin to uncover the extent and importance of the hidden networks which have operated throughout history, the influence of the secret societies upon the arts has yet to be fully explored. Considering that these organisations represent art-forms which germinate and then generate mythologies which partake of the nature of fiction, it is curious that the relationship between literature and the secret societies has not yet been more closely scrutinised.

Secrecy acts as a mechanism which enables the individual to retain a private fantasy world within the outer world.[6] In a primitive setting ostentatious secrecy functions through secret ritual to protect tribal taboos governing birth, death and the transition from childhood to adulthood. Modern society has demystified the land-marks of human existence by exposing them to public scrutiny. In compensation for the loss of traditional

1

mysteries the institutionalised secrecy of clandestine groups mirrors the complex secret life of every member through ritual and symbolism. The various secret societies create an artificial environment containing surrogate goals which often turn out to be ceremonial reworkings of ancient heroic quests. Yet the rituals, goals and value-systems inherent in the various secret societies cannot be dismissed as mere phantasy.

The trappings of ceremony and secrecy may be the legacy of precautions taken during a period of persecution when the society may have been founded. Secret organisations have frequently been banned by governments suspecting political subversion. During the eighteenth and early nineteenth centuries, legislation against oath-taking was implemented to outlaw workers' fraternities such as the Luddites and the predecessors of the modern Trades Unions. In the early decades of the nineteenth century, the penalty for illegal oath-taking was transportation. Perhaps the best recorded case is the "Dorchester labourers" or "Tolpuddle Martyrs" who were transported in 1834 for taking an oath of confederacy.[7]

The severity of the penalty for perjury gave it a corresponding significance. Jean-Paul Sartre speaks in this context of a fraternity of fear which characterises a group bonded in such a way by an awesome pledge.[8] In some cases spine-chilling oaths would literally depict the activities and obligations which membership of the society entailed. Thus the oath taken meant that secret societies such as the Assassins and allegedly the Illuminati could oblige members to carry out sacrificial or contractual murder. Coercive initiation and continuous indoctrination could, therefore, account for the allure of many brutal esoteric sects such as the eighteenth-century Russian sect called the *Skoptsi* or "Castrators" whose supreme rites of purification involved the act of castration![9] In a hostile social climate some secret societies only survive by imposing a greater terror on their members. Sartre points out that terror from an external threat determines the extent of terror generated from within the group itself. In this respect the initiation oath could involve a fearful pledge through which the initiate would literally authorise his own execution by fellow members in the event of any future betrayal. One might expect that in a less hostile climate, where the secret society approaches social acceptability, the significance of the oath will change. The fearful pledge may be retained after its literal meaning has been transformed into metaphor.

Thus secret societies not facing any external menace may include a terror ritual without intending any of their members to be subjected to acts of violence. Here the appeal to terror has a different role; that of reinforcing the values of the group. Consequently the consent of a neophyte to a horrific penalty for perjury contained within an oath of allegiance may be merely a metaphoric means of emphasising loyalty and secrecy as in the case of the following Masonic pledge:

2

> I Hereby solemnly Vow and Swear in the Presence of
> Almighty God and this Right Worshipful Assembly,
> that I will Hail and Conceal, and never Reveal the
> Secrets or Secrecy of Masons or Masonry, that shall
> be revealed unto me; unless to a True and Lawful
> Brother....All this under no less Penalty than to
> have my Throat cut, my Tongue taken from the Roof
> of my Mouth, my Heart pluck'd from under my Left
> Breast, them to be buried in the Sands of the Sea,
> the Length of a Cable-rope from Shore, where the
> Tide ebbs and flows twice in 24 Hours, my Body to
> be burnt to Ashes, my Ashes to be scattered upon
> the Face of the Earth, so there shall be no more
> Remembrance of me among Masons.[10]

This oath is primarily figurative. The awesome language is
designed to stress, in an exaggerated fashion, the values of
secrecy and group cohesion. Such secret societies may be described
as symbolic as they may not be striving for concrete social or
political goals. Furthermore their secrecy does not function to
protect them from persecution but may be maintained to satisfy
the emotional, psychological or creative needs of the members.

Membership of a secret society provides a communal identity
which cushions the individual from the external world partly by
satisfying deep-seated yearnings relating to self-knowledge. C.G.
Jung, who regarded secret societies as serving a legitimate role in
the development of the maturing individual, also described them
as "crutches for the lame, shields for the timid, beds for the
lazy, nurseries for the irresponsible" which equally serve as:

> shelters for the poor and weak, a home port for
> the shipwrecked, the bosom of a family for orphans,
> a land of promise for disillusioned vagrants and
> weary pilgrims, a herd and safe fold for lost sheep,
> and a mother providing nourishment and growth.[11]

The security of ritual ensures group continuity by enhancing
awareness of the solemnity and importance of its values. Likewise
symbolism, which unites the form of ritual with the content of
belief, provides members with "a sort of emotional furniture."[12]
The mythic ethos of these organisations fosters the individual's
sense of self by confirming him or her within an ideological
framework which either seeks to reproduce or repudiate the social
values outside. Initiates also experience the novelty of adjusting to
new moral codes and having to re-align boundaries of social
behaviour.

There is, however, another dimension to participation within
a secret society. This may be called the imaginative aspect which
appeals to the creative writer. It is likely that the poet would
have been stimulated by the importance attached to the

3

imagination and would have welcomed the opportunity to experiment in unfamiliar modes of communication conducted through rites and symbols. All these inventive features of secret societies open up an immediate affinity with the creative mind. Symbolism and ritual energise and intensify imaginative states, thus demonstrating that the experience of initiation is really induction into another mode of consciousness.

The foregoing discussion of the psychological function of secret societies may go some way in explaining why they attracted so many writers and artists. For example, the novelist, Laurence Sterne (1713-68), belonged to the Demoniacs,[13] a satanic sect which inspired John Hall-Stevenson's *Crazy Tales* (1762).[14] The Demoniacs were loosely associated with the Rabelaisian monks of Medmenham Abbey, an eighteenth-century hell-fire club which had recruited the poet, Charles Churchill, and the political agitator and poet, John Wilkes, who made Masonic history by being the first Freemason to be initated while still in gaol.[15] The poet, Dante Gabriel Rossetti (1828-82), helped found the Pre-Raphaelite Brotherhood in 1848 while the lyricist Henry Carey (1648?-1743) joined the Gregorians, a society which was dedicated to eating and drinking.[16] Clandestine fellowships such as the Freemasons boast of having recruited such eminent writers as Boswell, Trollope, Wilde, and among the poets, Smart, Burns and Kipling.[17] It is plausible to suggest that poets have been attracted to the secret societies in the belief that they would discover there a concealed symbolic language which would be compatible with the poetic sensibility. Often the language of ritual takes the form of verse while the hypnotic effects of ceremonial chants may be achieved through the rhythms of poetry. The following poem appears in one of the rituals for the Order of the Golden Dawn:

> I come in the Power of the Light.
> I come in the Light of Wisdom.
> I come in the Mercy of the Light.
> The Light hath healing in its Wings![18]

Esoteric sects also cultivate alternative modes of communication through secret signs, pass-words and hieroglyphics. For example, the Rosicrucians blend the hermetic mysteries with those of the Cabala, a strain of Jewish mysticism which incorporates a system of numerology. In some secret societies Cabalistic trance techniques were employed in order to induce visionary states. The magical orders often developed their own ciphers or occult alphabets in order to preserve a hidden wisdom. The mystical teaching of these societies was usually directed towards the acquisition of esoteric knowledge, often through an appeal to antiquity. Sometimes this involved initiation into the secrets of a lost civilisation; revelations of the Egyptian gods or of the ancient mystery religions. For the neophyte the society may even promise to unlock the tribal memory of some earthly paradise. This would represent a symbolic attempt to reverse the Fall of Man through a second encounter with the Tree of Knowledge in a recreation of the Garden of Eden. Ritual was the key to such mystical illumination which enabled initiates to make an imaginative leap towards discovering the arcana of ancestral wisdoms. In this sense secret societies are dynamos for the world of the imagination. Seekers after prohibited knowledge, both artistic and divine, may not only be searching for the secrets of the creation but also for the mysteries of creativity. Consequently the secret society has always held out a powerful appeal for the creative mind. Poets found that through these organisations they were able to explore occult traditions and actively engage in magic and mysticism which fired the poetic imagination. The suggestion that artistic inspiration may be derived from participation in a secret creative underworld may even undermine the popular image of the established poet as an interpreter of the predominant culture. The power of the language of art is contained within the poet's words which are etched upon the national consciousness and then enshrined in the form of great poetry. Perhaps it is disturbing to realise that from within the hidden contours of language, the poet may be communicating secrets of ritual and magical symbolism to the initiated. To some extent the existence of a hidden level of meaning within a poem violates the function of poetry as a medium for mass-communication. But poetry is as much a private as a public art-form. It may speak in strange incantations, draw on the arcana of the secret societies or borrow the language of ceremonial secrecy. For the creative writer the twilight world of the secret societies opens up a wealth of metaphor and allegory.

The five poets who will be investigated here drew on their knowledge of secret societies in a variety of ways. Christopher Smart discovered in Freemasonry a vehicle for the Christianity and mysticism which permeated his religious verse. In contrast, Burns applied Masonic ideas to secular ends throughout his life and work. He became the fraternity's unofficial ambassador and, it is claimed, the Poet-Laureate of the lodges. P.B. Shelley's attraction towards the Illuminati and the Assassins was yet another expression of Romantic idealism while Rudyard Kipling's allegiance to Freemasonry contributed towards the imperialism which had helped colonize the Masonic network on a world-wide basis. Finally W.B. Yeats's involvement with the Order of the Golden Dawn and other esoteric sects represents a nexus of the occult tradition within which the poetic self merges into the hidden orders of ritual and symbolism.

Smart, Burns and Kipling were members of the Freemasons who represent the largest and most influential secret society. It is therefore germane to chart its development here. Throughout its history Freemasonry has been a parent body spawning other organisations such as the Gormogons [19] and the Ancient Order of Druids.[20] Masonry developed out of the Medieval building trade which had received a great impetus after the Norman Conquest.[21]

During the early years of the eleventh century the Saxons began to build churches in the pre-Conquest style. The architects, builders and stone-masons involved in these building projects evolved rituals and ceremonies similar to the miracle plays performed by the craft guilds. The Masons, however, were not incorporated into any guild or municipal corporation since they were the workers of a scattered trade having to travel the country in search of construction work. Owing to the itinerant nature of the craft, a complex system of secret signs and pass-words emerged so that a Mason would be able to identify a fellow-craftsman amongst a group of strangers. This precaution was essential in order to preserve the secret techniques of the skilled workers from outside competition. Gradually the craft began to admit non-operatives as it developed into a purely mystagogical system. Freemasons pirated ethical systems such as Christianity and Judaism thus creating for themselves a hybrid code of virtuous behaviour and moral law. Consequently the workers' tools were transmuted into emblems of morality while the craftsman's signs evolved into symbolic gestures and handshakes, known as grips, which denoted grades of initiation. The operative hierarchy of apprentice, journeyman or fellow and master craftsman was largely replaced by three symbolic degrees of Entered Apprentice, Fellowcraftsman and Master Mason. The antiquarian, Elias Ashmole, was instrumental in turning the fraternity into a speculative organisation which "accepted" members. He was "made" a Mason at Warrington in 1646, the earliest recorded initiation of a speculative member in an English Lodge. During this period, Freemasonry completed its transition from an operative craft to a speculative or symbolic order. The United Grand Lodge of England was established in 1717 at a time which witnessed the rapid proliferation of social clubs and secret societies.[22] Masonic historians have made controversial claims that many well-known eighteenth-century writers became members such as Pope, Swift, Goldsmith, Cowper, and Smart.[23]

During the Enlightenment, poets and novelists such as Scott, Mackenzie, and Burns joined the lodges. They may have been attracted to the Masonic movement because it opened up an alternative form of patronage. By this time, Continental Freemasonry was evolving into a radical organisation which already had exhibited overtones of the anarchistic politics of France. Early historians such as the Abbé Barruel and John Robinson even attributed the outbreak of the French Revolution to the Masons and Bavarian Illuminés whom they denounced as agents of subversion.[24] The revolutionary brotherhood of the Illuminati, which was further discredited by various Gothic novelists,[25] greatly appealed to Shelley particularly since it was a secret society which blended mysticism with political reform. During the nineteenth century some political movements modelled themselves on the Illuminati, such as the Italian *Carbonari* or charcoal-burners who had recruited Byron. Other secret societies were content to absorb and then reproduce the social norms

Creative Underworlds

around them. As Kipling's life and work reveals, "colonial" Masonry fell into this latter category by becoming a bulwark of the social order. The pragmatism of the twentieth century engendered the desire for a Romantic revival. Secret societies such as the Hermetic Order of the Golden Dawn provided an arcana of ritual and romance, mysticism and folk-lore for seekers such as Yeats. Poets who transposed the living image of a secret society into poetic imagery did not always acknowledge their debt to these clandestine traditions. Hence there is the need for an exegesis of the secret systems of ritual and belief which are concealed in poetry. It is this forgotten heritage which should be restored to literary history and criticism. The importance of the secret societies to the creative imagination may be illustrated by the following survey of the influence they exerted on several eminent poets, beginning with Smart.

## Notes

1. George Crabbe, *The Borough*, 2 vols (London, 1810) I, pp.159-61.

2. Carl Gustav Jung, *Memories, Dreams, Reflections* recorded and edited by Aniela Jaffé, trans. Richard and Clara Winston (London, 1963), p.316.

3. *Rudyard Kipling's Verse: Definitive Edition* (London, 1945), p.237. All page references for quotations of Kipling's poetry will be taken from this edition.

4. J.M. Roberts, *The Mythology of the Secret Societies* (London, 1972), p.10.

5. John Saltmarsh, review of Douglas Knoop and G.P. Jones, *Introduction to Freemasonry*, in *Economic History Review*, VIII, (Nov., 1937), p.103.

6. See Georg Simmel, "The Sociology of Secrecy and Secret Societies", *The American Journal of Sociology*, XI, no. 4 (Jan., 1906), pp.441-98 and Sissela Bok's chapter on secret societies in *Secrets: Concealment and Revelation* (London, 1984), pp.45-58. See also Charles A. Blanchard, *Modern Secret Societies* (London, 1903) and William J. Whalen, *Handbook of Secret Organisations*, (Milwaukee, 1966).

7. See E.P. Thompson, *The Making of the English Working Class* (Harmondsworth, 1968), p.560.

8. See Jean-Paul Sartre, *Critique of Dialectical Reason*, ed.

7

Jonathan Rée, trans. Alan Sheridan-Smith (London, 1976), pp.428-44.

9. See Arkon Daraul, *Secret Societies Yesterday and Today* (London, 1961), pp.87-99.

10. Daniel Defoe, *The Perjur'd Free Mason Detected: and yet the Honour and Antiquity of the Society of Free Masons Preserv'd and Defended* (London, 1730), p.16.

11. Jung, *Memories, Dreams, Reflections,* pp.315-6.

12. E.J. Hobsbawn, *Primitive Rebels: Studies in Archaic Forms of Social Movement in the 19th and 20th Centuries* (Manchester, 1959), p.153.

13. See Wilber L. Cross, *The Life and Times of Laurence Sterne* (London, 1939), p.28 *passim*. See John Dickson Carr, *The Demoniacs* (London, 1962). In death Sterne was associated with Freemasonry since two Freemasons erected his headstone on 22 March 1768 at St George's Church, Hanover Square, which bears the following inscription:

> This Monumental Stone was erected by two Brother
> Masons; for although he did not live to be a member
> of their society, yet, as his incomparable performances
> evidently proved him to have acted by rule and square,
> they rejoice in this opportunity of perpetuating his
> high and irreproachable character to after ages.

14. See John-Hall Stevenson, *Crazy Tales* (Dublin, 1772).

15. See F. Pick and G. Norman Knight, *The Pocket History of Freemasonry* (London, 1977), p.101.

16. The Gregorians flourished in London before 1738. Alexander Pope defines the Gregorians and Gormogons as "A sort of Lay-brothers from the root of the Freemasons", in *The Works of Alexander Pope,* ed. Pope and William Warbuton, 9 vols (London, 1751), V, p.289. See Carey's anthem to the society, *The Merry Gregorians* (1729) in *The Poems of Henry Carey,* ed. F.T. Wood (London, 1730), p.249.

17. See Pick and Knight, *The Pocket History of Freemasonry,* p.327.

18. Israel Regardie, *The Golden Dawn: An Account of the Teachings, Rites and Ceremonies of the Order of the Golden Dawn* (Minnesota, 1971), p.x.

19. See J.L. Carr, "Gorgons, Gormogons, Medusists and Masons", *Modern Language Review,* LVIII (Jan., 1963), pp.73-8. The

Gormogons were a body of malcontent Masons who formed themselves into a society in order to mimic and disparage the parent society. The Order was founded by Sir Philip Wharton who had also established the society for the advancement of flirtation. Wharton, who had been Grand Master of the Grand Lodge of England, may have been the model for Lovelace in Richardson's *Clarissa Harlowe* (1747-8). See T.C. Duncan Eaves and Ben D. Kimpel, *Samuel Richardson: A Biography* (Oxford, 1971), p.267.

20.  For a discussion of the relationship between the Freemasons and the Druids see John Cleland, *The Way to Things by Words, and to Words by Things...On the Real Secret of the Freemasons* (1766) facsimile reprint (Yorkshire, 1968).

21.  For further information see Douglas Knoop and G.P. Jones, *The Medieval Mason* (Manchester, 1933).

22.  See Lewis C. Jones, *The Clubs of the Georgian Rakes* (New York, 1942). In his *Travels through France and Italy* (1766) Smollet reflects upon the growth of clubs and secret societies in England which he observes among the "fraternities of devotees" in Italy saying: "There is scarce an individual, whether noble or plebian, who does not belong to one of these associations, which may be compared to the Freemasons, Gregorians, and Antigallicans of England." See *The Works of Tobias Smollet*, ed. W.E. Henley and T. Seccombe, 12 vols (London, 1899-1901), XI, p.288.

23.  See Pick and Knight, *The Pocket History of Freemasonry*, p.327 and *A Treasury of Masonic Thought* ed. Carl Glick (London, 1961), p.XVII.

24.  See below chapter 4 (1) "The Bavarian Illuminati".

25.  See Christine Benedicte Eugenie Naubert, *Herman von Unna* (1794), Cajetan Tschink, *The Victim of Magical Delusion: A Magico-Political Tale* (1795) and Karl Grosse, *Horrid Mysteries* (1797).

# CHRISTOPHER SMART

"A MASON is great and respected"

Smart[1]

## Masonry and Madness

It has been universally accepted by scholars that Christopher Smart (1722-71) was a Freemason yet no record of his membership has been traced. The dominant view is that Smart joined the fraternity some time after 11 April 1747 since a candidate for admission during this period had to be at least twenty five years old.[2] Even though no documentation of his Masonic affiliation is available, evidence may be found in his poetry particularly the *Jubilate Agno* (1756-63) and *A Song to David* (1763) which contain many references to the craft and its symbolism. But there is no mistaking the Masonic leanings of the following lodge drinking-song which appeared in *A Collection of Masons' Odes and Songs* (1756) and has since been ascribed to the poet:

"Song" by Brother C. Smart

Tune, *Ye Frolicsome Sparks of the Game*

A MASON is great and respected,
    Tho' Cavillers wrangle and mock
His *Plan* is in *WISDOM* projected,
    His *Edifice* built on a Rock.
*Cho.* The attempts of his *Foes* miscarry,
    And ever in vain are found;
    Or so wide, that they need no Parry,
Or so weak, that they make no Wound.


GOOD-NATURE'S an *Englishman's* Merit,
    A Title all *Britons* desire;
But we claim the *Name* and the *Spirit,*
    From the CORNER-STONE up to
        the Spire,
*Cho.* The Attempts of our *Foes* miscarry, etc.


Tho' often decry'd and derided,
    No *Tyrant* our *Freedom* controuls,

With us mighty MONARCHS have sided,
And EMP'RORS are writ in our ROLLS.
*Cho.* The Attempts of our *Foes* miscarry, etc.

Then fill up the Glass and be funny,
Attend to due METHOD and FORM;
The *Bee* that can make the most *Honey,*
Is fairly the *Flow'r* of the *Swarm.*
*Cho.* The Attempts of our *Foes* miscarry, etc.[3]

Masonic symbolism pervades Smart's *Jubilate Agno* where he explicitly declares his Masonic allegiance: *"I am the Lord's builder and free and accepted MASON in CHRIST JESUS"* (B, 109).[4] Smart's claim that he is a *"free and accepted MASON"* is an acknowledgement of his speculative rather than operative Masonic identity. The prefix "free" came to be attached to the word "Mason" because of the medieval practice of emancipating skilled artisans from the restraints of the guild regulations. This freedom enabled the Masons to establish themselves nationally as an itinerant body which was later to prove an asset in their emergence as an organization of international importance. Non-operatives admitted into the craft were known as "accepted" Masons hence Smart's use of this speculative term. By stating that he is a "MASON *in* CHRIST JESUS" Smart emphasises that he is an advocate of a Christianised version of Freemasonry while his self-imposed role as *"the Lord's builder"* is derived from the Masons' building myths based on the Old Testament accounts of King Solomon's Temple.

Smart celebrates the Freemasons' craft in the *Jubilate Agno,* a strange fragmented poem through which he rehearsed his ideas for the great *Song to David.* The earlier poem was written during Smart's confinement in institutes for the insane from 1757-63.[5] Smart was confined initially in private lodgings after a commission of lunacy had been taken out against him under a writ of *de Lunatica Inquirendo.* He was later committed in May 1759 to a private mad-house[6] in Bethnal Green run by a Mr Potter until his release at the end of January 1763. Smart also spent a year at St Luke's Hospital for the insane where he was admitted to the curable ward in May 1757. St Luke's was run by the humane William Battie whose name, ironically, has become a synonym for madness on account of his enlightened approach to mental illness! Unlike many other eighteenth-century asylums, St Luke's prohibited members of the public from visiting the inmates for the express purpose of jibing and humiliating them. This peep-show practice had been most abused in the year 1707 when over 96,000 visitors passed through Bedlam or Bethlem Hospital which had come to symbolise the terrors of the mad-house in eighteenth-century England.[7] Dr Battie had been a governor of Bethlem since 1742 and was determined that St Luke's should be

11

based on a radical model of reform in mental health. In his *Treatise on Madness* (1758) he urged that "the impertinent curiosity of those who think it pastime to converse with madmen, and to play upon their passions, ought strictly to be forbidden".[8] Smart draws attention to such visits from the public in the *Jubilate Agno* where he notes *"For they pass by me in their tour"* (B, 63). Presumably he was referring here to a different establishment, since he goes on to criticise the brutalities taking place within asylums.

> FOR I pray the Lord JESUS that cured the LUNATICK
> to be merciful to all my brethren and
> sisters in these houses ....
> For they work me with their harping-irons, which
> is a barbarous instrument, because I
> am more unguarded than others.
>
> (B, 123-4)

Smart recorded his experiences in the *Jubilate Agno* which can be described as a panoramic compilation of ideas pirated from scriptural, Masonic, and mystical traditions. It may be the case that Smart had been advised to compose the *Jubilate* as part of his therapy for as Dr Johnson noted "such employment, as Dr Battie has observed, is necessary for madness".[9]

The poem was never published during his life-time. The first edition was produced by William Force Stead in 1939 who subtitled it *A Song from Bedlam*.[10] The preservation of the autograph manuscript had been due to the madness of another poet, William Cowper. Two of his friends, William Hayley and the Reverend Thomas Carwardine, found Smart's poem and decided to use it as a case history in poetic mania. In his essay on "The Madness of Christopher Smart", John Middleton Murry argues that the Age of Reason had prescribed notions of rationality which tended to exclude the poet and the prophet:

> From this angle the history of English poetry
> in the eighteenth century is a singularly depressing
> story. The real poets were all "mad". Chatterton,
> Savage, Collins, Smart, Cowper, were suicides or
> lunatics, or both. Even the equable Gray was on
> the verge of melancholia. At the end of the sombre
> procession comes John Clare, "the asylum poet," whom
> the doctor certified for the madhouse because he
> showed an inconquerable inclination to write verses
> .... In the old, old days before modern "civilisation"
> had begun its levelling, there was more room for the
> poets. They were mad, but their madness was "divine".
> The gods, nay, the very principle of the divine, visited
> them. But in the Age of Reason, they were simply mad.
> No more divinity about their delusions: no more reverence
> for the great unspeakable power which manifested through

them. Our modern civilisation is wonderful, tremendous, terrifying; but it has no room for these things. It does not want, and it will not have, the prophet and the seer. The poet, the authentic poet, is no less: he is the *vates sacer* now, as ever, for the truth he knows is eternal. But there is no room for it in the philosophy of modern civilisation, and modern civilisation will one day pay the penalty for trying to shut out what is older and more enduring than itself."[11]

Traditionally madness had been linked to the revelation of mystic truth which characterised Smart's visionary poetry. More recently madness has been viewed as a social construct which reflects a converse image of society itself. Michel Foucault's remarks in *Madness and Civilisation: A History of Insanity in the Age of Reason* are applicable to the *Jubilate Agno:* "where there is a work of art, there is no madness; and yet madness is contemporary with the work of art, since it inaugurates the time of its truth."[12] Since all appearances of irrationality had been exiled by the Augustan thinker, other outlets had to be found. The secret societies were underground channels which provided a means of expressing art forms which might otherwise be deemed modes of madness. Freemasonry, in particular, enabled its members to rationalise their irrational impulses by canalising regressive patterns of behaviour into the play-acting of Masonic ritual. Macabre ceremonies stirred deep superstitions while blood-curdling oaths intimidated the initiate. The fears activated by these rites would then be dispelled by the fellowship of the lodge. The solemnity of such occasions was enhanced by a religious veneer ransacked from the orthodox churches.

As a devout Christian, Smart would have valued the scriptural derivation of much Masonic ritual. The Freemasons' lodge had recaptured the piety of a more religious age. In doing so, the Masons were simulating a reality lost to the irreligious Age of Reason by restoring to their brethren the mysticism and symbolism which public rationality had robbed from the individual. Smart found that Masonry could accommodate his apocalyptic yearnings and evangelical zeal. Forces of millenarianism and mysticism were converging onto the Masonic scene which was attracting mystics and freethinkers. The mythologies of the craft filled the vacuum of disenchantment created by the demythologising spirit of the Enlightenment. According to Theodor Adorno and Max Horkheimer, the eighteenth century aspired towards an ideological state of "blank purity"[13] which set out to purge from the pervading reality the demons of medievalism. Inadvertently Smart had succeeded in recalling these demons who now wreaked their revenge in the mad house. Evidence suggests that Smart had erased the boundaries between fantasy and reality since he was subject to hallucinations. The Masonic world, itself, was suspended between fact and fiction with its apocryphal histories and emphasis upon ritualised make-believe. The activities of the lodge could have helped activate Smart's creative imagination, at the same time furnishing him with an environment where he could achieve a temporary liberation from the responsibilities of the world outside. Freemasonry may have indulged Smart's idiosyncracies but it could never have contained them indefinitely. Through his poetry he conveys a sense of pride in his Masonic membership which rested upon his conviction that "A MASON is great and respected". Indeed, he would have derived consolation from the craft while undergoing the indignities of his confinement. Smart was suffering from attacks of acute melancholia which resulted in mental disorientation and then violent paroxysms. According to W. Russell Brain in "Christopher Smart: The Flea that Became an Eagle", Smart was subject to cyclothymia, "a disorder characterized by recurrent attacks of depression and excitement or predominantly by one or the other".[14] Smart's mental condition was undoubtedly aggravated by his excessive consumption of alcohol though as Brain notes "in Smart's case the mental illness was not the result of his drunkenness, but he drank because he was mentally unstable".[15] Smart would have regarded his Masonic lodge as a drinking club since the consumption of alcohol had been sanctioned by the Freemasons as an expression of fraternal conviviality. In this respect his membership would have had a detrimental effect on his health since the socializing of the lodge while "at rest" opened up for Smart yet another avenue towards alcoholism. As Dr Johnson wryly recalled "before his confinement, he used for exercise to walk to the ale-house; but he was *carried* back again."[16] The expense of Smart's drinking habits added to his mounting debts. In view of these financial difficulties it is possible that the lodge contributed to the costs of his private confinements which would have been in accordance with the Masonic obligation to help brothers in distress. But such a fraternal solution could only have been effective in the short-term since Smart's inability to keep out of debt continued throughout his life until he became completely destitute, dying in a debtor's prison in 1771. His old tutor, Thomas Gray, had predicted that Smart's degenerate life-style would end in tragedy, saying "& for his Vanity & Faculty of lyeing, [sic] they are come to their full Maturity, all this, you see must come to a Jayl, [sic] or Bedlam, & that without any help, almost without pity."[17]

Smart had alienated many of his friends by subjecting them to the bizarre aspects of his religious mania. His insistence upon the practice of spontaneous and continuous prayer meant that he would even call his friends from their meals and out of their beds to pray with him. Yet this is more symptomatic of eccentricity than of madness. Johnson argued:

> I did not think he ought to be shut up. His infirmities were not noxious to society. He insisted on people

praying with him; and I'd lief pray with Kit Smart as
anyone else. Another charge was, that he did not love
clean linen; and I have no passion for it.[18]

According to Mrs Piozzi, Smart was considered sufficiently sane
to earn money by teaching Latin to the sons of the keeper of
the mad-house. She goes on to make a distinction between
madness and frenzy, delirium and mania before arguing that the
alarming and volatile nature of Smart's symptoms were grounded
in frenzy and delirium rather than in madness or mania.[19]
Johnson also challenged the prescribed notions of Augustan
rationality by means of which Smart had been judged insane:

> Madness frequently discovers itself merely by unnecessary
> deviation from the usual modes of the world. My poor
> friend Smart showed the disturbance of his mind, by
> falling upon his knees, and saying his prayers in the
> street, or in any other unusual place. Now, although,
> rationally speaking, it is greater madness not to pray
> at all, than to pray as Smart did, I am afraid there
> are so many who do not pray, that their understanding
> is not called in question.[20]

As a poet and prophet Smart's "preternatural excitement to
prayer"[21] was symptomatic of the waves of irrationality that
swept England during the 1750's and 1760's. It could be said that
Smart's religious enthusiasm was seen as tantamount to madness
during the irreverent Age of Reason. This was an unstable period
affecting both the external and internal states of English policies.
In this politically uncertain milieu the fatalistic creed of
millenarianism gained support throughout the country. Earthquakes
in London and Lisbon, together with a strange distemper which
raged among cattle, provoked an outpouring of prophecies which
swept the nation. These were the harbingers of a new religious
fervour manifested by the crowds of people who flocked to hear
the Wesleys at Moorfields. There was a widespread belief that a
cataclysmic disaster was imminent, for as the Reverend John
Brown pronounced: "We are rolling to the brink of a Precipice
that must destroy us."[22] Smart's contemporary, William Law, a
disciple of the mystic Jacob Boehme, predicted universal chaos
unless the population followed his advice to engage in continuous
prayer.[23] The opening of Smart's poem, "Prayer" (1775) likewise
recommends the reader to "Pray without ceasing" (II, p.344)
Smart firmly believed that prayer was the agency of mankind's
salvation and predicted in the *Jubilate Agno: "For I prophecy that
men will learn the use of their knees"* (C, 108). The poet developed
this theme in the "For" section of an earlier passage in the poem:

> *For it will be better for England and all the world in*
>     *a season, as I prophecy this day ....*
> *For I prophecy that they will obey the motions of the*

15

> *spirit descended upon them as at this day* ....
> For *they have seen the glory of God already come down*
>     *upon the trees*....
> For *I prophecy that it will descend upon their heads*
>     *also* ....
> For *I prophecy that the praise of God will be in every*
>     *man's mouth in the Publick streets* ....
> For *I prophecy that there will be Publick worship*
>     *in the cross ways and fields.*
>
> (C, 58-63)

Smart's predictions refer to the apocalyptic "Age of the Horn".[24]
This announced the second coming which would restore to man's
forehead the  horn of strength and to earth the cornucopia, the
horn of plenty:

> For *I prophecy that we shall have our horns again* ....
> For *in the day of David Man as yet had a glorious*
>     *horn upon his forehead.*
>
> (C, 118-9)

In the *Jubilate Agno* Smart is nostalgic for the "day of David",
the time before man lost his mystic insights and affinity with
nature:

> For *when Man was amerced of his horn, earth lost part*
>     *of her fertility.*
>
> (C, 156)

The millenial land of milk and honey was central to the
doctrine of the Freemasons while the cornucopia was included in
the arcana of Masonic symbolism.[25]  Possibly Smart had become
involved with the quasi-Masonic movement which was to
culminate in the establishment of the "New Church" in 1778 by
the Swedenborgians, the followers of the mystic Emanuel
Swedenborg.[26]  It may be no coincidence that Smart, who was so
receptive to the doctrines of millenarianism, should be committed
to St Luke's Asylum in 1757, the year of Swedenborg's "Last
Judgement":

> For *this is the twelfth day of the MILLENNIUM*
>     *of the MILLENNIUM foretold by the prophets.*
>
> (B, 382)

In becoming a Freemason Smart would have been in contact
with those quasi-Masonic mystics who may have impressed upon
him the urgency of their visionary quest to restore fallen
mankind to an earthly paradise. Smart's own missionary zeal is
apparent from his self-ordained task in the *Jubilate* as the *"Lord's
News-Writer-the-scribe-evangelist"* (B, 327). Smart believed that his
example of public prayer and adoration of Christ would inspire

people to "*learn to take pleasure in glorifying God with great cheerfulness*" (C, 69). He believed that through prayer the human race could save itself from the impending holocaust. Unfortunately Smart's eccentric admonitions were regarded as evidence of his lunacy. His committal for anti-social behaviour including religious mania suggests that his over-zealous reaction to Masonic mysticism may have indirectly brought about the circumstances which inspired the creation of the *Jubilate Agno*. Smart's declaration in the poem that he was a Christian Mason deserves some comment. It was partly a response to the virtual abolition of the Christian character of the craft which prescribed that the religious duty of the Freemason was to embrace the Deistic belief in a supreme being known as the Great Architect of the Universe. Outside the lodge a Mason might profess one of the creeds of his country but, once in the Masonic meeting-place, he must abide by the Religion on which all men agree. The official voice of Masonry was careful to condemn "stupid" atheists and "irreligious" libertines in order to dispel any doubts that it might be at variance with public opinion. Nevertheless speculative Freemasonry reflected the beliefs of its Hanoverian founders who included Freethinkers, Newtonians and Deists. The latitudinarianism of the Masons had been officially sanctioned by Grand Lodge and then formulated by James Anderson in the first charge or ordinance of his Masonic *Constitutions*:

> A Mason is obliged, by his tenure, to obey the moral
> law; and if he rightly understands the art, he will
> never be a stupid atheist, nor an irreligious
> Libertine.... it is now thought more expedient only
> to oblige them [the Freemasons] to that religion in
> which all men agree, leaving their particular opinions
> to themselves; that is, to be good men and true, or
> men of honour and honesty, by whatever denominations
> or persuasions they may be distinguished.[27]

The implementation of enlightened religious toleration in the lodges was interpreted as opening the craft to men of non-Christian faith which was described as the "de-Christianization of Freemasonry".[28] It led to internal dissension which erupted into a long and bitter quarrel between the two factions known as the Antients [sic] and the Moderns. In 1751 the Antients defected to set up a rival Grand Lodge in an attempt to restore many of the Christian traditions which had lapsed over the years. Prayers during lodge meetings had been neglected while traditional Saints' days were generally ignored. The Antients tried to rekindle the spirit of Christianity back into the lodges through the introduction of a fourth Masonic degree known as the Holy Royal Arch. This new degree, which was allegedly disliked by the Moderns, revitalized the Christian doctrines and symbols which had characterised earlier forms of Freemasonry.

Yet Smart's insistence that his brand of Freemasonry was
firmly implanted in Christianity was more than a response to an
internal wrangle between the Antients and the Moderns.  He was
also retaliating against the official condemnation of the society in
1745 by the Presbyterians, who formalized their objections in a
synod which passed an act denouncing the Freemasons' oath in
1757.  By coincidence this was the year that Smart was first
committed to the asylum.  In view of his evangelical outlook, he
would have been disconcerted to have discovered that a branch
of the Nonconformist Church had denounced Freemasonry as an
abuse of Christian and Biblical teaching.  In the first fragment of
the *Jubilate*, Smart's persistent allusions to Old Testament
characters who also figure in the history of Masonry may have
been written in defiance of the conclusion reached by the
Presbyterian Synod that Masons "pretend to take some of these
secrets from the Bible".[29]
Smart, whose Masonic allegiance was essentially Christian,
would have naturally supported the Antients.  Consequently the
blend of Masonic and Christian imagery throughout his poetry can
be attributed to this period of turmoil in the history of
Freemasonry which is crystallized in his description of himself in
the *Jubilate Agno* as a "*free and accepted* MASON *in* CHRIST
JESUS" (B, 109).

*Jubilate Agno:*  **A Song from Bedlam** [30]

In this poem Smart exposes the roots of eighteenth-century
irrationality which were embedded in mysticism and Masonry.  The
*Jubilate Agno* should not be read as a document attesting to the
diseased mind of the author but as a specimen of ecstatic writing
which reveals Smart to be a poet of the idiosyncratic.  By
preserving in verse certain Masonic mysteries Smart would have
regarded himself as a custodian of mystic truth.  To the Augustan
mind which prescribed that the poet concentrate upon the general
and generic, Smart's subjective focus on the particular and
obscure would have been sufficient to testify to his madness.
Since Smart, like John Donne, chose to see with a "telescopic
eye",[31] his contemporaries would have considered the poem to be
a regression to the eclecticism of the Metaphysical poets.  The
heterogeneity of the poem partly stemmed from Smart's dissolution
of the lines of demarcation separating expressions of the private
consciousness from those of the public self and the secrets of
esoteric knowledge from the dissemination of open information.
For the modern reader the epistemic concerns are more pragmatic.
The difficulties in deciphering some of the erudite and often
intractable passages in the poem are compounded by the loss of
over half the original manuscript.  The remnants consist of thirty
two pages made up of ten single leaves and three pairs of

conjunct leaves with lines beginning with either "For" or "Let". The antiphonal nature of the poem suggests that Smart was experimenting with the principles of Hebraic verse.[32] The most recent editor, Karina Williamson, has divided the poem into four fragments, A, B, C, D. The *Jubilate Agno* is a cosmic anthem which celebrates the Creation through imagery adopted from Christian, Masonic, and occult sources. It reflects Smart's esoteric inclinations and his commitment to Christianity and Freemasonry which he merged together as a buffer to the hostility displayed towards the craft by the established churches. This antagonism was levelled largely against the Freemasons' appeal to scriptural authority for the validation of their central mythology. One of their fundamental motifs concerned the building of King Solomon's Temple which was considered to be the chief architectural feat of ancient operative Masonry. The Masons supplemented the Biblical accounts of this undertaking with a wealth of legends and traditions. The *Dowlands* Masonic manuscript (circa 1500) refers to the principal architect and builder who is named in the *Inigo Jones* manuscript (1607) as the craft's legendary founder, Hiram Abif. Speculative Masons identified themselves with Hiram hence Smart's description of himself as "the Lord's builder". The Hiramic tradition that King Solomon's chief builder and Master Mason had been assassinated by treacherous workmen seeking to discover the secrets of the temple-building was first indicated in 1730,[33] though it is believed to have a much earlier origin.[34] The established churches objected to Masonry invoking Biblical authority because they suspected that the brotherhood was trying to establish itself on a pseudo-religious base.

The Catholic hierarchy objected to Freemasonry because it represented a rival belief-system dividing loyalty between the Church and the craft, the lodge and the confessional. During the eighteenth century, the Roman Catholic church condemned the Masons in two papal Bulls. The first of these, *In Eminente*, was issued in 1738 by Clement XII who announced that assemblies of Freemasons "have become to the faithful such objects of suspicion that every good man now regards affiliation to them as a certain indication of wickedness and perversion." [35] He also accused Masons of "perverting the minds of the incautious, and shooting down innocent people from their hiding places."[36] Here Clement X11 was referring to the papal agents who spied on lodge meetings. The second papal indictment was *Providas Romanorum* released by Benedict X1V on 18 May 1751.[37] This document restated the objections made in *In Eminente*. It goes on to argue that Masonic organisations were contrary to civil and canonical interests. Benedict XIV was also concerned that the religious pluralism of the Masons would, in some way, jeopardize the homogeneity of the Catholic Church. He claimed that the Masonic oath was designed to protect members from legitimate authority by keeping any criminal activity secret.

Smart refers to these Vatican condemnations in the *Jubilate* through his word-play on "Bull", *"For there are many words under Bull"* (B, 678). Robert Brittain suggests that in his poetry Smart expressed the antagonism between the Roman Catholic Church and the Freemasons:

> The only unpleasant theme in Smart's later poetry is a certain antipathy to the Roman Church; it may owe its existence to his Masonic connections, and have been aggravated by the conversion of his estranged wife.[38]

Smart may have been thinking of his wife when he wrote in the *Jubilate*, "A papist hath no sentiment" (B, 295). Later in the poem he attacks the Catholic Church while referring to the strained relations existing between the Venetian Republic and the Vatican state:

> *For I prophecy that the Reformation will make*
> *great way by means of the Venetians.*
>
> (C, 98)

As an autocratic institution the Vatican regarded the Freemasons as politically subversive. During the 1770s some lodges in France were composed entirely of Catholic clergy and monks,[39] even though the Church objected to Masonic doctrine on theological grounds. For example, ecclesiastics interpreted the unholy trinity of Jehova, Baal and Osiris of the higher degrees as a sacrilegious parody of God the Father, God the Son and God the Holy Spirit.[40] Not surprisingly many Christians regarded Freemasonry as a pagan alternative to Christianity. This was mainly because the Masons revered a godhead known as the Great Architect of the Universe and paid homage to the messianic Hiram Abif whom some churchman regarded as a surrogate Christ.

Hiram was martyred by three apprentices for refusing to divulge the secrets of Masonry. Coincidently the title, *Jubilate Agno*, which translates into Stead's original title, *Rejoice in the Lamb*, has Masonic connotations relating to Hiram's murder. According to John Fellows:

> The names Jubela, Jubelo, Jubelum, given to the
> pretended assassins of Hiram, I take to be a
> play upon the word *Jubilum*, the Latin term
> answering to jubilee. They were of course formed
> at the time freemasonry was first established.[41]

Masons had adopted the lamb as the symbol of the innocence of the martyred Hiram. In commemoration of their founder each Freemason during lodge meetings wore a white lamb-skin apron which had been presented to him on his initiation:

> I now present to you, by command of our Worshipful
> Master, a White Lambskin Apron, the original
> garment that our Almighty Father presented to our
> first parents after their fall. It is a Badge of
> the most ancient as well as the most honourable,
> for while it reminds us that we are members of a
> fallen race, it also teaches us that by the
> sacrifice of the lamb, we are clothed with
> innocence. Be therefore humble, yet honourable
> in all your labours. Operative Masons always
> wear an apron to protect their garments from dirt
> and soil, so let ours remind us to keep always
> our consciences clean and unspotted.[42]

Since Smart's mention of the lamb in the first line of the *Jubilate Agno,* "give the glory to the Lord, and the Lamb" refers specifically to Christ, the custom of wearing a white lamb-skin must have been a vivid reminder to him of the interchangeability of Masonic and Christian symbolism.

In view of the scriptural foundation for many legends and customs of Freemasonry, the problem arises in Smart's poetry of distinguishing Biblical from Masonic sources. For example, W.H. Bond claims that the opening lines of the poem are based on the titles of the Psalms 66 and 100 in the Psalter of the *Book of Common Prayer* and from "The Book of Revelation" 7.9-10:

> Rejoice in God, O ye Tongues; give the glory
> to the Lord, and the Lamb.
> Nations, and languages, and every Creature, in
> which is the breath of Life.
>
> (A, 1-2)

Arthur Sherbo, however, suggests that Smart derived these lines from Anderson's Masonic *Constitutions* "we are also of all *Nations, Tongues, Kindreds* and *Languages.*"[43] Sherbo goes on the point out that the fourth line of the *Jubilate Agno:*

> Let Noah and his company approach the throne of
> Grace, and do homage to the Ark of their Salvation.
>
> (A, 4)

may be translated into Masonic language as follows:

> Let the Masons (descendants of Noah and sometimes
> called Noachidae) approach the seat of the Grand
> Master in the Grand Lodge of England (called the
> throne) and do homage to the Ark of Safety (part
> of the ritual in the American Royal Arch Degree).[44]

The ambivalence between Christian and Masonic sources is appropriate in view of Smart's Christianised version of Freemasonry. Even Smart's Biblical reference to "Nimrod, the mighty hunter" (A, 9) has Masonic significance for as Bernard E. Jones reveals:

> An eighteenth-century tradition, as extra-ordinary as it was foolish, was to the effect that Ham's eldest son, Nimrod (in Scripture: "a mighty hunter before the Lord"), was Grand Master of all masons and a builder of many cities in Shinaar. But its existence is one more indication that Noah and his family had masonic associations in the minds of at least some early speculatives.[45]

Freemasons have claimed that many Old Testament figures were recruited into the Brotherhood. Accordingly, it has been estimated that at least twenty-one of the Biblical personages named in fragment A of the *Jubilate Agno* are mentioned in Masonic history and legend.[46]

A more specific example of Masonic symbolism may be found in Smart's references to the bee in fragments A and C of the poem.[47]

> Let Pedaiah bless with the Humble-Bee, who loves
> himself in solitude and makes his honey alone.
> Let Maaseiah bless with the Drone, who with the
> appearance of a Bee is neither a soldier nor
> an artist, neither a swordsman nor smith.
> (A, 97-8)

The likelihood that these lines relate to Freemasonry is suggested by Smart's lodge drinking song, where he refers to the bee in a specifically Masonic context:

> The *Bee* that can make the most *Honey*,
> Is fairly the *flow'r* of the *Swarm*

The bee was a popular symbol in eighteenth-century Masonry, and one of the earliest references to it as such may be found in the spoof "Letter from the Grand Mistress of the Female Freemasons" (1724) which has been attributed to Swift:

> A *Bee* has in all Ages and Nations been the Grand
> *Hierogliphick* of *Masonry*, because it excels all
> other living Creatures in the Contrivance and
> Commodiousness of its *Habitation* ... *Masonry* or
> *Building* seems to be of the very Essence or Nature
> of the *Bee*.[48]

Swift discusses the historical implications of this emblem to the craft in a manner which parodies the exaggerated claims made by Masonic historians such as Dr Anderson in his *Constitutions*. Swift concludes his digression with the following exposition of "bee" metaphors:

What *Modern Masons* call a *Lodge* was for the above Reasons by Antiquity call'd a HIVE of *Free-Masons*, and for the same Reasons when a Dissension happens in a *Lodge* the going off and forming another *Lodge* is to this Day call'd SWARMING.[49]

To a Freemason, Smart's concluding line to fragment C of the *Jubilate Agno* has Masonic connotations:

*For I pray God be gracious to the Bees and*
*the Beeves this day.*

(C, 162)

Within Masonic iconography the bee was a symbol of the industrious Mason since, as Swift points out, this imagery was specifically associated with building. Smart engages in word-play in Fragment A by identifying the wasp with architecture:

Let Zorobabel bless with the Wasp, who is the Lord's architect, and buildeth his edifice in armour.

(A, 101)

The name "Zorobabel" is the New Testament spelling for "Zerubbabel", who helped carry out the rebuilding of King Solomon's Temple after it had been ransacked by rebels. This incident, as recounted by the prophet Haggai, forms one of the motifs of the fourth Masonic degree, the Holy Royal Arch. During this ritual the Grand Masters and Past Grand Masters assume the identity of Zerubbabel and Joshua the High Priest, who are mentioned by Smart in the *Jubilate Agno* (A, 101, 26, B, 99).[50]

The catenarian arch was the central symbol of the Holy Royal Arch which had emerged during the early eighteenth century.[51] It had been instituted by the Antients who claimed to have salvaged it from a then discarded version of the Master's degree. Unexpectedly, the Moderns resisted the implementation of the additional degree on the grounds that it represented an unwarranted departure from the original trigradal system. They were not convinced by the Antients' counter-arguments which stressed the antiquity of the degree. Headway was made towards resolving the dispute when Thomas Dunkerley, the illegitimate son of George II and a Mason of the Modern persuasion, was initiated or rather "exalted" into the Royal Arch in 1754. The degree gained much support because of its Christian content which, as mentioned earlier, would have

23

appealed to Smart.

In his poetry Smart drew on another off-shoot of the craft associated with the Royal Arch known as Mark Masonry.[52] Records for 1758 confirm that this system was made up of two degrees, the Mark Man and the Mark Mason. The Mark Man's degree was intended for Fellowcraftsmen while the Mark Master was for Master Masons. The distinguishing feature of this order was that every member possessed a Mason's Mark. The satirical poem, *The Free-Masons* (1722-23) mentions this custom:

> They then resolv'd no more to roam,
> But to return to their own Home;
> Tho' first they Signs and Marks did frame,
> To Signify from whence they came.[53]

The tradition stems from the operative craft when workmen carved their mark upon a finished stone. Much of the ritual for Mark Masonry is based upon the symbolism of sacred stones derived from the Old Testament. The degree of Mark Man incorporated a legend which Smart may be referring to in the *Jubilate Agno:*

> *For there is a blessing from the STONE of JESUS*
> *which is founded upon hell to the precious*
> *jewell on the right hand of God* (B, 31)

This concerns the laying of the foundation-stone of King Solomon's Temple. On the morning that the King attended the ceremony, a precious stone fell from his crown which was recovered by the Senior Master of the Order of Mark Men. The precious stone was then set into the *Tetragrammaton*, the sacred name of God, which was engraved on the royal diadem. The language of Smart's image of Christ as the *"precious jewell on the right hand of God"* overlaps with that of Mark Masonry. Sherbo has interpreted Smart's *"STONE of JESUS"* as a reference to the Freemasons' Foundation Stone which was inscribed with the Tetragrammaton.[54] The importance of the Foundation Stone to Royal Arch Masonry is revealed in Dunkerley's version:

> The foundation-stone was a block of pure white marble,
> without speck or stain, and it alluded to the chief
> corner-stone on which the Christian Church is built,
> and which, though rejected by the builders, afterwards
> became the head of the corner. And when Jesus Christ,
> the grand and living representative of this stone, came
> in the flesh to conquer sin, death and hell, He proved
> Himself the sublime and immaculate corner-stone of man's
> immortality.[55]

The typology of Christ as the corner-stone was celebrated by Masons in a rudimentary form of the modern-day "rejection rite".

Smart employs messianic-Masonic stone symbolism in "The Headstone in the Corner":

> The Lord did thus bespeak the throng,
> Have ye not read in David's song?
> What scoffing builders could disown
> Is of the church the corner-stone,
> The work of God, supremely wise. (II, p.282)

Smart reworks the metaphor of the disowned corner-stone in his *Translation of the Psalms* where he writes:

> That rock neglected and unknown
> Is now become the corner stone
> E'ven of the house of God;
> Which all the builders to a man
> Refus'd, from him that drew the plan,
> To him who bore the hod.
> (Callan, II, p.695)

The last two lines draw attention to the hierarchy of operative Masonry from the Master Mason drawing the plan down to the Apprentice carrying the hod who refuse the corner-stone which Smart, in Psalm XXVIII, specifically identifies with Christ:

> The works omniscient love design'd
> And hands almighty skill'd,
> Yet may they for their crimes atone,
> And all on Christ the corner stone
> In clemency rebuild.
> (Callan, II, p.447)

Smart's Christianised approach to Freemasonry is taken up by Thomas De Quincey who describes Christ as the corner-stone in his *Historical-Critical Inquiry into the Origin of Rosicrucians and Freemasons:*

> Free-masonry was represented under the form of Solomon's Temple - as a type of the true Church, whose corner-stone is Christ. This Temple is to be built of men, or living stones .... Christ is the Grand-Master; and was put to death whilst laying the foundation of the temple of human nature.[56]

Smart approached the concept of Christ as a Grand Master in his version of Psalm CXI, where he writes: "Dispos'd in Christ the Master's skill" (Callan, II, p 681) while the idea of Christ as a master-builder is implied in his poem "Immortality":

> Sure Immortality was known
> To few, but very few,

> Before I came, the corner-stone
> To build my work anew.
>
> (II, p.361)

De Quincey's account of Christ building a temple of living stones recalls Robert Samber's metaphor in his highly rhetorical Masonic address in his novel *Long Livers* (1722): "Ye are Living Stones, built up [into] a spiritual House, who believe and rely on the chief *Lapis Angularis*, which the refractory and disobedient Builders disallowed."[57] Here the "Living Stones" are the individual Freemasons who "polished by the Master's hand" grow towards spiritual and moral perfection until they became smooth stones known as perfect ashlars. During the eighteenth century the broached thurnel, a pointed conical-shaped stone, was sometimes used as a substitute for the perfect ashlar. Some Masonic historians have claimed that the broached thurnel was symbolic of a church spire.[58] Smart's reference to a spire in his Mason's drinking song: "From the CORNER-STONE up to the SPIRE" demonstrates how the Christian images of the corner-stone and the spire may be used in a specifically Masonic context.

A blend of Biblical and Masonic imagery surfaces in Smart's reference to thunder and lightning in the *Jubilate Agno:*

> For THUNDER is the voice of God direct in verse
> and musick....
> For LIGHTNING is a glance of the glory of
> God. (B, 271-2)

These lines are relevant to initiation into Freemasonry, the *"School-Doctrine of Thunder and Lightning"* (B, 269) at the moment when the blindfolded candidate is alarmed by loud noises, representing thunder. Eventually his ritual ordeal ends and the blindfold, known as a cable tow, is removed which dramatically exposes him to light, the symbolic equivalent of lightning.[59] In fragment B Smart refers to the lightning before death which is re-enacted in the preparation of the candidate for the degree of Entered Apprentice:

> For The Lightning before death is God's
> illumination in the spirit for preparation
> and for warning. (B, 467)

During a more advanced stage of initiation, the cycle of life, death and rebirth is graphically illustrated as in the dramaturgical mime relating to Hiram's murder in the Master's degree.

In *A Song to David*, Smart transposes into poetry these mysteries of initiation along with the creed and iconography of the Freemasons. As we have seen, the blend of Masonic and Christian ideas in the *Jubilate Agno* incorporated many of the poet's most sacred and personal beliefs. Smart's identity as a

Mason coloured his spirituality by adding another dimension to his verse. Furthermore the interpretation of parts of the *Jubilate* in the light of Freemasonry provides a degree of coherence and continuity to its otherwise fragmented and heterogeneous appearance which takes us one step further to seeing the poem as evidence of Smart's genius rather than of his madness.

## The Lord's Builder: *A Song to David*

> You are called from Darkness to Light you are a
> chosen Generation, a royal Priesthood.
>
> Robert Samber[60]

The *Jubilate Agno* provided Smart with the raw material of poetic inspiration which was later refined into *A Song to David*. The importance of Freemasonry to this poem will be analysed through two groups of stanzas. The first set (XXX-XXXVIII) deals with the seven days of creation which are symbolized by seven pillars each named after a letter of the Greek alphabet. A Masonic interpretation will be made of this section which, according to Smart's synopsis, "Shews [sic] that the pillars of knowledge are the monuments of God's works in the first week". Next Smart's closing stanzas to the poem will be investigated in terms of Christianity and Masonry. The emphasis here will be upon the interaction between the poet's dual identities as a Christian and Freemason.

*A Song to David* was written shortly after Smart's release from Mr Potter's mad-house. The poem met with mixed reactions for as the Freemason and poet, William Mason, remarked to Thomas Gray: "I have *seen* his *Song to David* & from thence conclude him as mad as ever".[61] Smart's nephew, Christopher Hunter, agreed with this verdict since he politely omitted the poem from his edition of Smart's work on the grounds that it provided "melancholy proofs of the recent estrangement of his mind."[62] The greatness of the *Song to David* was eventually recognised by later generations who perhaps realised that the gods had bestowed a divine madness on Smart. D.G. Rossetti, a member of the nineteenth-century Pre-Raphaelite Brotherhood was so impressed by the work that he even praised it as "the only great *accomplished* poem of the last century".[63] Browning, while comparing Smart's poetry to parts of a building, marvelled:

> So - thus it is thou deck'st,
> High heaven, our low earth's brick-and-mortar work?

He visualised *A Song to David* as a chapel, describing it as "Art's response/ to earth's despair":

Christopher Smart

> from floor to roof one evidence
> Of how far earth may rival heaven.[64]

Browning's response to the architectural structure of the poem is consistent with Smart's description of himself as "the Lord's builder," one who builds in words a sacred edifice of verse. Thus it is appropriate that for the *Song to David* Smart should have borrowed imagery from the builder's art through his use of Masonic symbolism.

Smart's masterpiece is a hymn to Creation which is communicated through his own blend of Christian Freemasonry. There can be little doubt that Masonic influences constituted an important train of thought in Smart's development as a poet of sacred verse. Nevertheless critics have tended to overlook the influence of Masonry on the poem. This is, indeed, puzzling. It is possible that the omission has been due to the widespread assumption that only members of the fraternity can detect hidden references to the secrets of the craft. Certainly access to Grand Lodge archives is restricted to Masons but most published Masonic material, including hand-books and exposures, is available to outsiders. Contrary to popular belief, the secrecy of the society does not extend to the ritual, symbolism and workings of the lodge. Yet critical commentators, such as Edward G. Ainsworth and Charles E. Noyes have insisted that Smart's use of Masonic "symbols must be meaningful to the enlightened" and that the exact meaning of parts of the poem is "necessarily unintelligible to the uninitiated."[65] Even Sherbo who admitted that the *Jubilate Agno* abounds with Masonic references believed that the effect Freemasonry had on the *Song to David* was minimal.[66] It would now appear that this was not, in fact, the case as I shall argue that Smart actually made fairly extensive use of Masonry in the poem.

The very hero of the *Song*, King David, is a figure who stands at the crossroads of both Christian and Masonic traditions. Indeed, David was prominent within the historiography of early speculative Masonry. Some Masonic writers even claimed that it was David rather than Solomon who actually began the building of the temple.[67] According to the *Roberts Constitutions* (1722):

> King David loved Masons well and cherish'd them,
> for he gave them good Payment, and gave them a
> Charge, as Euclydes had given them before in Egypt,
> and further, as hereafter followeth: and after the
> Decease of King David, Solomon his Son finished
> the Temple that his Father had began.[68]

Smart, however, does not deviate from the scriptural version that Solomon began the building of the temple since, in the *Song*, he refers to David: "'Twas he the famous temple plann'd" (VII). David, as the planner of the temple, is mentioned again in the

28

later poem "The Presentation of Christ in the Temple" (1765). Here Smart acknowledges the chief architect and builder, Hiram Abif, who, like King David, was venerated by the Freemasons:

> When Hiero built, from David's plan,
> The house of godlike style,
> And Solomon, the prosp'rous man,
> Whose reign with wealth and fame began,
> O'erlaid with gold the glorious pile.
>
> (II, p.41)

The Freemasons believed that they were building a temple of thought which was the spiritual counterpart to the archetypal temple of King Solomon. In the *Song to David*, Smart describes this figuratively through an image of a temple of the imagination constructed by the brethren's pledges of allegiance to the craft:

> Beauteous the temple deck'd and fill'd,
> When to the heav'n of heav'ns they build
> Their heart directed vows. (LXXIX)

In the same way, Smart's description of himself in the *Jubilate Agno:* "*I am the Lord's builder and free and accepted MASON in CHRIST JESUS*" (B, p.109) suggested that he was building in words and poetry towards this spiritual goal. The "architectural" symmetry of the *Song to David* evokes the structure of the Masons' spiritual temple while the last two lines of the poem anticipate the completion of this task:

> And now the matchless deed's atchiev'd, [sic]
> DETERMINED, DARED, and DONE. (LXXXVI)

The poet employed Masonic symbolism and ideas in the *Song* because the memory of the King was honoured and enshrined by Masons in contrast to the controversy over David's character which raged amongst academics and divines. Smart believed that Freemasons should aspire to the virtues exemplified by King David which would transform the craft's system of morality into a ministry of virtue. In stanzas IV - XVII Smart attributes to David the following virtues:

> Great, valiant, pious, good, and clean.
> Sublime, contemplative, serene,
> Strong, constant, pleasant, wise!

These are similar to the inventory of Masonic moral imperatives contained in an eighteenth-century lodge drinking song:

> Great, noble, generous, good, and brave,
> Are titles they most justly claim.[69]

These lines may be compared to the following chorus taken from the ballad opera, *The Generous Freemason* (1731):

> Great, generous, virtuous, good, and brave,
> Are Titles they most justly claim;
> Their Deeds shall live beyond the Grave,
> And ev'ry Age their Fame proclaim.[70]

David was not only a key figure in the early Masonic tradition but also a type of Christ and, as "Israel's sweet Psalmist", the prototype of the divine artist. Consequently Smart, as a Freemason, devout Christian and religious poet, used the figure of King David as a point of consolidation. His thanks to David as the author of the *Psalms* are conveyed in his advertisement to the *Song to David* which he declares to have been "composed in a Spirit of Affection and thankfulness to the great Author of the Book of Gratitude, which is the *Psalms* of DAVID the King."[71] As a Mason, Smart, in the *Song to David*, expressed the gratitude Freemasons owed to King David as the man who had planned the Temple of Solomon, which contained the heart of their most sacred beliefs.

## Degrees of Initiation

In *A Song to David* Smart makes the greatest use of the esoteric symbolism of Freemasonry in nine stanzas relating to the seven pillars of wisdom (XXX-XXXVIII). The seven pillars are named after letters of the Greek alphabet and represent the six days of creation followed by one day of rest. Each of the seven stanzas begins with one of the following Greek letters: *alpha, gamma, eta, theta, iota, sigma* and *omega*. Why Smart chose these particular letters remains a mystery which has puzzled critics since the *Song to David* first appeared in 1763.[72]

One explanation may be found through a Masonic interpretation of this section. Odell Shepard and Paul Spencer Wood were the first critics to suggest that Freemasonry was influential in determining Smart's choice of the seven Greek letters.[73] They claimed that the letters had a visual significance through their physical resemblance to the emblems of Masonry. Shepard and Wood interpreted five of the Greek letters along the following lines: alpha (A) corresponded to the compass; gamma ($\Gamma$) to the square; eta (H) to Jacob's ladder; theta ($\Theta$) to the All-Seeing Eye and iota (I) to the plumb line (see plate I). Although they omitted sigma ($\Sigma$) and omega ($\Omega$) from this scheme, it is possible to include them in this visual pattern of Masonic symbolism. Sigma represents the three-jointed, four-cubit rule which was used by operative Masons during the Middle Ages [74] while omega bears a physical resemblance to the "Royal Arch" and the dome of the temple. The "Royal Arch" was the symbol of the fourth degree mentioned earlier which would have been of topical interest to Smart since it had been introduced recently into the craft. The dome was the name given to the ceiling of the lodge which brethren sometimes called the temple. Masonic writers often referred to King Solomon's Temple as "the dome". In this context, Smart's mention in the *Song* of "ADORATION in the dome/Of Christ" (LXXI) demonstrates his tendency to put a Masonic reference into a Christian context.

The majority of Smart's visual symbols such as alpha (A), gamma (Γ), iota (I), sigma (Σ) and eta (H) are structural devices associated with the Freemasons's emblematic tools. These were the heirlooms inherited from operative Masonry where they had served as the working tools for builders and stone-masons. In speculative Masonry the tools were used symbolically in their application to the moral character of the individual Mason as illustrated by the following lines from a Masonic song:

> Our plumb-line and compass, our square and
> our tools
> Direct all our actions in virtue's fair rules.[75]

The tools also played a part in the Masonic version of the Creation myth which incorporated a belief in the Great Architect of the Universe. In his *Hymns for the Amusement of Children* (1770), Smart refers to the Freemasons' concept of God who created the cosmos with the working tools:

> The stars, the firmament, the sun,
>      God's glorious work, God's great design,
> All, all was finish'd as begun,
>      By rule, by compass, and by line.
>
>                               (II, p.335)

This stanza has a striking resemblance to the following verse from a contemporary Masonic song:

> Since God himself I'll prove to be
> The first great Master of Masonry...
> He took up his compass with masterly hand,
> He stretched out his line and he measur'd the land,
> He laid the foundation, of Earth and Sea
>      By the first rules of Masonry.[76]

It is hardly surprising that Smart uses the symbols of the compass (alpha), line (iota) and rule (sigma) in a set of stanzas dealing with the creation. The image of a mechanistic god measuring out the cosmos with compass and line is graphically displayed in Blake's *Ancient of Days* (see plate 2). The Freemasons' Great Architect of the Universe reveals the Newtonian presupposition within Masonic ideology. The doctrines of the craft had been established by the Hanoverian Freethinkers, James Anderson and John Theophilus Desauguliers, who were both disciples of Newton. The latter had even written a poem, *The Newtonian System* (1728) while Anderson formulated regulations for the fraternity in a way which reflected the influence of the Baconian scientific method. The development of speculative Freemasonry coincided with the emergence of the Scientific Revolution whose radical epistemologies were in the process of questioning orthodox theologies. Even though the lodges were the harbingers of the new science they still hankered back to the past. In this way they expressed the polarization in Enlightened thought between the past and the present. The Masons were intent upon creating a sense of their own history by generating fables relating to their own antiquity. As Ainsworth and Noyes point out, "Grave legend in Smart's day put the origin of Freemasonry coeval with the creation of the world".[77] In his *Constitutions*, Anderson mentions that Masons dated their calendar from the year of light, *anno lucis*, the "Year of Masonry", which they claimed marked the beginning of time when Freemasonry began. Accordingly the Masonic system of dating predates the Christian *anno Domini* by four thousand years. Thus it is not inappropriate that Smart should employ a Masonic level of meaning in his account of the seven days of creation as the following analysis will reveal.

*Alpha*

In the first stanza of the seven pillars section, Smart announces his theme:

> The pillars of the Lord are sev'n,
> Which stand from earth to topmost heav'n;
> His wisdom drew the plan;
> His WORD accomplish'd the design,
> From brightest gem to deepest mine,
> From CHRIST enthron'd to man (XXX)

Smart visualised the universe as a great temple supported by pillars stretching from the earth to heaven, which ostensibly represented the seven days of creation. Yet the image of seven pillars illustrating the seven orders of architecture appears within the arcana of Freemasonry during the 1760's (see plate 3).[78] Even the Masonic fraternity had been compared to a group of pillars, as the following lodge song reveals:

> Like pillars we stand,
> An immoveable band,
> Cemented by power from above;
> Then freely let pass
> The generous glass

To Masonry, friendship, and love.[79]

The association between "pillars" and "seven" was significant since, according to the Masons' catechism, seven was the number of people required for a "Just" and "Perfect" lodge.[80] The pillars which stand from earth to heaven in line two metaphorically extend from the floor to the ceiling of the lodge room which was decorated appropriately with pictures of the sun, clouds, moon and stars. In the next line "His wisdom drew the plan" Smart draws attention to the concept of God as the "Great Architect of the Universe" who was represented in the lodge by the Master Mason. In operative Masonry the Master drew up plans for the builders on a board supported by a trestle table which in speculative Masonry was replaced by a tracing board depicting the emblems of the craft. The idea of a plan or design is continued in line four with "His WORD accomplish'd the design". Here Smart venerates the creative power of the Christian *Logos*. The subordinate Masonic meaning relates to the legendary lost word which was the object of a ceremonial quest in the ritual of the Royal Arch. The search extended from the upper to the lower reaches of the lodge as a microcosm of the world which Smart describes as spanning "brightest gem to deepest mine". The polarity between "gem" and "mine" as represented on the "Great Chain of Being" is echoed in the final line: "From CHRIST enthron'd to man".

The following seven stanzas document the six days of creation followed by one day of rest which are inscribed upon the seven pillars of wisdom. In Masonic terms, the Alpha (XXXI), Gamma (XXXII) and Eta (XXXIII) stanzas refer respectively to the three degrees of Entered Apprentice, Fellowcraftsman and Master Mason. The first of these stanzas describes the initial impulse of creation when God created light:

> Alpha, the cause of causes, first
> In station, fountain, whence the burst
> Of light, and blaze of day;
> Whence bold attempt, and brave advance,
> Have motion, life, and ordinance,
> And heav'n itself its stay. (XXXI)

The name of the first pillar, alpha, bears a physical resemblance to the compass which Masons believed was used by the Great Architect to divide the day from the night. Through this imagery Smart draws a parallel between the creation of light and the initiation of a candidate into the first degree of Freemasonry who will be "first/In station". The prospective Entered Apprentice, who must pass from darkness into light, prepares for his admission ceremony by meditating alone in a dark room for several hours.[81] After this, he is blindfolded and led into the lodge room by a noose or cable-tow. The candidate is then asked what he is seeking and his reply to this question is "light". After undergoing various ritual ordeals, the blindfold is removed and he is rewarded by light, "whence the burst/Of light, and blaze of day". The setting for this symbolic illumination is physically dramatic since the lodge room is brightly lit up and the entire company are dressed in white, holding shining swords. After receiving the light, the initiate is told of the dangers he encountered while he was led blindfolded around the lodge with a cable-tow. In the alpha stanza, the following lines refer to this stage of the initiation ceremony:

> Whence bold attempt, and brave advance,
> Have motion, life, and ordinance.

The first line refers to the advice given to the candidate who must avoid reacting in fear and panic to his blind ordeal. During his circumambulation of the lodge, he is instructed to make a "bold attempt" (XXXI) for should he retreat, the noose will tighten around his neck. The second part of the line refers to another warning which relates to part of the ritual when the point of a poniard is placed on the candidate's left breast. He is advised to make a "brave advance" to the point of the sword for if he rushes forward rashly, he will pierce his own heart. Both of these actions, the "bold attempt" and the "brave advance", require "motion" and, if the wrong steps are taken, the candidate literally endangers his "life". The neophyte must learn to avert all danger by adhering to the Masonic code of virtue laid down in the "ordinances" of the lodge. In this way he will be able to combat evil by practising the qualities of bravery and boldness which he demonstrated during his initiation.

## Gamma

The next stanza is concerned with the second day of creation when God created the firmament by separating the waters above, from the waters below:

> Gamma supports the glorious arch
> On which angelic legions march,
> And is with sapphires pav'd; (XXXII)

The opening line "Gamma supports the glorious arch" announces a stanza containing symbols relevant to the second degree Freemason, the Fellowcraftsman. In the operative workings, the Fellowcraftsman was given the responsibility of carrying out independent work on arches while, in speculative Masonry, this degree of independence is achieved symbolically. In Smart's stanza, the capitalised form of gamma (Γ) resembles the physical shape of the carpenter's square and is symbolic of the Fellowcraftsman's pledge to live honestly "on the square" with his fellow man. The square is also related to the sign of the Fellowcraftsman through which he physically imitated the shape of a square by standing in a perpendicular position with his arm extended outwards to form a right angle. This could account for Smart's choice of the Greek letter gamma, signifying the second degree Mason, for the name of the pillar recording the second day of creation. After describing the heavens in the first half of stanza XXXII, Smart goes on to depict the sky:

> Thence the fleet clouds are sent adrift,
> And thence the painted folds, that lift
> The crimson veil, are wav'd.

Here he is referring to the interior of a lodge room since "fleet clouds" were painted on the ceiling. Samuel Prichard in his exposé, *Masonry Dissected* (1730), reveals the following "secret" from a Freemason's *viva voce* which states that the lodge ceiling was known as the "clouded Canopy":

> Q. What covering have you to the lodge?
> A. A clouded Canopy of divers colours (or the clouds).[82]

In the concluding line, the "crimson veil" is symbolic of the curtain of darkness which is drawn aside so that the Fellowcraftsman may have a further glimpse of the light of Freemasonry. Dorothy Griffiths suggests that the "crimson veil" might be a reference to the veil of Solomon's temple,[83] but in view of Smart's Christian outlook it would seem more likely that the image refers to the moment of the Crucifixion when "the veil of the temple was rent in twain" (Matthew 27: 51).[84] Early Freemasons had attached a Christian significance to the veil as indicated by the section "Questions concerning the Temple" in the Masonic *Dumfries* M.S. (circa 1710):

> 7  What doth the vaill signiffie?
> The son of god our lord jesus christ hanging upon y[e]
> alter of y[e] cross is y[e] true vaill yt is put betwe
> god & us shadowing w[t] his wounds and blood y[e] multitud
> of our offences.[85]

The image of the "crimson veil" must have been welcome to Smart who, as we have seen, took every opportunity to combine Christian and Masonic symbolism.

## Eta

In the following stanza (XXXIII) Smart deals with the third day of creation when God separated the land from the sea and created the vegetation. Eta is the name of the third pillar whose Masonic motif is that of the third degree, the Master Mason:

> Eta with living sculpture breathes,
> With verdant carvings, flow'ry wreathes
> Of never-wasting bloom;
> In strong relief his goodly base
> All instruments of labour grace,
> The trowel, spade, and loom.

The "living sculpture" refers to the trees and plants "Of never-wasting bloom" decorated on the pillar while the "instruments of labour" depicted on the base include the trowel, spade and loom. The nature-nurture theme of the pillar is explored through Masonic symbolism in a counterpoint between the human and divine. Eta is the eighth letter of the Greek alphabet, which bears a physical resemblance to Jacob's ladder, a Masonic emblem appearing on many breast jewels of the 1760 period.[86] It is a symbol of spiritual ascent illustrating the link from God to mankind which Smart refers to in the *Jubilate Agno:* *"For Jacob's Ladder are the steps of the Earth graduated hence to Paradise and thence to the throne of God"* (B, 392). Jacob's Ladder was traditionally associated with the Master Mason who was believed to have reached the highest rung of spiritual attainment. The illumination of the Master who was known as "darkness visible"[87] is symbolized by one of three candles in the lodge room called the three lesser lights. These represent the sun, moon, and Master while the three greater lights are emblematic of the Bible, the square and compasses. Smart's mention of the "sculpture", "carvings" and "flow'ry wreathes" refers to the decoration on the candle signifying the Master. As Jones points out "The candles that lit up the eighteenth-century lodges were thick and heavy, ornamented sometimes with "symbolic reliefs in white wax pressed on to the candle".[88] He also notes that the candles were sometimes supported by miniaturized pillars which were themselves Masonic symbols standing for wisdom, strength and beauty. These were miniature versions of the eta pillar described by Smart:

> In strong relief his goodly base
> . All instruments of labour grace,
> The trowel, spade, and loom.

The "goodly base" of the pillar alludes to the moral stabiliy of the Master Mason. Such didacticism was popular in contemporary Masonic songs as the following extract reveals:

> A glorious pillar rais'd on high,
>   Integrity its base.
> Peace adds to olive boughs, entwin'd,
>   An emblematic dove,
> As stamp'd upon the mason's mind,
>   Are unity and love.[89]

The "trowel, spade, and loom" mentioned in the last line are all emblematic working tools associated with the third degree.[90] The trowel symbolizes charity with which the Master "cemented" brotherly love in the lodge, while the spade is the implement he used to remove all traces of worldliness from his soul. Finally, the loom represented purity since it evoked the memory of Hiram Abif weaving fine linen and fine wool for the hangings of King Solomon's temple who would:

> Keep from commixtures foul and fond,
> Nor work thy flax with wool. (XLV)

Smart advocated the purity practised by Hiram who wove the wool and the linen (flax) separately so that the fibres would remain fine or pure.


*Theta*

The theta stanza occupies a central position in the series of Greek letters perhaps because its shape (Θ) resembles two Masonic symbols for God, the All-Seeing Eye and the point-within-the-circle.[91]

> Next Theta stands to the Supreme -
> Who form'd, in number, sign, and scheme,
>    Th' illustrious lights that are;
> And one address'd his saffron robe,
> And one, clad in a silver globe,
>    Held rule with ev'ry star. (XXXIV)

The first line acknowledges Christ's position on the right hand of God - "the Supreme" - who, on the fourth day, created the sun, moon and stars in order to separate the day from the night. Smart's stanza corresponds closely to the description of the fourth day of creation given in Genesis. Despite this overt level of meaning, it is also possible to make a Masonic interpretation of this stanza. In this case the word "sign" may be decoded as a reference to the secret signals used by a Freemason as a means of communication. Smart's mention of "number" refers to a "charge" or "order" to all Masons to add to their knowledge of the craft by progressing through the various degrees. The third word of the trilogy "number, sign, and scheme" alludes to the Great Architect's plan for mankind which the Master Mason mimes with the aid of a tracing-board. The sun and moon are "Th' illustrious lights that are" which are represented in the lodge by the three lesser lights mentioned earlier which denote sun, moon, and the Master of the lodge.[92] Two of these lights, the sun and the moon, are described in the second half of the stanza:

> And one address'd his saffron robe,
> And one, clad in a silver globe,
> Held rule with ev'ry star.

The final line refers in terms of Freemasonry to the "blazing star" which was painted on the ceiling of every lodge room. The line "Held rule with ev'ry star" may be another way of saying "Held rule with ev'ry lodge".

Even though the archetypal images of the sun and moon are Masonic symbols, Smart's metaphors belong to the language of alchemy which betrays the transmission of Rosicrucian teaching into the craft. In the *Jubilate Agno* (B, p.111) Smart refers to the sun and the moon in the context of marriage. Hermetically this represented the fusion between the solar and lunar principles of sulphur and mercury which were vital ingredients in the alchemical process. Another link with alchemy in stanza XXXIV arises out of Shepard and Wood's claim that theta (Θ) physically resembles the symbol of the All-Seeing Eye [93] which, according to Jones, was derived from the alchemists:

> Some masonic symbols were almost certainly introduced by the alchemists, as, for instance, the all-seeing eye, a symbol of very great antiquity representing the ever-watchful and omnipresent Deity and, as a Christian symbol, supported by a host of biblical references. Even in its Masonic form of an open eye within a triangle it has been used as a Church emblem, but it came to Freemasonry much more probably from alchemy than from Christian symbolism.[94]

Smart makes direct reference to the image of the All-Seeing Eye in one of his *Hymns for the Amusement of Children* (1775):

> These cloaths, of which I now divest
> Myself, ALL-SEEING EYE,
> Must be one day (that day be blest)
> Relinquish'd and laid by.
> (II, p.365).

Despite Shepard and Wood's assertion that theta refers to the All-Seeing Eye, there is very little resemblance between the two figures. It is more likely that theta relates to the other Masonic symbol for God, the point-within-the-circle. Once again it is possible that this figure was imported into Freemasonry from alchemy since it is identical to the hermetic symbol for gold which is also the astrological sign for the sun, the planet which ruled gold. Whether Smart is referring to the All-Seeing Eye or the point-within-the-circle is not of paramount importance since both Masonic symbols refer to the Creator, and even the letter theta (Θ) is the initial of the Greek word for God, Θεοϗ.

## *Iota*

The name of the next stanza, iota, describes the fifth day when God created "those that fly" and swim. Smart compares this Greek letter to the string of a musical instrument, an image which is highly appropriate in a poem about David the harpist:[95]

> Iota's tun'd to choral hymns
> Of those that fly, while he that swims
> In thankful safety lurks. (XXXV)

A Masonic reading suggests that iota symbolizes the plumb-line which is another working tool associated with the Fellowcraftsman. The plumb-line represented the moral rectitude of the second degree Mason who was known figuratively as the pillar of his lodge. This relates to the second part of Smart's stanza since the "foot...chapitre and niche" of the fourth line refer to parts of a pillar. It may be significant that the secret password for the Fellowcraftsman was "Jachin", the name for one of the two pillars, Jachin and Boas, which had stood at the porch of King Solomon's Temple. Smart mentions the two pillars which were cast in bronze by Hiram Abif in Psalm LXXVIII:

> There pillar'd up with molten brass,
> His temple stands secure,
> Made like the earth's continual mass
> For ever to endure.
> (Callan, I, p.579)

According to the *Old Charges* or early Masonic manuscripts the pillars were made hollow "to serve as archives to Masonry, and to hold the Constitutional Rolls".[96] This suggests an additional meaning to the second part of stanza XXXV where Smart ostensibly describes the pillar which records the fifth day of creation:

> And foot, and chapitre, and niche,
> The various histories enrich
> Of God's recorded works. (XXV)

For Freemasons, the "various histories" would refer to the constitutions and official histories of the craft while God's "recorded works" allude to the archives which consisted of early documents appertaining to operative Masonry. In this context the "niche" is the recess in the pillar where these "Constitutional Rolls" were stored. The "foot" mentioned in the fourth line is the base of the pillar which contrasts with the "chapitre" or top.

### Sigma

The sixth pillar commemorates the creation of mankind and the land animals on the sixth day:

> Sigma presents the social droves,
> With him that solitary roves,
> And man of all the chief;
> Fair on whose face, and stately frame,
> Did God impress his hallow'd name,
> For ocular belief. (XXXVI)

The "social droves" presented by sigma indicate the gregariousness of the animal kingdom in contrast to the individualism of human beings. Towards the end of the stanza, Smart reveals how God made man in His own image which is described in Genesis, 1: 26-7.

> And God said, "Let us make man in our image after our likeness: and let them have dominion over the fish of the sea, and over the fowl of the aire, and over the catell, [sic] and over all the earth, and over every creeping thing that creepeth upon the earth." So God created man in His own image, in the image of God created He him.

In a Masonic interpretation of stanza XXXVI, he "that solitary roves" is the itinerant Master Mason who is free to travel in search of labour being "man of all the chief." William Hauser suggests that the end of the stanza is an evocation of the well-known Masonic emblem, the compasses superimposed on the square and surrounding the letter "G" which is the initial of God.[97] He states that this emblem, which was emblazoned on the Master's apron, becomes the "ocular belief" of the final line of the stanza. The Greek letter beginning this stanza is sigma ($\Sigma$) which resembles the three-jointed four-cubit rule used in the operative trade. In speculative Masonry this working tool was employed as a symbol of moral rectitude and is mentioned by Smart in his poem "Reason and Imagination": "Take thou this compass and this rule" (Callan, I, p.81).

### Omega

Omega ($\Omega$) is the name given to the pillar in the next stanza (XXXVII) of this section which commemorates the day of rest following the six days of creation:

> OMEGA! GREATEST and the BEST,
> Stands sacred to the day of rest,

> For gratitude and thought;
> Which bless'd the world upon his pole,
> And gave the universe his goal,
> And clos'd th' infernal draught.    (XXXVII)

The shape of omega resembles the dome of King Solomon's Temple, the name given to the ceiling of the lodge room. Omega may also represent the symbol of the Grand Pontiff, a nineteenth degree, which was in existence by 1758.[98] Since it is unlikely that Smart advanced to such a high degree it is more probable that he was referring to the insignia of the fourth degree of the "Royal Arch" which had been implemented during this period. Significantly, Freemasons describe the "Royal Arch" as the alpha and omega of the craft. Stanza XXXVII completes Smart's series of Greek letters from alpha to omega, a symbolism traditionally associated with Christ who declared "I am the Alpha and Omega, the beginning and the end, the first and the last (Revelation 22:13)." In the *Jubilate Agno* Smart wrote "*For Christ being* A *and* Ω *is all the intermediate letters without doubt*". (C, 18) The idea of spiritual regeneration is conveyed through alpha and omega as representative of the cycle of death and rebirth engineered by the Creator who

> bless'd the world upon his pole,
> And gave the universe his goal,
> And clos'd th' infernal draught.

In Smart's metaphor, the world is the circle symbolizing the female principle of fecundity while the pole represents the male. Like alpha and omega, the circle represents eternity since it has neither beginning nor end. Its perfect figure is achieved by means of a compass which is signified by alpha in stanza XXXI. The enigmatic last line of the stanza "clos'd th' infernal draught" refers to the attainment of salvation when the plan of creation and man's mortal state of sin will be discarded forever. Theologically "th' infernal draught" refers to Christ's hallowing of hell by way of analogy with the parable of the draught of fishes where the Messiah is represented as a fisher of souls (Matthew, 13: 47-50). In terms of Freemasonry the "draught" is directly related to the tracing-board, the chart of secret emblems drawn on the floor of the lodge with chalk and charcoal. At the close of a lodge meeting, the tracing-board was ceremoniously wiped off the floor to ensure that "the profane might not ... gain any insight into [the] mysteries".[99] This final ritual constitutes the Freemasons' equivalent of omega, signifying the end of a Masonic gathering.

According to Ainsworth and Noyes, the next stanza, which concludes the seven pillars section, continues the idea of David the Mason:[100]

> O DAVID, scholar of the Lord!

41

> Such is thy science, whence reward
> And infinite degree;
> O strength, O sweetness, lasting ripe
> God's harp thy symbol, and thy type
> The lion and the bee! (XXXVIII)

In Masonic terms this stanza is a reminder of the amount of study required for a Mason wishing to progress through the various degrees of the craft. In his hymn, "Taste" (1770) Smart makes the Socratic equation between knowledge and virtue:

> Who reads the most, is most refin'd,
> And polish'd by the Master's hand.
> (II, p.341)

The spiritual state of a newly-initiated Freemason is symbolized by a rough ashlar or unhewn stone which will be "polish'd by the Master's hand". Eventually through the study of the Scriptures and the teachings of Freemasonry, he will become a perfect ashlar or polished stone. The perfect ashlar was also represented by the precious stone or gem set into the Master's signet ring which Smart describes as "The jasper of the master's stamp" (XXVI).[101]

The theme of learning in the first line of the poem is continued with reference to knowledge through the word "science" derived from the Latin *scientia*, (knowledge):

> O DAVID, scholar of the Lord!
> Such is thy science, whence reward
> And infinite degree.

In early Masonic songs, the lodge was often valued as a centre for scientific pursuits:

> On Virtue's tablet marks HER moral rule,
> And forms her lodge an universal school;
> Where Nature's mystic laws unfolded stand,
> And Sense and Science join'd, go hand in hand.[102]

The "infinite degree" in the third line of stanza XXXVII is a compliment to Smart's Masonic hero whose wisdom has enabled him to progress beyond the trigradal system to the highest of all degrees. Smart also flatters David by describing him as a lion, a popular heraldic emblem which appeared on the coat of arms of the Grand Lodge of England.[103] Smart's reference to the lion and the bee are metaphors for strength and sweetness based on the account in Judges 14: 8 of how Samson found a swarm of bees and honey in the carcass of a lion which he had recently slain. This typology of death and rebirth, destruction and regeneration in the last line makes an appropriate conclusion for a set of stanzas dealing with the Creation.

## The Glory of God and Freemasonry

The structure of the *Song to David* has Masonic significance since Smart used key-words and groups of stanzas to formulate numerical patterns. The most obvious example of this may be seen in the repetition of the word "adoration" which appears in twenty one consecutive stanzas (LI-LXXI). In the libretto and score of *The Magic Flute* (1791) Mozart employed Masonic number systems, mainly threes, fives and sevens, which may be traced back to Pythagorean numerology.[104] Sequences of numbers would be used in Masonic rites of initiation. The novitiate Mason ceremonially gained admission to the lodge by knocking on the door in a series of threes. Smart builds up his *Song* on stanzas grouped in threes and sevens and their multiples.[105] This strategy turns the poem into a sacred chant which underlies the rhetoric of ritual. The reiteration of the word "Glorious" in the last three verses (LXXXIV-LXXXVI) is a refrain which subdivides the final section of the poem.

The prominence Smart has given to the word "Glorious" in his litany suggests that it is a trigger-word serving as a common denominator for both his Christian and Masonic affinities. In a climactic ending to the poem Smart lists his priorities in ascending order since the first stanza contains veiled references to Freemasonry, the second to the worship of God while the third is wholly concerned with the adoration of Christ. In Freemasonry the word "Glorious" is abbreviated by the letter "G" which was always visible in the centre of the ceiling of the lodge room. According to the Mason's catechism it signified three things: "Glory, Grandeur and Geometry" which were expounded as "Glory is to God, Grandeur to the master of the lodge, and Geometry, which is ranked as the fifth science, for all the brothers."[106] Smart would have been aware that in Masonic circles the word "Glory" or "Glorious" was also an epithet for God particularly since the letter "G" designated his sacred initial.

In the Masonic stanza LXXXIV, the first of the eulogistic trio, Smart ostensibly glorifies the cosmos:

> Glorious the sun in mid career;
> Glorious th' assembled fires appear;
> Glorious the comet's train;
> Glorious the trumpet and alarm;
> Glorious th' almighty stretch'd-out arm;
> Glorious th' enraptur'd main;
>
> (LXXXIV)

To a Freemason, line one points to the time when a Masonic initiation traditionally took place "when the sun is at its meridian" or "in mid career". The second line "Glorious th' assembled fires appear" praises the beauty of the stars. The imagery is also applicable to the moment in the ceremony when the neophyte is exposed to light:

> The lights, the glitter of the swords, the fantastick
> ornaments borne by the grand officers, the appearance
> of all the Brethren in white aprons, all this together
> makes a dazzling sight for a person who had been two
> hours in the dark.[107]

Maybe Smart was recalling his own admission into Freemasonry since the blinding revelation of his brethren, "th' assembled fires," imprinted on him a vivid memory of the event. In this context the "trumpet and alarm" in line four refers to the devices used to frighten the candidate while he is blindfolded and in a state of darkness. The "almighty stretch'd out arm" of God is represented by the Master of the lodge who ritually embraces the neophyte kneeling before him. The iconography of the lodge room is mentioned in the third line where Smart writes "Glorious the comet's train". Like the letter "G", the "blazing star" with its comet's tail was drawn on the ceiling of the lodge. According to Walton Hannah, the "blazing star" symbolized the bright morning star whose rising brings peace and salvation to the faithful and obedient of the human race.[108] He goes on to claim that the star represents the Luciferianism of the Freemasons who seek to rekindle the spiritual light extinguished by the Fall of Mankind.

Within the symphonic structure of the *Song to David* Smart has orchestrated a Masonic level of meaning which provided him with another means of praising God and the Creation. The poet's cryptic references to the craft would suggest that he was still abiding by his vow of secrecy to the brotherhood. This analysis of the influence of Freemasonry on the poem is not intended to imply that *A Song to David* is an exclusively Masonic work. On the contrary, Freemasonry is just one of many intricate patterns which make up this devotional lyric. Through verse Smart transmitted his experiences both as a Christian visionary and as the initiate of a secret society. Perhaps only through the aesthetic imagination of poetry could he communicate his revelationary knowledge of the mysteries of Masonry. The poetic idea that the fraternity guarded a hidden code of communication is expressed in a Masonic song:

> The use of accents from thy aid is thrown,
> Thou forms't a silent language of thy own:
> Disdain'st that records should contain thy art,
> And only liv'st within the faithful heart.[109]

This verse refers to the silent and symbolic language of Masonry which may only be relayed to the outside world through the poetic truth of the "poet's lays". Smart's celebration of the craft through his poetry was both clandestine and ostentatious.

craft through his poetry was both clandestine and ostentatious. Along with Burns he would have agreed with the poet who once wrote of the Freemasons:

> Heroes and kings revere their name,
> While Poets sing their lasting fame.[110]

**Notes**

1. "A Collection of Masons' Odes and Songs", added to *A Defence of Freemasonry* (London, 1765), p.64.

2. See Arthur Sherbo, *Christopher Smart: Scholar of the University* (Michigan, 1967), p.279n.

3. "A Collection of Masons' Odes and Songs", p.64.

4. *The Poetical Works of Christopher Smart*, ed. Karina Williamson (Oxford, 1980), I, p.29. This edition of the *Jubilate Agno* will be used throughout. References to Smart's other poems including *A Song to David* will be from vol. II edited by Karina Williamson and Marcus Walsh (Oxford, 1983). Other quotations will be taken from *The Collected Poems of Christopher Smart* (London, 1949) hereafter referred to as Callan.

5. See Sherbo, *Christopher Smart: Scholar of the University*, pp.266-9.

6. For a useful background see chapter 23 "Private Madhouses: A Fine Trade" in Ida Macalpine and Richard Hunter, *George III and the Mad-Business* (London, 1969), pp.322-8.

7. See Michael Macdonald, *Mystical Bedlam: Madness, anxiety and healing in Seventeenth-Century England* (Cambridge, 1981), p.122

8. Sherbo, *Christopher Smart: Scholar of the University*, pp.266-9

9. Sherbo, "The Probable Time of Composition of Christopher Smart's *Song to David, Psalms*, and *Hymns and Spiritual Songs*", *Journal of English and Germanic Philology*, LV (Jan.,1956), p.54.

10. See *Rejoice in the Lamb: A Song from Bedlam*, ed. William Force Stead (London, 1939).

11. John Middleton Murry, *Discoveries* (London, 1930), pp.198-9. See also Charles David Abbott, "Christopher Smart's Madness," *Publications of the Modern Language Association of America*, XLV (Dec., 1939), pp.1014-22.

12. Michel Foucault, *Madness and Civilization: A History of*

*Insanity in the Age of Reason* (London, 1967), pp.288-9.

13. Theodor Adorno and Max Horkheimer, *Dialectic of Enlightenment*, trans. J. Cumming (London, 1973), p.28.

14. W. Russell Brain, "Christopher Smart: The Flea that Became an Eagle", *Medical Bookman and Historian*, II, no. 7 (July, 1948), p.297.

15. Ibid, p.298.

16. *Boswell's "Life of Johnson"*, ed. G.B. Hill revised L.F. Powell, 6 vols (Oxford, 1934-50), I, p.397.

17. Thomas Gray wrote this in a letter to Wharton dated March 1747, no. 135 in *Correspondence of Thomas Gray*, ed. Toynbee Paget and Leonard Whibley (Oxford, 1935), I, p.275. Sherbo points out that between 1753-1754, the poet gave benefit performances for "Decay'd and Antient Masons" and for "a Free Mason". See *Christopher Smart: Scholar of the University*, p. 81.

18. *Boswell's Life of Johnson*, ed. G.B. Hill, 1, p.397.

19. See Hester Lynch Piozzi (Mrs Thrale), *British Synonymy; or, An Attempt at Regulating the Choice of Words in Familiar Conversation*, 2 vols (London, 1794), II, pp.5-6. Here she suggests that "LUNACY seems to be the legal term, INSANITY, and sometimes MELANCHOLY, the medical ones; while PHRENZY, MADNESS and DISTRACTION are the poetical expressions of what we call MENTAL DERANGEMENT, Ibid, II, p.6.

20. *Boswell's "Life of Johnson"* ed. G.B. Hill, I, p.397. See also chapter 5 "Irrationality and Madness in seventeenth and eighteenth-century Europe" in George Rosen, *Madness in Society* (London, 1968) pp.151-71.

21. *Thraliana: The Diary of Mrs Hester Lynch Thrale* (later Mrs Piozzi) 1776-1809, ed. Katherine C. Balderston, 2 vols (Oxford, 1951), 11, p.728.

22. John Browne, *An Estimate of the Manners and Principles of the Times* (London, 1757), p.15.

23. See *The Spirit of Prayer: or The Soul rising out of the Vanity of Time, into the Riches of Eternity* (1949) in *The Works of William Law*, ed. G.B. Morgan, 9 vols (Brockenhurst, 1892-93), VII.

24. Albert J. Kuhn, "Christopher Smart: The Poet as Patriot of the Lord," *English Literary History*, XXX (June, 1963), p.123.

25. See Charles I. Paton, *Freemasonry: Its Symbolism, Religious*

*Nature and Law of Perfection* (London, 1873) pp.444-5.

26. For further information see Samuel Beswick, *The Swedenborg Rite and the Great Masonic Leaders of the Eighteenth Century*, (New York, 1870).

27. See James Anderson, *Constitutions of the Ancient Fraternity of Free and Accepted Masons* (1723), ed. John Noorthouck (London, 1748), p.35. Hereafter cited as *Constitutions* (1723).

28. Pick and Knight, *History of Freemasonry*, p.88.

29. "Act concerning the Mason Oath", *Scots Magazine,* XIX (Aug., 1757), p.432.

30. The Latin main title is taken from William H. Bond's edition, *Jubilate Agno* (London, 1954). The English subtitle is derived from Stead's edition, *Rejoice in the Lamb: A Song from Bedlam.*

31. Alexander Pope, "Essay on Man", *The Poems of Alexander Pope*, ed. John Butt (London, 1963), p.511.

32. It is widely believed that Smart was influenced by Robert Lowth's *De Sacra Poesi Hebraeorum* (Oxford, 1753) which draws attention to the technique of parallelism used in Hebrew poetry. W.H. Bond argues that Smart's "For" section in the *Jubilate Agno* is really a response to a corresponding "Let" section. See *Jubilate Agno* ed. Bond, pp.17-18. Karina Williamson, "Christopher Smart's Hymns and Spiritual Songs," *Philological Quarterly,* XXXVIII (1959), p.423.

33. See Samuel Prichard, *Masonry Dissected* (London,1730), pp.26-7.

34. See Alex Horne, *King Solomon's Temple in the Masonic Tradition,* (Wellingborough, 1972), p.289. The development of the Hiramic tradition may be traced through three anonymous pamphlets; *Hiram: or, the Grand Master-key to the door of both Antient and Modern Freemasonry. By a member of the Royal Arch*, 2nd ed. (London, 1766), *Jachin and Boaz or an Authentic key to the Door of Free-Masonry — both ancient and modern,* (London, 1797) and *The Three Distinct Knocks or The Door of the Most Antient Free-Masonry opening to all Men, neither Naked nor Cloath'd, Bare-foot nor shod* (London, 1785).

35. Walton Hannah, *Darkness Visible: A Revelation and Interpretation of Freemasonry* (London, 1952), p.68.

36. Loc. cit.

37. See A.E. Waite, *A New Encyclopaedia of Freemasonry and of*

*Cognate Instituted Mysteries: Their Rites, Literature and History,* 2 vols (London, 1925), II, pp.265-66.

38. *Poems by Christopher Smart,* ed. Robert E. Brittain (New Jersey, 1950), p.50.

39. See Robert Shackleton, "The Encyclopédie and Freemasonry," *The Age of Enlightenment,* ed. W.H. Barber, J.H. Brumfitt, R.A. Leigh, R. Shackleton and S.S.B. Taylor (London, 1967), p.224.

40. See Hannah, *Darkness Visible,* pp.34-5.

41. John Fellows, *The Mysteries of Freemasonry* (London, 1877), p.283.

42. *Rite Ancien de Bouillon: An Old English Ritual* (1740), ed. John T. Thorp (Leicester, 1926), p.18.

43. Quoted by Sherbo in "Christopher Smart, Free and Accepted Mason", *Journal of English and Germanic Philology,* LIV (Oct., 1955), p.665.

44. Loc. cit.

45. Bernard E. Jones, *The Freemasons' Guide and Compendium* (London, 1956), p.317.

46. See Sherbo, "Christopher Smart, Free and Accepted Mason", p.665.

47. For a further discussion of the bee as a Masonic emblem see George W. Bullamore, "The Beehive and Freemasonry", *Ars Quatuor Coronatorum,* XXXVI (1923), pp 219-33.

48. Jonathan Swift, *Prose Works,* ed. Herbert Davis, 14 vols (Oxford, 1939-68), V, p.327. Regarding the uncertain authorship Davis admits that the letter "was printed among Swift's works in the eighteenth century, and is still accepted in some quarters", V, p.358.

49. Ibid, V, p.328.

50. See Ezra 3:2 and Haggai 1:12-14, 2:2-5, 21-23.

51. See Bernard E. Jones, *Freemasons' Book of the Royal Arch* (London, 1957).

52. See John A. Grantham, "An Introduction to Mark Masonry", *Transactions of Manchester Association for Masonic Research,* XXIII (Nov., 1933), pp. 124-96.

53. Pick and Knight, *The Pocket History of Freemasonry*, p.214.

54. See Sherbo, "Christopher Smart's knowledge of Occult Literature", *Journal of the History of Ideas*, XVIII (April, 1957), p.234.

55. Quoted by Jones, *The Freemasons' Guide and Compendium*, p.504.

56. Thomas de Quincey, *Works*, ed. David Masson (Edinburgh, 1880), XVI, pp.413-4.

57. *Early Masonic Pamphlets*, ed. Douglas Knoop, G.P. Jones and Douglas Hamer (Manchester, 1945), p.44.

58. See Jones, *The Freemasons' Guide and Compendium*, pp.413-14.

59. The sophisticated thunder and lightning machines devised for this purpose were later innovations which were used in the American lodges of the nineteenth century.

60. *Early Masonic Pamphlets*, ed. Knoop, Jones and Hamer, p.44.

61. This appears in a letter from William Mason to Thomas Gray dated June 1763. See Letter 371 in *Correspondence of Thomas Gray*, ed. Toynbee and Whibley, II, p.802.

62. Christopher Devlin, *Poor Kit Smart* (London, 1961), p.13.

63. *The Poetical works of Christopher Smart*, ed. Walsh and Williamson, II, p.103.

64. See Robert Browning, *Works* (London, 1912), X, p.181.

65. Edward G. Ainsworth and Charles E. Noyes, *Christopher Smart: A Biographical and Critical Study* (Columbia, 1943), pp.121-2.

66. See Sherbo, "Christopher Smart, Free and Accepted Mason", p.664.

67. See Horne, *King Solomon's Temple in the Masonic Tradition*, p.99.

68. *Early Masonic Pamphlets*, ed. Knoop, Jones and Hamer, p.77.

69. *The Free-Masons' Melody, Being A General Collection of Masonic Songs* (Bury, 1818), p.222.

70. *Early Masonic Pamphlets*, ed. Knoop, Jones and Hamer, p.263.

71. *Proposals for Printing, by Subscription, a New Translation of the*

*Psalms of David*, 8 September 1763.

72. See *Monthly Review*, XXVIII (April, 1763), pp.320-21.

73. See *English Prose and Poetry, 1600-1800*, ed. Odell Shepard and Paul Spencer Wood (Boston, 1934), p.1020.

74. See William Hauser, "An Analysis of the Structure, Influences and Diction of Christopher Smart's *A Song to David*", unpublished Ph.D. thesis (University of Pittsburg, 1963), p.128.

75. William Preston, *Illustrations of Masonry* (London, 1778), no. xxxvii.

76. Ibid., no. xviii.

77. Ainsworth and Noyes, *Christopher Smart*, p.121.

78. "A Masonic Engravings of 1769", *Transactions of Leicester Association for Masonic Research*, XXI (1912-13), p.138. For a Talmudic interpretation of the seven pillars see Katherine M. Rogers, "The Pillars of the Lord: Some Sources of *A Song to David*," *Philological Quarterly*, XL (Oct., 1961), pp.525-34.

79. *The Free-Masons' Melody*, p.206.

80. See Prichard, *Masonry Dissected*, p.10.

81. See *Solomon in all his Glory: or, The Master-Mason being a True Guide to the inmost recesses of Free-Masonry* (London, 1768), p.6.

82. *Masonry Dissected*, p.13.

83. See Dorothy Griffiths, "The Poetry of Christopher Smart", unpublished Ph.D. thesis (University of Leeds, 1951), p.402.

84. The edition used throughout chapter 2 is *The King James Bible* (1611) (Cambridge, 1624).

85. *Early Masonic Catechisms*, (Manchester, 1943), p.59.

86. See Jones, *Freemasons' Guide and Compendium*, p.405.

87. See Hannah, *Darkness Visible*, ii.

88. Jones, *Freemasons' Guide and Compendium*, p.360.

89. *The Free-Masons' Melody*, p.102.

90. See Hauser, "An Analysis of ... *A Song to David*", pp.134-5.

91. Ibid., pp.135-6.

92. See Jones, *Freemasons' Guide*, pp.360-1.

93. See *English Prose and Poetry*, ed. Shepard and Wood, p.1020.

94. Jones, *Freemasons' Guide and Compendium*, p.121.

95. See Christopher M. Dennis's discussion of the harp in "A Structural Conceit in Smart's *Song to David*", *Review of English Studies*, XXIX, no. 115 (1978), pp.257-66.

96. Horne, *King Solomon's Temple*, p.218.

97. See Hauser, "An Analysis of ... *A Song to David*", pp.138-9.

98. See Albert G. Mackey, *An Encyclopaedia of Freemasonry*, 2 vols. (New York, 1912), I, p.308.

99. *Solomon in all his Glory*, p.25.

100. See Ainsworth and Noyes, *Christopher Smart*, p.122.

101. Another example appears in Psalm CXLV, "Truth is the signet of thy ring" (Callan, II, p.773).

102. Preston, *Illustrations of Masonry*, p.278.

103. See Jones, *Freemasons' Guide*, p.551.

104. See Jacques Chailley, *The Magic Flute, Masonic Opera* (London, 1972), p.160.

105. See Raymond D. Havens, "The Structure of Smart's *Song to David*", *Review of English Studies*, XIV (April, 1938), pp.178-82.

106. *Solomon in all his Glory*, p.22

107. *A Master-key to Freemasonry* (London, 1760), p.16.

108. Hannah, *Darkness Visible*, p.60n.

109. *The Free-Masons' Melody*, p.309.

110. Ibid., p.222.

# 3 ROBERT BURNS

"To MASONRY and SCOTIA dear!"

Burns[1]

## The Freemasons' Poet-Laureate

Robert Burns (1759-96) who is renowned as "the prince o' poets an' o' ploughmen"[2] was also a bard of the Freemasons. He rose through the Masonic ranks to become an ambassador for the fraternity earning the accolade of being the first Poet-Laureate of the lodges. In view of the importance which Burns attached to his Masonic membership, it is curious that the influence of Freemasonry on his life and work should have been underestimated by so many of his biographers and critics.[3] Masonry actively furthered Burns's career by bringing him into contact with a number of writers and patrons who helped establish his reputation as a poet.[4] In turn, Burns derived poetic inspiration from the craft and conveyed through his poetry his sense of commitment and loyalty to the Freemasons.

Burns's Masonic career began on 4 July 1781 when, at the age of 23, he was initiated into St David's lodge, no. 174, Tarbolton. He had been introduced to the fraternity by John Ranken of Adam Hill to whom he dedicated a number of poems including "Epistle to John Ranken" and "Lines to John Ranken". In compliance with the entrance requirements of the lodge, Ranken would have vouched for the poet's good character. Burns was then admitted into the order by Alexander Wood, a local tailor, who charged him an entrance fee of twelve shillings and sixpence. His initiation was recorded in the lodge minutes as "*sederant* for July 4th (1781) Robert Burns in Lochly was entered an apprentice."[5] According to tradition the ceremony took place in Mason's Tavern, situated in what is now known as Burns Street. From then on Burns progressed rapidly through the tripartite system of Masonic degrees even though he spent much of his time at Irvine where he was learning the craft of flax-dressing.[6] Three months after his initiation as an Entered Apprentice, he advanced to the second degree of Fellowcraftsman and then to the third degree of Master Mason. Burns's progress was registered in the minutes of the lodge meeting for 1 October which announced "Robert Burns in Lochly was passed and raised."[7]

Burns's involvement with Scottish Freemasonry coincided with a turbulent period in its history. Ten years earlier, the Grand Lodge of Scotland had been seeking to centralise the craft. The original St James's Kilwinning lodge, Tarbolton, had resisted this move with the result that twenty malcontent members who had wanted the sanction of Grand Lodge left in protest to form a new lodge called St James, no. 174. Eventually, the former dissenting Tarbolton lodge agreed to be affiliated with Grand Lodge whereupon it was renamed St James, no. 178. Inevitably, rivalry grew up between the two lodges until the Scottish Grand Lodge authorised them to merge together under the name of St David on 25 June 1781. But the wrangles were not yet over. Members who had originally belonged to the St James's lodge complained about losing their former identity through the merger. Burns, who had been initiated into the united lodge, sympathised with the St James's faction and defected with them in 1784 to form a new lodge. Less clear was the attitude of officials at Grand Lodge. Had they sanctioned the manoeuvre or did it constitute Masonic mutiny? Burns wrote to the Master of the lodge, Sir John Whitefoord, of Ballochmyle who had been the Senior Grand Warden of Scotland, urging him to investigate the matter:

> We have considerable sums in bills which lye by without being paid, or put in execution, and many of our members never mind their yearly dues, or anything else belonging to the Lodge. And since the separation from St David's, we are not sure even of our existence as as [sic] a Lodge.- Their [sic] has been a dispute before the Grand Lodge, but how decided, or if decided at all, we know not.[8]

By helping to rescue St James's Lodge from bankruptcy Burns was instrumental in preventing it from being outlawed by the Grand Lodge of Scotland. Hans Hecht mentions the role Burns played in preserving a lodge which had contributed to the local community "St James was resuscitated through a secession in which Burns took part, and from that time onward exercised considerable influence on the intellectual life of Tarbolton and its immediate vicinity."[9] Burns's concern for his Masonic brethren during this period of uncertainty was an important factor in his election to Depute-Master of the lodge on 27 July 1784, an office which he commemorated in his poem, "The Farewell. To the Brethren of St James's Lodge, Tarbolton" (1786). As Depute-Master Burns was effectively in charge since the office of Worshipful Master tended to be an honorary position usually reserved for an absentee member of the aristocracy. Nevertheless the head of St James's, Sir John Whitefoord, was not such a remote figure since he was a close friend of Burns who remembered him as follows:

> Thou, who thy honour as thy God
>     rever'st,
> Who, save thy *mind's reproach*, nought
>     earthly fear'st
> To thee this votive off'ring I impart,
> The tearful tribute of a broken heart.

> The *Friend* thou valued'st, I, the *Patron* lov'd;
> His worth, his honour, all the world approv'd.
> We'll mourn till we too go as he has gone,
> And tread the shadowy path to that dark world
>      unknown   (II, p.585)

Burns proved to be such a popular Depute-Master that he was re-elected to the post in July 1786 until St John's Day in 1788. While Burns was in office, the brethren expressed dissatisfaction with their meeting-place in Mason's Tavern. Burns supported their campaign for a purpose-built Freemason's lodge which was described in the minutes of 5 June as follows:

> It was proposed by the Lodge, that as they much
> wanted a lodge-room, a proposal be laid before
> the heritors, who are intending to build a
> steeple here, that the lodge shall contribute to
> the building of a *lodge-room as the basis of a
> steeple*, and that from the funds of the lodge they
> offer fifteen pounds, besides what will be advanced
> from the particular friends of the lodge; in order
> that this proposal be properly laid before the
> heritors, five persons - namely, the Right Worshipful
> Master, Brother M'Math, *Brother Burns*, Brother
> Wodrow, Brother William Andrews - are appointed to
> meet on Saturday at one o'clock, to draw up a
> proposal to lay before the heritors on Friday
> first.[10]

There is no indication that this proposal ever materialised. But an adequate meeting-place was essential for the fraternity's social functions and rituals particularly those of initiation. By all accounts Burns presided over these ceremonies with great enthusiasm. According to Robert Chambers, Burns was "so keen a mason, that he would hold lodges for the admission of new members in his own house."[11] During one Masonic gathering, Burns even initiated his own brother, Gilbert.[12] But the first man Burns is believed to have admitted into the craft was Matthew Hall, a musician who accompanied James M'Lauchlan, the violinist of traditional Scottish music. Burns mentions M'Lauchlan in his poem, "The Brigs of Ayr", which commemorates the building of a bridge across the river Ayr:

> While arts of Minstrelsy among them rung,
> And soul-ennobling Bards heroic ditties sung.
> O had *M'Lauchlan*, thairm-inspiring Sage,
> Been there to hear this heavenly band engage.
>                               (I, p.288)

Burns extended his Masonic contacts by gaining admittance into another lodge, the Canongate Kilwinning, Edinburgh, in 1787.

Earlier that year, on 6 February, the Prince of Wales was initiated into Freemasonry at the Star and Garter, London. The Canongate Kilwinning lodge responded by calling a meeting for the purpose of sending him their congratulations. According to popular myth, it was upon this occasion that the Master of the Lodge, Ferguson of Craigdarroch, decided to confer upon Burns the title of "Poet-Laureate of the Lodge." Burns had already called himself "Laureate" in a stanza written on 3 May 1786 which predates his admission into Canongate Kilwinning:

> To phrase you, an' praise you,
> Ye ken your LAUREATE scorns:
> The PRAY'R still, you share still,
> Of grateful Minstrel Burns.
> (I, p.242)

In January 1787, two months before the alleged inauguration, the Grand Master of Scotland, Francis Charteris, proposed a toast for the members of St Andrew's Lodge to "Caledonia, and Caledonia's Bard, brother Burns!"[13] Burns described his reaction to this toast in a letter to his friend and patron, John Ballantine:

> As I had no idea such a thing would happen, I was downright thunderstruck, and, trembling in every nerve, made the best return in my power. - Just as I had finished, some of the Grand Officers said so loud as I could hear, with a most comforting accent, "Very well indeed!" which set me something to rights again.-[14]

The investiture of Burns as Poet-Laureate on 1 March 1787 is commemorated in a painting by Steward Watson, a Masonic artist who was also the Grand Lodge secretary (see frontispiece). Nevertheless it would appear that Watson's painting is anachronistic since it contains portraits of Masons in attendance who had not even seen Burns until two years after the alleged ceremony.[15] Furthermore it is curious that the event is not mentioned anywhere in the lodge records despite the existence of first-hand accounts. More perplexing still is that Burns, himself, never made any direct reference to the Laureateship or to the ceremony. The controversy is explored by David Murray Lyon who initially had believed in the authenticity of Burns's inauguration:

> The poet Burns was a member, and was elected Poet Laureate of Lodge Canongate Kilwinning, to which many of his friends belonged. He was not installed as represented by Bro Stewart Watson's picture, but there may have been some ceremony on the occasion. Probably there was. There is evidence for it.[16]

Yet in his *History of the Lodge of Edinburgh*, Lyon retracts his original view and concludes:

> The whole subject has been recently carefully investigated, with the result that there can be no doubt that Burns was never elected to, and never held the office of, Poet-Laureate of the Lodge, and that the alleged ceremony of his installation into that office never took place . . . .There are many other facts which all go to show that the poet's election and inauguration as Poet-Laureate of this Lodge is a myth![17]

Even so, the tradition persists that Burns had been elected the Freemasons' Poet-Laureate at Canongate Kilwinning Lodge. Twenty years after this legendary event, James Hogg, the "Ettrick Shepherd" succeeded Burns as the Masons' bard. In the minutes it was recorded that the post had been "in abeyance since the death of the immortal brother, Robert Burns."[18]

The Kilwinning Lodge, which had been associated with the Knights of Malta, was said to be the oldest in existence. This claim had been made by a native of Kilwinning, Michael Ramsay, known as the Chevalier Ramsay.[19] He was a Freemason and exiled Scottish Jacobite living in France where he had been trying to raise funds for the restoration of the Stuart dynasty. In the poem, *The Muses Threnodie* (1638) the Scottish poet, Henry Adamson, makes a connection between the Masons and the Stuarts:

> For we have brethren of the *Rosie Crosse*;
> We have the *Mason word* and second sight,
> Things for to come we can foretell aright....
> But for King Charles, his honour we are back.[20]

Some branches of Scottish Masonry which had supported the Stuarts were sympathetic towards the Jacobite cause. After 1715, several Masonic lodges canalized the surges of Scottish nationalism which followed the suppression of the Jacobite rebellion. The current Whig administration created some new offices including that of "the king's mason".[21] This title formalised the relationship between the monarchy and the Masons. Burns, himself, harboured a sentimental attachment to the Stuart kings when he visited the ruined Stirling Castle where he scratched out the following verse on a window pane:

> Here Stewarts once in triumph reign'd,
> And laws for Scotland's weal ordain'd;
> But now unroof'd their Palace stands,
> Their sceptre's fall'n to other hands;
> Fallen indeed, and to the earth,
> Whence grovelling reptiles take their birth.

> The injur'd STEWART - line are gone,
> A Race outlandish fill their throne;
> An idiot race, to honor lost;
> Who know them best despise them most.
>
> (I, p.348)

Because Burns was not a Jacobite he renounced his action some months later through an act of even greater vandalism. He returned and smashed the window. His reverence for the Stuarts as the founders of Scottish independence did not extend to supporting the restoration of a Jacobite Catholic heir to the throne even though the Vatican's support of the Jacobite cause had led to an alliance between the Jesuits and the "Scottish" Freemasons. Ramsay, who had helped orchestrate these political manoeuvres, was dismissed by James Stuart, the "Old Pretender", as a madman. Nonetheless Ramsay continued to profit from the conspiratorial milieu of Italian Freemasonry. In Rome and Florence intrigue was the hall-mark of the lodges which were attracting religious dissidents, political subversives, and foreign spies. Pope Clement XII reacted to this political threat by issuing a Bull in 1738 which banned Catholics from becoming Freemasons on pain of excommunication. He condemned Masonry as "depraved and perverted", dangerous to the "well-being of souls", and as a result "most suspect of heresy".[22]

Ramsay's method for building up support had been to recruit members for the Scottish or Blue Rite which he may have introduced. Despite its Scottish associations the Blue Rite was never as popular in Scotand as in Europe. The Rite, which continues up to the present day, consists of thirty degrees including the basic triadic system of Entered Apprentice, Fellowcraftsman, and Master Mason. Burns progressed along the path of the Blue Rite through his initation into the fourth Masonic degree, the Royal Arch, which was reserved for Master Masons. His installation took place on 19 May 1787, at St Abb's lodge, no 70, at Eyemouth. It was customary for the candidate to pay a guinea as an admission fee but, because Burns had become such a celebrity, his fee was waived. The lodge minutes record this event as follows:

> Eyemouth, 19 May, 1787. At a general encampment
> held this day, the following brethren were made
> Royal Arch Masons: namely, Robert Burns, from the
> Lodge of St James, Tarbolton, Ayrshire, and Robert
> Ainslie, from the Lodge of St Luke, Edinburgh....
> Robert Ainslie paid One Guinea admission dues,
> but on account of Robert Burns' remarkable poetic
> genius, the encampment unanimously agreed to admit
> him *gratis*, and considered themselves honoured by
> having a man of such shining abilities for one of
> their companions.[23]

As an active Freemason, Burns was a valuable asset to the Masonic community since his fame helped to attract recruits. Many people who joined the craft probably did so in the hope that they would be mentioned in his verse since this was where Burns often commemorated his Masonic brethren. Some, however, were lampooned such as James Humphrey of Mauchline who had acted as Senior Warden during the poet's initiation. In his epitaph, Burns addressed Humphry as the "Noisy Polemic" and even goes on to denounce him as "a bleth'ran bitch" (I, p.47). One of Burns's patrons was Tam Samson, a prominent member of the lodge. Burns responded ambivalently to his patronage by writing a mock elegy for him nearly ten years premature entitled "Tam Samson's Elegy" which contained the following lodge lament:

> The brethren o' the mystic *level*
> May hing their head in wofu' bevel,
> While by their nose the tears will revel,
>       Like ony bead;
> Death's gien the Lodge an unco devel,
>       Tam Samson's dead! (I, p.273)

The lodge secretary, the school teacher, John Wilson, was ridiculed by Burns as "Dr Hornboòk". The animosity between Burns and Wilson erupted during a lodge meeting which provoked Burns to revile his rival in "Death and Doctor Hornbook":

> The Clachan yill had made me canty,
> I was na fou, but just had plenty -
>                   (I, p.79)

Unfortunately the poet's willingness to attack a rival-brother in verse meant that the private disputes within the lodge could be amplified into the public forum of his poetry. This was contrary to the regulations governing the lodge which specified:

> Whereas a Lodge always means a company of worthy men
> and circumspect, gathered together in order to promote
> charity, friendship, civility and good neighbourhood,
> it is enacted that no member of this Lodge shall speak
> slightingly, detractingly or calumniously of any of
> his Brethren behind their backs, so as to damage them
> in their professions or reputations without any certain
> grounds, and any member committing any such offence
> must humble himself by asking on his knees the pardon
> of such person or persons as his folly or malice hath
> aggrieved.[24]

It was more usual to find Burns unashamedly using his poetic licence to praise his fellow-Masons. The tone of his Masonic poetry is joyful and hymnal as in the poem "To Dr John Mackenzie" (A.D. 1786). This is also dated "An. M. 5790" which refers to the calendar used in the Ancient and Accepted Scottish Rite. "An. M." is an abbreviation of *Anno Mundi*, "In the Year of the World", a Hebraic system of dating which involves adding 3760 to the A.D. year. Though Burns claims to be using an An. M. date, he is actually using the A. L. (*Anno Lucis*) "Year of Light" system which is found by adding 4004 to the ordinary calendar year. It is appropriate that Burns has used a Masonic date in a verse-epistle inviting Dr Mackenzie of Mauchline to the Freemasons' annual procession which traditionally took place on Midsummer Day, 24 June:

> Friday first's the day appointed
> By our Right Worshipful Anointed,
> To hold our grand Procession,
> To get a blade o' Johnie's Morals,
> And taste a swatch o' Manson's barrels,
> I' the way of our Profession:
> Our Master and the Brotherhood
> Wad a' be glad to see you;
> For me, I wad be maier than proud
> To share the MERCIES wi' you
> If Death, then wi' skaith then
> Some mortal heart is hechtin,
> Inform him, an' storm him,
> That SATURDAY ye'll fecht him.
> (I, p.270)

The Mason's parade had been banned by Grand Lodge in 1747 in order to deter the derisive mock-Masonic processions which were conducted by rival organisations such as the Gormogons. In Hogarth's engraving of a parade, *The Mystery of the Masons brought to Light by the Gormogons* (1724) (see plate 4), a monkey is dressed in apron and gloves as a visual pun on the Gormogons aping Freemasonry![25] A further regulation issued in 1754 expressly prohibited a brother from attending any public procession dressed in his Masonic regalia.[26] The Antients, however, only forbade parades in 1799 for a few years and then gave permission before for them to continue. This is one indication that Burns was aligned with the Antients since his poem was written in 1786 at a time when processions had been outlawed by the Moderns. One cause of dissension between the two factions had been the neglect of saints' days which the Antients had re-instated within the Masonic calendar. One of the most important festivals was June 24, the traditional birthday of St John the Baptist which, as Burns indicates in his epistolary verse, was celebrated by a ceremonial procession:

> Tarbolton, twenty-fourth o' June,
> Ye'll find me in a better tune. (I, p.413)

The date was also commemorated as the day on which Grand Lodge had met to appoint the first Grand Master in 1717. The

Antients continued to install his successors on this feast-day. The reason why St John was such a prominent Freemasons' saint remains unclear. During the seventeenth century English Masons had been called "St John's Men" or "St John's Masons" while in Scotland the connection between craft Masonry and the celebration of St John was even more pronounced.[27]

Burns's "St John's Day" invitation suggests that he was an active participant in these proceedings. And by appearing publicly as a Mason, Burns demonstrated that he was not in any way secretive about his membership. Indeed, through his poetry he openly acknowledged the benefits he derived from the fellowship of the lodge by exhibiting pride in his Masonic allegiance.

## The Patronage of the Lodge

During the eighteenth century, Freemasonry increased its sphere of influence by becoming accessible to a cross-section of trades and professions. In becoming a speculative order, Masonry could now admit both the artist and the artisan. Grand Lodge was determined to diminish its more sinister role as a secret society by stressing the craft's commitment to public life. Gradually Masonry emerged as a benevolent and charitable body which was also a source of patronage for the arts. In Burns's day, Freemasons who were patrons of the Drama appeared at theatrical performances in full Masonic regalia. Artists and writers such as Hogarth and Defoe may have been among those commissioned to rebuild the face of Freemasonry so that it could eventually project a public image which would make it acceptable as a social institution. By 1743 there was particular urgency for reform since Masonry had fallen into disrepute. The popularity of the Freemasons had waned so drastically that Walpole concluded that "nothing but a persecution could bring them into vogue again".[28] The "persecution" materialised in the form of a pamphlet war waged against the fraternity during the 1740s. Some pamphlets were exposés produced in response to the growing public curiosity concerning the activities of the brotherhood. Other anti-Masonic pamphleteers alleged that the craft promoted bribery and corruption, drunkenness and debauchery. Though many of these accusations were groundless, the society was certainly in need of reorganisation and general improvement.

It has been suggested that Hogarth had been encouraged by his Masonic superior, James Thornhill, to satirise the craft in order to stimulate much needed reform.[29] Through paintings and engravings, such as *The Mystery of the Masons brought to Light by the Gormogons* (1724), and *Night*, from the series *The Four Times of Day* (1738), Hogarth graphically presented the social abuses associated with the fraternity. He was able to reach a wide audience by exhibiting his work at Vauxhall Gardens which effectively became an early public art gallery. Therefore, Hogarth was able to communicate to fellow-Masons by incorporating within his art secret codes and signals taken from craft ritual and myth which would be intelligible to the initiated. Early speculative Masons were anxious to preserve the secrecy of their rites and symbolism under threat from the vogue for exposures pouring from the press. The most effective of these was a pamphlet entitled *Masonry Dissected* written by a renegade Mason called Samuel Prichard. It is likely that Defoe had been assigned by Grand Lodge to reply to Prichard's exposé. Defoe's pamphlet, *The Perjured Freemason Detected* (1730), attacks Prichard as a perjurer and sets out to invalidate his findings.[30] Undoubtedly lodge officials recognised the importance of the artist and writer as a spokesman who would help legitimise Masonic activities toward social acceptability. Strategically the cultivation of the arts was useful in spreading Masonry to all branches of society. Indeed the potential power of the poet to influence public opinion would have favourably disposed Grand Lodge to patronise Burns as a future ambassador for Freemasonry.

Ideologically, the lodges represented an important alternative to the system of aristocratic patronage. Freemasonry provided a platform for the assertion of bourgeois values during the Enlightenment which helped free the poet and painter from subservience to the ruling classes. Ironically, the aristocracy had established itself within this system of equality and fraternity from the onset. Stephen Knight suggests that the installation of Anthony Sayer, a non-aristocrat as the first Grand Master, was a tactic intended to play down the extent of aristocratic influence:

> The upper classes kept a low profile. They backed the creation of a central organization welding individual Lodges together, but evidently wanted this done before they assumed control. Of the four original London Lodges, the first three contained not one "Esquire" between them, whereas Lodge Original No 4 was made up of seventy-one members of whom, in 1724, ten were nobles, three were honourable, four were baronets or knights, and two were generals.[31]

The first noble to be installed Grand Master was the Duke of Montague in 1721. Throughout the next decade he was followed by ten Grand Masters, seven of whom were members of the aristocracy. Among these was Lord Byron (the great-uncle of the poet) who became Grand Master in 1747. The headship of the English Freemasons was even extended to royalty when the younger son of George II, the Duke of Cumberland, took up the office in 1782. A royal precedent had already been set by Frederick, Prince of Wales, who in 1737 became an accepted Mason. Fifty years later Burns was amongst those who celebrated the initiation of the future kings, George IV and William IV, into the craft. Burns recognised the central importance of the monarch to Masonry and even described King George III in Masonic language as "the sacred key-stone of our royal Arch Constitution." But when George was treated for insanity in 1788 Burns revised his views and confessed "it is altogether impossible that [he is] such a man as I can appreciate."[32] Surprisingly the Masonic spirit with its revolutionary values of liberty, equality and fraternity did not militate against an aristocratic leadership. Smart typified such traditionalism by boasting of the fraternity's regal and imperial connections in his lodge song:

> With us mighty MONARCHS have sided,
> And EMP'RORS are writ in our ROLLS.

For Burns, aristocratic and Masonic patronage converged. An example of this occurred when James Dalrymple of Orangefield introduced him to his future patron, Lord Glencairn, during a meeting of the Canongate Kilwinning Lodge in 1786.[33] Other aristocrats Burns encountered through Masonry included; Lord Torphichen, Lord Pitsligo, Lord Elcho, the Earl of Eglinton and the Earl of Glencairn. In being flexible enough to accommodate the Masonic fraternity, the British ruling classes were instrumental in converting this former quasi-craft guild into a bulwark of the social hierarchy. The protean character of Freemasonry enabled it to assimilate and then reproduce the social values outside. In France, during the welter of social upheaval the lodges provided a focal point for the bourgeois Revolution whereas in Britain Masons mirrored and then reinforced the class-system itself. The middle classes were attracted to Masonry because it fostered Enlightened individualism. Self-interest was enshrined within the Mason's insurance scheme which was guaranteed to help brethren in distress. The fraternity also had a kinship with the friendly societies.[34] These working-class combines, out of which developed the trades' union movement, bore a family resemblance to the Masonic underground co-operatives which set out to provide collective support for the individual.

In Burns's case, Freemasonry had put him into contact with influential people such as Gavin Hamilton and James Dalrymple. The lodges helped to launch his poetic career as a poet by campaigning for subscribers in order to meet the publishing costs of his volumes of poetry. Gavin Hamilton, a fellow Mason, was influential in getting St James's lodge to provide funds for the publication of Burns's first book, *Poems Chiefly in the Scottish Dialect* (1786). The poet dedicated the edition to Hamilton, his "Friend and Brother", who he described as:

> ...the poor man's friend in need,
> The GENTLEMAN in word and deed.
> (I, p.244)

The book was published in Kilmarnock where the local brethren

admitted Burns into St John's lodge on 26 October 1786. This was
the first time in Masonic circles that Burns was acknowledged as
a poet since he was described in the lodge minutes as "Robert
Burns, poet, from Mauchline, a member of St James".[35] The
Kilmarnock members accepted 350 copies of the book which
became known as the Kilmarnock edition.[36] The Right Worshipful
Master subscribed to 35 copies and another brother to 75.
Unfortunately, the Kilmarnock publishing venture was not
sufficent to ensure Burns's financial stability so, in 1787, another
edition of the poems was brought out. From this Burns earned
500 pounds though he forfeited copyright. The book was
published in Edinburgh under Masonic patronage. The printer,
William Smellie, and the engraver, Alexander Nasmith, were both
Masons while the publisher, John Wilson, was a member of the
Kilmarnock Lodge. The volume, which was known as the
Edinburgh edition, was a reprint of the Kilmarnock version with
a hundred pages more including twenty-two additional poems not
all of which were new. The publisher of the Edinburgh edition
was William Creech who Burns had met at a Masonic meeting.
Creech became the subject of two of Burns's poems including a
satirical lament for his absence. Since the majority of Burns's
friends and business acquaintances were Freemasons, it is likely
that the moral imperative to help a fellow-Mason operated to
Burns's advantage. For example, some enthusiastic brothers even
bought volumes of his poems to swell book-sales. Robert Aiken,
mentioned in "Holy Willie's Prayer" and dubbed "Orator Bob" (I,
p.471) in the poem "The Kirk of Scotland's Garland - a New
Song" boasted of having "read Burns into fame" by obtaining 145
subscribers for the Kilmarnock edition.[37] In the literary world,
Henry Mackenzie, the author of *The Man of Feeling* (1771) was
also a Freemason who favourably reviewed his first volume of
poems in *The Lounger* (9 December 1786).[38] The poet was also
admired by Walter Scott, another Mason, who on seeing Burns's
portrait in a lodge room remarked:

> I am much gratified by the sight of the portrait
> of Robert Burns.I saw that distinguished poet only
> once, and that many years since, and being a bad
> marker of likenesses and recollector of faces, I
> should in an ordinary case have hesitated to offer
> an opinion upon the resemblance, especially as I
> make no pretension to judge of the fine arts. But
> Burns was so remarkable a man that his features
> remain impressed on my mind as I had seen him only
> yesterday, and I could not hesitate to recognise
> this portrait as a striking resemblance of the poet,
> though it had been presented to me amid a whole
> exhibition.[39]

Like Burns, Scott's work had been influenced by the craft. In
*Ivanhoe* (1819) Scott is concerned with the Knights Templar who

figured in legendary histories of the craft from which developed
Templar Masonry. The later novel, *Anne of Geierstein* (1829) also
deals with a secret society which is loosely based on the
Freemasons.[40] These literary examples illustrate that Freemasonry
not only furnished the writer and artist with a source of
patronage but also provided material and inspiration for works of
art. In addition to this a beneficial reciprocity operated between
Burns and the brotherhood. As he indicated through his poetry,
any system of patronage works best when it is of mutual
advantage to both parties *"sic Poet* an' *sic Patron"* (I, p.243).


The Mason's Apron


The literary influence of Freemasonry on the Scottish
Enlightenment is best demonstrated through Burns's poetry. An
explicitly Masonic poem, attributed to Burns, is "The Master's
Apron" which appeared in *The Freemason* for October 1902:

> Ther's mony a badge that's unco braw;
>     Wi' ribbon, lace and tape on;
> Let kings an' princes wear them a'
>     Gie me the Master's apron!
>
> The honest craftsman's apron,
> The jolly Freemason's apron,
> Be he at hame, or roam afar,
> Before his touch fa's bolt and bar,
> The gates of fortune fly ajar,
> 'Gin he but wears the apron!
>
> For wealth and honour, pride and power
>     Are crumbling stanes to base on;
> Fraternity suld rule the hour,
>     And ilka worthy Mason!
> Each Free Accepted Mason,
> Each Ancient Crafted Mason.
>
> Then, brithers, let a halesome sang
> Arise your friendly ranks alang!
> Guidwives and bairnies blithely sing
> To the ancient badge wi' the apron string
> That is worn by the Master Mason![41]

The poem is filled with references to Masonic symbolism and
craft ritual which would be instantly intelligible to the initiated.
Through the secret figurative language of the lodge, Burns
venerated the "badge" of Freemasonry, the Mason's apron. The
antiquity of this item of Masonic regalia is evident from the last

two lines where Burns refers to "the ancient badge" worn by the "Master Mason". The Mason reader would be reminded here of the apron worn by Hiram Abif, the legendary founder of the brotherhood, who was also the chief architect of King Solomon's Temple. The importance of the apron to Freemasonry had emerged from its use in the operative craft as protective clothing for the "Ancient Crafted Mason". From this functional origin the apron, which was traditionally made out of lamb-skin, had taken on an emblematic significance which evoked the purity and moral integrity of the craftsman.

As an apprenticed tradesman, Burns would have appreciated the operative purpose of the apron which functioned in the lodge-room to identify a member's rank and duties within the order. This information was communicated by the "ribbon, lace and tape" which also served to decorate the apron. In the first line of the poem, Burns voices his disapproval of elaborate aprons as "unco braw". Yet, towards the end of his life in 1790, Burns modified his ascetic tastes sufficiently to accept a decorative apron from the composer and lyricist, Charles Sharpe. In the presence of his fellow-Masons at the Globe Tavern, Dumfries, Burns was presented with the apron of

> chamois leather, very fine, with figures of gold,
> some of them relieved with green, others with a
> dark-red colour [while] on the under side of the
> semi-circular part which is turned down at the
> top is written in a bold, fair hand: "Charles
> Sharpe, of Hotham, to Rabbie Burns. Dumfries,
> Dec. 12, 1791."[42]

By appropriating the elaborate apron to Kings and Princes in line three of the poem, Burns demonstrates his awareness of the link between royalty and the craft. Nevertheless, he acknowledged the egalitarian ideals of Freemasonry by praising the Master and honest craftsman above kings and princes. In doing so he pays homage to the second and third degrees of the brotherhood, that of the Fellowcraftsman and Master Mason.

The apron was symbolic of the fraternal spirit of the craft expressed through the hospitality which was extended to every member. The Masonic network which was spreading throughout Europe came close to translating into actuality the Enlightenment concept of Universal Benevolence. As Burns notes in "The Master's Apron":

> Be he at hame, or roam afar,
> Before his touch fa's bolt and bar,
> The gates of fortune fly ajar
> 'Gin he but wears the apron!

The apron signified the secret knowledge possessed by the Freemason which enabled him to gain access into any Masonic lodge through the use of grips, pass-words and signs. According to Burns, the power and influence of the fraternity ranked before "wealth and honour, pride and power". These secular goals are dismissed as "crumbling stanes" which provide powerful metaphors for Freemasonry whose legendary past had cultivated the skills of the stone-mason. King Solomon's Temple stood at the heart of Masonic mythology having been transmuted into the spiritual ideal of the temple of "living stones".[43] The vitality of the Freemason as a living stone eager to rebuild the temple of mystical Enlightenment contrasted with the false values of wealth, honour, pride, and power which are seen as crumbling stones. The revolutionary message of Freemasonry as a vast edifice which encompassed an alternative system of morality signified a movement intent upon reforming the spiritual destiny of mankind through the central image of the builder. Hence Burns's attempt to arouse his fellow-Masons, their wives and children, to sing a hymn of praise to the uniform of the master - builder, the Mason's apron.

Burns may be seen wearing an apron in a portrait painted after his election to the office of Depute-Master of St James's lodge (see plate 5). His apron is distinguished by a flap which in the operative craft was designed to protect the worker's clothing. Speculative Masons disputed whether or not to wear the triangular bib inside or outside their apron. Jones draws attention to an expose of 1772 where the initiate was reported to say: "I tied the apron round my waist, with the flap on the inside, an apprentice not being entitled to wear it otherways".[44] The portrait of Burns shows that he had exercised his right as Master Mason to wear the flap externally. Emblazoned on this bib is his Mason's Mark, a reminder of the society's operative roots when stone-masons inscribed their signature or mark onto the part of a building they had completed. For Burns the Mason's Mark was synonymous with his word of honour as inscribed in the Bible which he gave to his sweetheart, Mary Campbell.[45] Burns dedicated to Campbell the song, "Highland Lassie O", where he wrote:

> She has my heart, she has my hand,
> By secret Truth and Honor's band.
>
> (I, p.253)

The "secret truth" may refer to the Masonic pledge represented by his Mason's Mark which he reproduced along with his autograph and texts from Leviticus and Matthew in Highland Mary's Bible (see plate 6). According to tradition the couple exchanged bibles, and Mary's Bible in two volumes, which originally belonged to Burns, is now preserved at the poet's monument in Alloway. It is interesting to note that a number of records reveal how Burns failed to reproduce his Mason's Mark consistently. One controversial reason for this has been put forward by Peter Watson who, after examining the Minute Book of Burns's lodge, came to the conclusion that, when the poet wrote out his name

came to the conclusion that, when the poet wrote out his name
and Mason's Mark, alcohol had impaired his judgment:

> Amongst a long list of signatures of members, many
> of them having their Mason's marks attached, we find
> Burns signing himself in full "Robert Burns", and
> adding his Masonic mark of nine points in the same
> line. This signature had less resemblance to the
> familiar and undoubtedly genuine form than many of
> the others, but there is no date to it, and it is
> just possible that the conditions under which he
> signed were what the lodge might term "unfortunate".[46]

**"Tis wine ye masons makes you free"[47]**

As the "unfortunate" conditions mentioned above suggest, Burns
may have been intoxicated at the time when he signed the
Minute-Book. Such indulgences were certainly exacerbated by the
conviviality of his fellow-Masons. In the "Epistle to J. Lapraik,
An Old Scotch Bard", Burns celebrates the fellowship of the
lodge:

> But ye whom social pleasure charms,
> Whose hearts the *tide of kindness* warms,
> Who hold your *being* on the terms,
> "Each aid the others,"
> Come to my bowl, come to my arms,
> My friends, my brothers!
> (I, p.89)

The Masonic authorities had been alerted to the problems caused
by drunkenness during lodge meetings. For example, one of the
rules of St James's lodge even attempted to curb some of the
more adverse effects of excessive drinking:

> If any Brother be so unfortunate as to have
> disordered his senses by strong liquors and
> thereby rendered himself incapable of behaving
> himself decently, peaceably and kind towards those
> around him, such Brother coming to the Lodge in
> that condition to the disturbance and disgust of
> his Brethren, shall be prudently ordered away to
> some place of safety in the meantime, and at the
> next meeting shall submit to such censure and
> admonition from the Chair, and to such a fine
> inflicted by the Lodge on him as to them may
> appear proper to his crime, and deter him from
> it in all time coming.[48]

Burns's drinking habits were well established outside the lodge. During his youth he had helped found the all male "Bachelors' Club" which levied a threepenny subscription for drinks, supplemented further by fines for non-attendance. Later, while visiting Edinburgh, Burns found that he preferred the atmosphere of the tavern to that of society's drawing rooms. Consequently he began to patronise Dawney Douglas's tavern in Anchor Close where the drinking club known as the Crochallan Fencibles met.[49] But Burns recalled it was at St Oswald's where he really seasoned his drinking habits so that he could "look unconcernedly on a large tavern bill, and mix without fear in a drunken squabble".[50] In the Bacchanalian eulogy, "Scotch Drink", Burns praises Scotland's national drink, whisky:

> Fortune, if thou'll but gie me still
> Hale breeks, a scone, an' *Whisky gill*,
> An' rowth o' *rhyme* to rave at will,
> Tak a' the rest,
> An' deal't about as thy blind skill
> Directs thee best. (I, p.176)

Burns even campaigned through his poetry for reforms to the drinking laws as in "The Author's Earnest Cry and Prayer," to the Scotch Representatives in the House of Commons", where he begged for a repeal of the heavy taxes on whisky. Bouts of excessive drinking marked the period of dissipation which had been triggered off by his personal problems with Jean Armour, the daughter of a Master Mason. In his "Second Epistle to Davie", Burns celebrates the love of women and the fellowship of men, specifically the Freemasons' fraternity:

> Whyles daez't wi' love, whyles daez't wi'
> drink,
> Wi' jads or masons; (I, p.240)

The connection between wine, women and Masonry during the eighteenth century is evident from a number of bawdy Masonic drinking songs. Invariably the Masons' working tools were subject to sexual innuendo while aspects of ritual and symbolism were used to evoke erotic imagery. Perhaps saucy lyrics were intended to compensate for the exclusion of women from the lodge-room. But it is more likely that the brotherhood hoped to counter their enemies' accusations of sodomy by asserting their heterosexual virility. A bawdy poem attributed to Burns called "A Masonic Song", describes how a Mason provides evidence of his initiation through his sexual prowess:

## A Masonic Song

It happened on a winter night
    And early in the season
Some body said my bonny lad
    Was gone to be a Mason.
        *Fal de ral etc.*

I cryed and wailed but nought availed
    He put a forward face on
And did avow that he was now
    A free accepted Mason.

Still doubting if the fact was true
    He gave me demonstration
For out he drew before my view
    The Jewels of a Mason.

The Jewels all baith great and small
    I viewed with admiration
When he set his siege and drew his gage
    I wondered at my mason.

His compass stride he laid it wide
    I thought I guessed the reason
But his mallet shaft it put me daft
    I longed to be a Mason.

Good plumets strong he downward hung
    A noble jolly brace on
And off a slant his broacher sent
    And drove it like a mason.

But the tempered steel began to fail
    Too soft for the occasion
It melted plain he drove so keen
    My galant noble Mason.

So pleased was I to see him ply
    The tools of his vocation
I beg'd for once he wuld dispense
    And make a Maid a mason.

Then round and round in mystic ground
    He took the middle station'
And with halting pace he reached the place
    Where I was made a mason.

Then more and more the light did pour
    With bright Illumination

> But when the grip he did me slip
> I gloried in my mason.
>
> What farther past is here lock fast
> I'm under obligation
> But fill to him up to the brim
> Can make a maid a mason.[51]

Throughout this poem Masonic terms are used as sexual metaphors. These include "jewels" which denote rank and office and the broacher or broached thurnel which is a conical stone chisel. Burns also exploits the phallic symbolism of the plummet or plumb-line, the "gage" referring to the 24-inch gauge used by the Entered Apprentice and the shaft of the "mallet" or hammer associated with the Master of the lodge. The Masons' clandestine communication through the use of body language is parodied by the image of the "compass stride" in stanza five while the secret "grip" or handshake is ridiculed in stanza ten. The poem culminates in a description of the sexual act which caricatures Masonic initiation by punning on the expression "made a Mason". G. Legman dismisses the homosexual undertones of the poem as factitious "homoerotic mummery"[52] which may have been intended to clash with its feminine perspective for comic effect.

Apparently Burns composed the "Masonic Song" extempore at a lodge meeting. The Masonic environment provided Burns with poetic inspiration because it was able to accommodate his defiance of the social and moral order outside. On another occasion at St Andrew's lodge in Irvine, he added a stanza to his song "No Churchman am I" which eulogised the drinking habits of the Freemasons:

### A Stanza added in a Mason Lodge

> Then fill up a bumper and make it o'erflow,
> And honours masonic prepare for to throw;
> May ev'ry true Brother of th' Compass and Square
> Have a big-belly'd bottle when harass'd with care.
>
> (I, p.39)

According to William Harvey, such drinking appliances as the "pint-stoup and the toddy-ladle were the working-tools of all the Degrees"[53] which suggests that Freemasonry had degenerated into a drinking club. Even the initiation fee for a candidate admitted by Burns was donated towards "defraying the expenses of the night".[54] For Burns imbibing was essential to social conviviality and as such the most apt expression of the fraternal bond. He communicated these beliefs in verse:

> But a club of good fellows, like those that are here,
> And a bottle like this, are my glory and care.
>
> (I, p.38)

Henry Mackenzie, however, took a more sombre view of the effect of alcohol on Burns believing that the poet had been "seduced by dissipated companions" and after he got into the Excise addicted himself to drunkenness" [55] Throughout his life, Burns cultivated his drinking habits within Masonic lodges. During the eighteenth century, Freemasons had acquired a reputation for excessive drinking. In the treatise, *Ebrietatis Encomium or the Praise of Drunkenness* (1723), chapter fifteen is dedicated to "Free masons and other Learned Men that used to get Drunk". Opponents of the craft suggested that the Masons had derived their epiphet "free" from their cult of imbibing. One comic couplet traces the semantics of "free" to a Bacchanalian source:

'Tis Wine, ye Masons, makes you free,
Bacchus the father is of Liberty.[56]

By the 1730s the public image of Freemasonry reeled towards one of institutionalised drunkenness. Hogarth caricatured the popular view of the drunken Mason returning from the excesses of a lodge-meeting in his engraving *Night* (see plate 7). In the fore-ground is Sir Thomas De Veil, a past Master of Hogarth's lodge.[57] De Veil is being physically supported by Sir Andrew Montgomery who was the Grand Tyler of the Grand Lodge of England. Ironically, De Veil who was a reputed drunkard was also a magistrate whose duties included the enforcement of the Gin Act (1736)![58] The drinking habits of the brotherhood were also ridiculed in "A Letter from the Grand Mistress of the Female Free-Masons" (1724). As the contents of the letter reveal, the Grand Mistress of the Female Freemasons has been misinformed about Freemasonry by the male Mason who formed and instructed the womens' lodge. The reason why his knowledge of Masonry is so erroneous was because his initiation at the lodge in Omagh, Ulster, had been abruptly curtailed. Apparently the brethren were so "far gone in *Punch* and *Whisky*"[59] that they had been unable to proceed with the ceremony.

Burns promoted the typological view of the "merry mason" throughout his verse. He referred earlier to the relationship between Masonry and drinking in the rhyming invitation to Dr Mackenzie where he invites him to "taste a swatch" or sample "o' Manson's barrels" which he proclaims to be "I' the way of our profession." A more subtle link appears in a Scots poem, described by William Harvey as "a symposium of fun, Freemasonry, and whisky"[60] which begins:

Frae wast to south, tell ilka callan'
The corps maun anchor at Crochallan.
"And wha gaes there" thrice Millar gruntit;
"I," rattlin' Willie roared and duntit.
As twal is Tron'd we a' link out;

> The moon - a ragged washin' clout -
> Glints shame-fac'd to ae wankriff starrie;
> The nicht's been wat - the caus'y's glaurie.
> In Davie's straucht, and numbering aicht,
> A bowl's filled to the rarest
> For sang or story; - or wha glory
> In drinkin' to the fairest.

These verses commemorate how Burns and Jo Millar, the Junior Warden of Canongate Kilwinning Lodge, celebrated the initiation of John Gray. In this poem Burns manages to convey the drunken atmosphere of these festivities through word-play on Hiram Abif and King Hiram of Tyre. The content of the "sang or story" is a retelling of one of the "tales of Tyre" narrated by William Cruickshank who was one of Burns's drinking companions:

> Now tales o' Tyre, for buikless billies,
> Are tauld by rival pedant Willies;
> How Thebes' King, when tir'd o' Sidon,
> Erected Tyre-folk to reside in;
> Nic Willie wond'rin wha could hire him,
> If't hadna been the first King Hiram,
> "O ye donnerill!" cried the Coronel,
> "Twas the hindmost King o' Tyre,
> "Twas nae Hiram, but King Iram,
> For he *finished* it - wi' fire.

In the last two lines Burns puns on the burning of Tyre and the fires of whisky. The poem was written as a reply to Cruickshank whose friendship Burns declared was as "dear to me as the ruddy drops that warm my heart".[61] The beginning of the final stanza suggests that Cruickshank had witnessed the poet's inauguration as Poet-Laureate which allegedly had taken place at the same time as Gray's initiation:

> But Latin Willies reck noo raise,
> He'd seen that nicht Rab croun'd wi' bays.

In recognition of Cruickshank's reputation as a Classics scholar, Burns concluded his poem with a Latin joke:

> If ye wad tell, *Cruik*, speer at hell
> *Pro* Iram *coram* Draco.

He continued the theme through a Masonic couplet:

> When Draco and when Iram flourished
> And if they baith freemasons nourished?

Burns viewed the temple-building period of the ancient world mentioned in the poem as a golden age for the Freemasons hence his attempt to unite past and present by celebrating the conviviality of the craft through the images of its own antiquity. The institutionalised festivities of the lodge which sanctioned the consumption of alcohol enabled Burns to indulge in a bacchanalian forgetfulness by overlooking the warning he once wrote on a tumbler at Ryedale:

> There's death in the cup - sae beware!
> Nay, more - there is danger in touching;
> But wha can avoid the fell snare?
> The man and his wine's sae bewitching! (II, p.827)

**Brothers of the Mystic Tie** [62]

Burns praises the fraternal spirit in two of his Masonic songs, "The Sons of old Killie" (1786) and "The Farewell. To the Brethren of St James's Lodge, Tarbolton". In the latter his fellow-Masons are praised as "Companions of my social joy!" while the lodge meeting takes place on "a chearful [sic] festive night" attended by a "social Band". For Burns Freemasonry was a compound of mysticism and conviviality which he presents in his address to his "brothers of the *mystic tye!*"

# The Farewell. To the Brethren of St. James's Lodge, Tarbolton

*Tune, Goodnight and joy be wi' you a'*

ADIEU! a heart-warm, fond adieu!
   Dear brothers of the *mystic tye*!
Ye favour'd, ye enlighten'd Few
   Companions of my social joy!
Tho' I to foreign lands must hie,
   Pursuing Fortune's slidd'ry ba',
With melting heart, and brimful eye,
   I'll mind you still, tho' far awa'.

Oft have I met your social Band,
   And spent the chearful, festive night;
Oft, honor'd with supreme command,
   Presided o'er the *Sons of light*:
And by that *Hieroglyphic* bright,
   Which none but *Craftsmen* ever saw!
Strong Mem'ry on my heart shall write
   Those happy scenes when far awa'!

May Freedom, Harmony and Love
   Unite you in the *grand Design*,
Beneath th' Omniscient Eye above,
   The glorious ARCHITECT Divine!
That you may keep th' *unerring line*,
   Still rising by the *plummet's law*,
Till *Order* bright, completely shine,
   Shall be my Pray'r when far awa'.

And *You*, farewell! whose merits claim,
   Justly, that *highest badge* to wear!
Heav'n bless your honor'd, noble Name,
   To MASONRY and SCOTIA dear!
A last request, permit me here,
   When yearly ye assemble a',
One *round*, I ask it with a *tear*,
   To him, *the Bard, that's far awa'*.
             (I, p.271)

The mood of these verses is sorrowful since they concern Burns's farewell to Scottish Freemasonry. He had recently completed all his arrangements for emigration to Jamaica where he intended to start work on a plantation as a book-keeper. The reason for his hasty departure was to escape the scandal involving Jean Armour, who was going to give birth to Burns's illegitimate twins. Burns was determined to escape the disapproval of the Kirk whom he pictured as a clan of "holy beagles" and a "houghmagandie pack" who would "sniff the scent" of the "old fox" Burns who intended "to earth among the mountains of Jamaica".[63] Though glad to leave behind the Kirk, Burns regretted abandoning his Fellow-Masons:

> Tho' I to foreign lands must hie,
> Pursuing Fortune's slidd'ry ba',
> With melting heart, and brimful eye,
> I'll mind you still, tho' far awa'.

Burns's paternalistic tone in "I'll mind you still, tho' far awa'." reflects his sense of responsibility as the Depute-Master of the lodge. The Master was Major-General James Montgomerie whose constant absences from Masonic gatherings meant that Burns had often been in sole command. Consequently he reminds the brethren in stanza two of the times when he was "honor'd with supreme command" and "presided o'er the *Sons of light*". In turn, the poet claims that after his departure he will remember the lodge through the Masonic symbol of the compass and square "that *Hieroglyphic* bright/ Which none but *Craftsmen* ever saw!" Since the Freemasons' code of ethics was symbolized by the craftsman's working tools, Burns urged his fellow-Masons to follow the plummet's "*unerring line*" so that order may reign over the lodge. This symbolism is derived from the Masonic version of the creation myth. As mentioned earlier the "Great Architect of the Universe was believed to have measured out the cosmos with the craftsman's working tools. Thus Freemasons unite in the grand design of their craft as a tribute to the Creator. As a microcosm of the divine harmony, the lodge room is watched over by the Masonic-Christian insignia of the "Omniscient Eye" which is displayed on the ceiling. In the last stanza Burns addresses his final farewell to a secular overseer, William Wallace, Sheriff of Ayr, the Grand Master-Mason of Scotland:

> And *You*, farewell! whose merits claim,
> Justly, that *highest badge* to wear!
> Heav'n bless your honor'd, noble Name,
> To MASONRY and SCOTIA dear!

Departure is also the key-note of the Masonic song "The Sons of old Killie" which Burns wrote shortly before leaving Kilmarnock for Edinburgh in 1786. At a lodge meeting held at the Old Commercial Inn, Croft Street, Burns sang this lyric in gratitude to the brethren of Kilmarnock lodge for making him an honorary member.

*Robert Burns*

# The Sons of old Killie

*Tune—Shawnboy*

**Lively**

Ye sons of old Killie, assembled by Willie,
    To follow the noble vocation;
Your thrifty old mother has scarce such another
    To sit in that honoured station.
I've little to say, but only to pray,
    As praying's the ton of your fashion;
A prayer from the Muse you well may excuse,
    'Tis seldom her favourite passion.

Ye powers who preside o'er the wind and the tide,
    Who marked each element's border;
Who formed this frame with beneficent aim,
    Whose sovereign statute is order;
Within this dear mansion may wayward contention
    Or withered envy ne'er enter;
May secresy round be the mystical bound,
    And brotherly love be the centre!

                        (I, p.299-300)[64]

In the first line of the song Burns addresses the brethren of
"Killie" (a contraction of Kilmarnock) who have been assembled
by "Willie" or William Parker, the Master Mason. The metaphor

76

"sons" has Masonic significance since Freemasons were known traditionally as "Widow's sons" in imitation of Hiram Abif. A sense of tradition was important to those who had chosen "To follow the noble vocation" of Freemasonry. The "thrifty old mother" mentioned in line three refers to Kilmarnock as a mother-lodge which is the term given to the place of a brother's initiation. Family imagery is continued towards the end of the poem through an invocation of brotherly love which is represented by the Masonic symbol of the point - within - the - circle. This image of harmony would have reminded Burns of the problems caused by internal discord which had split up the Tarbolton lodge in 1773. The point - within - the - circle was also symbolic of the Creator as a configuration of the finite within the infinite signified by the circle, the figure of eternity. The Masons had derived their mystical teaching from the Hermetic tradition of the Renaissance. The point-within-the-circle had been transmitted from alchemy where it had functioned as the chemical symbol for gold.[65] The four elements of earth, fire, water and air which were essential to the process of transmutation of base metal into gold are mentioned at the beginning of the second stanza:

> Ye powers who preside o'er the wind and the
> tide,
> Who marked each element's border.

The spiritual dimension of alchemy signified the process towards purity and the integration of fallen man with nature, the goal of the Freemasons preserved through the "secresy" of the "mystical bond".

The mysticism and paganism of Freemasonry would suggest that Burns had rebelled against his own religious upbringing by belonging to an organization which contained anti-Christian elements. Nevertheless, in "Address to the Deil" he ridicules the rumours that Masons conjured up the devil in their ceremonies:

> When MASONS' mystic *word* an' *grip*,
> In storms an' tempests raise you up,
> Some cock, or cat, your rage maun stop,
>   Or, strange to tell!
> The *youngest Brother* ye wad whip
> Aff straught to *H-ll*. (I, p.171)

Burns's father, William, had been a devout Christian who had written for his children *A Manual of Religious Belief for the Instruction of Children* (1875). Perhaps Burns was thinking of his father when he wrote in "A Masonic song":

> It happened on a winter night
>   And early in the season
> Some body said my bonny lad

Was gone to be a Mason.
(II, p.931)[66]

As a Presbyterian, Burns would have been subject to the influence of a powerful religious body, the Kirk.[67] In 1707 the Treaty of Union posed a threat to the power of the Kirk through moves on the part of the "heritors" to appoint officials of the Church of Scotland by patronage instead of by election. At a time when the Kirk was struggling to maintain a grip on the community Burns may have sought in Freemasonry an alternative to the authority of these Scottish patriarchs. Even though there must have been an overlapping membership, Burns's defection to the Masons could be interpreted, in symbolic terms at least, as an act of betrayal in view of the official complaint made against the fraternity by the Presbyterian Church. After a Synod held in 1745, the Presbyterians passed an act of the assembly in 1757 repudiating the Masons' oath. This they denounced as a mixture of "sinful, profane and superstitious devices: "Whereas an oath is one of the most solemn acts of religious worship, which ought to be taken only upon important and necessary occasions; and to be sworn in truth, in judgment, and in righteousness." [68] The Synod also objected to the penalty for perjury as well as to the tenet that the neophyte was swearing allegiance to a set of principles which were, as yet, unknown to him:

If that oath was not administered to them, without
letting them know the terms of it, till in the act
of administering the same to them? If it was not an
oath binding them to keep a number of secrets, none
of which they were allowed to know before swearing
the oath? If, beside a solemn invocation of the
Lord's name in that oath, it did not contain a capital
penalty about having their tongues and hearts taken
out in case of breaking the same? If the said oath was
not administered to them with several superstitious
ceremonies; such as, the stripping them of, or
requiring them to deliver up, any thing of metal which
they had upon them, - and making them kneel upon their
right knee bare, holding up their right arm bare, with
their elbow upon the Bible, or with the Bible laid
before them, - or having the Bible, as also the square
and compasses, in some particular way applied to their
bodies? and, if among the secrets which were
bound by that oath to keep, there was not a passage
of scripture read to them, particularly 1 Kings vii,
2i with or without some explication put upon the same,
for being concealed.[69]

Freemasonry had been condemned by orthodox Christians as a Gnostic heresy mainly because Grand Lodge had excluded

Christianity from Masonic ritual. The craft's first official historian, the Scottish Mason, James Anderson, only mentions Christianity during a passing reference to the historical Christ as the Messiah and the great Architect of the Church who was born during the reign of the Emperor Augustus. Eighteenth-century thinkers strongly identified with this period of Ancient Rome which may be why Anderson makes the outlandish claim that the Emperor Augustus was an early Grand Master. Freemasonry drew on the classical characteristics of the Augustan world-picture which developed into the cultural panoply of the Enlightenment. Deism, which attracted Enlightened thinkers, was adopted as the creed of the Freemason. In Anderson's *Constitutions*, the section dealing with the "Charges of a Free-Mason" opens: "It is now thought more expedient only to oblige them [the Freemasons] to that religion in which all men agree, leaving their particular opinions to themselves".[70] The Deistic belief in a supreme being was galvanised by the Masons into a veneration for the Great Architect of the Universe. Philosophers such as Locke and Voltaire having become Deists made overtures towards Freemasonry as a uniform belief-system [71] which in some respects was a microcosm of the Enlightenment. Burns addresses his brothers of the mystic tie as "Ye favour'd, ye enlighten'd few" which points to the relationship between mystical initiation and illumination through the light of reason which had already begun to dawn in the lodges:

Where scepter'd Reason from her Throne,
Surveys the Lodge and makes us one.[72]

The paradigm of *Aufklarlîng* built upon the paradox between elitism and egalitarianism was contained within the deeper structures of the secret societies which proliferated during the Golden Age of the Scottish Enlightenment. Appropriately it was a secret society which set out to define the term "Enlightenment" in 1783.[73]

In an analogy of universal Enlightenment, every candidate for Masonic initiation was taken out of the darkness and received into the light of Freemasonry. The metaphor of Enlightenment was realised through ritual illumination since the initiate was blindfolded before being dazzled by brilliant artificial lights. The privileges of Freemasonry were then extended to the neophyte. Paradoxically, the Enlightenment spawned elitist sects and attitudes which set out to diffuse egalitarian ideals. According to Herbert Grierson and J.C. Smith, Burns encapsulated the development of the democratic spirit, yet he chose to be one of the "favour'd" and "enlighten'd few"[74] of a secret society. His social poetry had christened him the poet of the people even though his Masonic verse was addressed to a highly selective audience, his fellow-Masons. Burns's career as a poet reflected the polarized forces of equality and exclusivity contained within Freemasonry which in turn mirrored the culture of the Enlightenment itself.

Even though the Masonic network represented an ideological alternative to society it also intensified and endorsed some of its values such as aristocratic patronage and the existing social hierarchy. The impact of Masonry upon Burns's career may be seen as a mixed blessing. While the lodge might have indulged Burns's weakness for hard drinking, membership also provided patrons and contacts who helped to further his career. The lodge ensured that Burns would never have to endure the solitary life of the garreted poet who was without friend or patron. Freemasonry also helped cultivate Burns as a poet of the Anglo-Scottish vernacular by encouraging him to continue writing Scots poetry. In this way the Masons kept Burns in touch with his cultural roots which helped him retain his identity as the ploughman poet. Burns was an active Mason until the end of his life. He became an honorary member of Loudon Kilwinning Lodge at Newmilns on 27 March 1786, and of St John's Kilwinning, Kilmarnock Lodge on 26 October 1768. On St Andrew's Day (30 November) 1792 he was elected Senior Warden at St Andrew's lodge, no. 179 in Dumfries which he frequented from December 1791 to April 1796 just three months before his death.[75] Eventually the lodge was named after Burns in recognition of his contribution to Freemasonry. In view of the poet's circumstances and immediate environment it was inevitable that he would be attracted to the Masons. According to one commentator:

> One prime factor which assisted to unite all classes
> in eighteenth-century Scotland into a recognised brother-
> hood, and provided the opportunity and sanction for
> voluntary co-operation, was the bond of Freemasonry;
> not Freemasonry as we know it to-day with all its modern
> trappings and symbolic teaching, but the earlier jolly
> Brotherhood with its gatherings at the local inn. There
> is no cause for wonder or surprise that in the fulness
> of time Robert Burns became a Freemason: the wonder
> would have been if he had not.[76]

Freemasons themselves have little doubt that the craft exerted a considerable influence on the life and work of Burns and that in his "best and most serious writings, in the highest flights of his genius, the spirit of Masonry is ever present, leading, directing, dictating, inspiring."[77]

## Notes

1. Burns, *The Poems and Songs of Robert Burns*, ed. James Kinsley, 3 vols (Oxford, 1968), I, p.271. All references following quotations will be taken from this edition which will be referred

to hereafter as Burns, *Poems*. A version of this chapter was submitted to the *Scottish Literary Journal* for inclusion in a special Burns issue for 1986 to commemorate the bicentenary of the Kilmarnock edition.

2. James Gibson, *Robert Burns and Masonry* (Liverpool, 1873), p.11.

3. An exception to this is L. M. Angus Butterworth, *Robert Burns and the eighteenth-century revival in Scottish Vernacular Poetry*, (Aberdeen, 1969), pp.246-56. Hereafter cited as Butterworth, *Robert Burns*.

4. Burns's fellow-Masons in Ayrshire included Sir John Whitefoord, Sheriff Wallace of Ayr, John Ballantine, Professor Dugald Stewart, Dr John Mackenzie of Mauchline, William Parker of Kilmarnock, Alexander Wood, James Humphry and John Wilson, the schoolmaster. Burns also joined the Canongate Kilwinning Lodge no. 2 in Edinburgh whose members included Patrick Miller of Dolswinton, Alexander Cunningham the lawyer, William Nicol the school master, Alexander Namyth the painter, William Creech the publisher and Henry Mackenzie the author of *The Man of Feeling*. See Maurice Lindsay, *The Burns Encyclopaedia*, (London, 1980), p.137.

5. Dudley Wright, *Robert Burns and His Masonic Circle* (London, 1929), p.8.

6. For an account of Irvine see Charles S. Dougall, *The Burns Country* (London, 1904), pp.232-3.

7. Wright, *Robert Burns and his Masonic Circle*, p.10.

8. *Letters of Robert Burns*, ed. J. De Lancey Ferguson, 2 vols (Oxford, 1931), I, p.13.

9. Hans Hecht, *Robert Burns: The Man and his Work* (London, 1936), p.32.

10. *The Life and Work of Robert Burns*, ed. Robert Chambers, revised William Wallace, 4 vols (London, 1896), I, pp.377-8.

11. Ibid., p.129.

12. William Harvey, *Robert Burns as a Freemason* (Dundee, 1921), pp.17-18.

13. See David Daiches, *Robert Burns*, (London, 1966), p.214.

14. *Letters of Robert Burns*, ed. Ferguson, I, p.67.

15. See frontispiece which has been included by kind permission

of The Grand Lodge of Scotland. For an account of those who attended the ceremony including Boswell see James Marshall, *A Winter with Robert Burns* (Edinburgh, 1846). Unfortunately this booklet is unreliable. For example, the antiquarian, Francis Grose, is mentioned as present but he did not become a Mason until 1791.

16. Harvey, *Robert Burns as a Freemason*, p.39.

17. David Murray Lyon, *History of the Lodge of Edinburgh*, (Mary's Chapel) no. 1 (London, 1900), pp.365-7. For a contrasting view see Hugh C. Peacock and Allan Mackenzie, *Robert Burns Poet-Laureate of Lodge Canongate Kilwinning: Facts Substantiating his Election and Inauguration on 1st March 1787* (Edinburgh, 1894).

18. Wright, *Robert Burns and Freemasonry* (Paisley, 1921), p.72.

19. See *Secret Societies*, ed. Norman Mackenzie (London, 1967), p.166.

20. *Early Masonic Pamphlets*, p.31. See Tom Crawford, "Political and Protest Songs in Eighteenth-Century Scotland 11 : Songs of the Left" in *Scottish Studies*, XIV (1970), pp. 105-31.

21. Margaret C. Jacob, *The Radical Enlightenment: Pantheists, Freemasons and Republicans* (London, 1981), p.127. For an earlier example of this practice see Douglas Knoop and G.P. Jones, *The Scottish Mason and the Mason Word* (Manchester, 1939), pp.49-50.

22. *Secret Societies*, ed. Mackenzie, p.166.

23. Wright, *Robert Burns and Freemasonry*, p.73.

24. Fred J. Belford, "Robert Burns - Freemason", *Year Book of the Grand Lodge of Antient, Free and Accepted Masons of Scotland* (Edinburgh, 1955), p.87.

25. The engraving was advertised in the *Daily Post*, 2 December 1724 as: "a curious print, engrav'd on a copper plate, by Ho---ge, taken from an original painting of Matachauter, by order of the Mandarin Hang-Lhi, grav'd at Pekin, and a number of them brought over from thence, by a merchant in the ship Cambridge". This is a response to a contemporary hoax concerning Gormogon satires of the Masons which took the form of two letters signed by the "illustrious *Mandarin* Hang Chi" appended to an essay on the subject by Aaron Hill in his journal, *The Plain Dealer*, 14 September 1724. The verses accompanying Hogarth's engraving highlight the mock-rivalry between the Masons and Gormogons:

> From Eastern Climes, transplanted to our coasts,
> Two Oldest Orders that Creation boasts

Here meet in miniature, expos'd to view
That by their Conduct, Men may judge their due.
The Gormogons, a Venerable Race
Appear distinguished with peculiar Grace.
What Honour! Wisdom! Truth! & Social Love!
Sure such an order had its birth above.
But mark Free Masons! What a farce is this?
How wild their myst'ry! What a bum they kiss
Who would not laugh when such occasions had?
Who should not weep, to think ye World so Mad.

26. See Pick and Knight, *The Pocket History of Freemasonry*, p.86.

27. See Jones, *The Freemasons' Guide and Compendium*, p.338.

28. Horace Walpole included this remark in a letter to Horace Mann dated 4 May 1743, no. 113 in the *Letters of Horace Walpole*, I (London, 1886), p.244.

29. See Ronald Paulson, *Hogarth: His Life, Art and Times*, 2 vols (London, 1971), I, p.130.

30. This Masonic pamphlet has been ascribed to Defoe. See John Robert Moore, *A Checklist of the Writings of Daniel Defoe* (Bloomington, 1960), p.227.

31. Stephen Knight, *The Brotherhood: The Secret World of the Freemasons* (London, 1984), p.25.

32. J. De Lancey Ferguson, *Robert Burns: Pride and Passion*, (New York, 1939), pp.296-7.

33. See the poem Burns dedicated to Glencairn, "Verses intended to be written below a noble Earl's picture" in Burns, *Poems*, I, p.312.

34. See E.P. Thompson, *The Making of the English Working Class*, pp.460-1.

35. Wright, *Robert Burns and Freemasonry*, p.45.

36. For a discussion of the Kilmarnock edition see Robert T. Fitzhugh, *Robert Burns: The Man and the Poet* (London, 1971), pp.107-23.

37. Harvey, *Robert Burns as a Freemason*, p.61.

38. See *Robert Burns: The Critical Heritage*, ed. Donald A. Low, (London, 1974), pp.67-71.

39. Belford, *Robert Burns - Freemason*, p.91.

40. See Henry Lovegrove, "Three Masonic Novels", *Ars Quatuor Coronatorum*, xxxii (1919), p.79.

41. *A Treasury of Masonic Thought*, ed. Glick, p.85.

42. Harvey, *Robert Burns as a Freemason*, pp.54-5.

43. De Quincey, *Works*, ed. Masson, XVI, p.413.

44. Jones, *The Freemasons' Guide and Compendium*, p.459.

45. See Hugh Douglas, *Robert Burns: A Life* (London, 1976), p.80 and Yvonne Helen Stevenson, *Burns and Highland Mary* (Ayr, 1979) and Fitzhugh, *Robert Burns*, pp.98-107.

46. Harvey, *Robert Burns as a Freemason*, pp.51-2.

47. *Early Masonic Pamphlets*, p.109.

48. Belford, *Robert Burns - Freemason*, p.87.

49. See Hecht, *Robert Burns*, pp.142-3.

50. Harvey, *Robert Burns as a Freemason*, pp.64-5.

51. G. Legman, *The Horn Book: Studies in Erotic Folklore and Bibliography* (London, 1970), pp.140-41.

52. Ibid., p.142.

53. Harvey, *Robert Burns as a Freemason*, p.65.

54. Loc. cit.

55. *Burns as Others saw Him* (Edinburgh, 1959), p.3.

56. *Early Masonic Pamphlets*, p.109.

57. In the Engraved List of 1729, De Veil is listed as a member of the Vine, Holborn in 1729, a lodge which Hogarth joined in 1731. See Derek Jarrett, *The Ingenious Mr Hogarth* (London, 1976), pp.53-5.

58. De Veil's hypocrisy was sharply criticized in the anonymous pamphlet *The Justice and the Footman* (London, 1744) which in turn gave rise to the defence by Taswell, *The Deviliad: An Heroic Poem* (London, 1744).

59. Swift, *Prose Works*, V, p.325.

60. Harvey, *Robert Burns as a Freemason*, p.71. Here the poem is quoted in full on pp.71-2.

61. Ibid., p.70.

62. Burns, *Poems*, I, p.271. The music accompanying "The Farewell. To the Brethren of St James's Lodge, Tarbolton" is reproduced from ibid., I, p.270 with kind permission of Oxford University Press. The poem inspired the following imitation by A. Glass of the Ayr Operative Lodge which appeared in *The Freemason* of 5 August 1871 and was then reproduced by Wright, *Robert Burns and his Masonic circle*, pp.24-5.

> I've sat beneath the old rooftree
>     Where Burns oft spent the festive night,
> As happy as a king could be
>     Amang the honoured Sons of Light.
> To me it was as Mecca's shrine
>     To ardent Eastern devotee,
> Where Scotias's minstrel passed langsyne
>     So many hours of joyous glee.
>
> What hallowed recreations throng
>     Around that spot, endeared to fame?
> What happy scenes of love and song
>     Are conjured up in Burns's name?
> What mystic fane, however grand,
>     Can with the lowly Lodge compare,
> Where, honoured with supreme command,
>     Presided Fame's eternal heir?
>
> Along the corridors of Time
>     For ever sweep his deathless lays,
> And Scotia's sons, in every clime,
>     Sing sweetly of their native braes;
> In fancy rove whaur Lugar flows,
>     Where hermit Ayr delights to stray
> Or bonny Doon in beauty goes
>     Past hoary, haunted Alloway.
>
> Nor sylvan bower, nor tiny flower,
>     That blooms where wimplin' burnie strays
> But he possessed the innate power
>     To twine around them fadeless bays.
> In Nature's Lodge, supreme and grand,
>     He sat as Master in the chair
> And shed a glory o'er the land
>     That time nor change can e'er impair.
>
> His was the keen, prophetic eye,

Could see afar the glorious birth
Of that Great Power, whose mystic tie
Shall make One Lodge of all the earth;
Shall usher in the reign of light,
Ring out the false, ring in the true,
Cause man to walk square and upright,
And wisdom's path of peace pursue.

63. J.G. Lockhart, *Life of Robert Burns* (London, 1976), pp.61-2.

64. The music is reproduced from Burns, *Poems*, I, p.299 with kind permission of Oxford University Press. Burns quotes the end of his poem in a letter to St James's lodge, Tarbolton, where he apologises for not being able to attend the quarterly meeting saying "If I must be absent in body, believe me I shall be present in spirit....

> Farewell!
> Within this dear Mansion may wayward Contention
> Or withered Envy ne'er enter
> May Secrecy round be the mystical bound,
> And brotherly Love be the Center!!!"

See *Letters of Robert Burns*, ed. Ferguson, I, p.118.

65. See F. Sherwood Taylor, *The Alchemists* (London, 1976), p.51.

66. Burns's eldest son became a Mason at the Old Lodge of Dumfries. See Dudley Wright, *Robert Burns and his Masonic Circle*, pp.128-9.

67. See A. Burns Jamieson, *Burns and Religion* (Cambridge, 1931), pp.14-26, 35-6, and Alexander Webster, *Burns and the Kirk* (Edinburgh, 1888).

68. "Act concerning the Mason-Oath", p.433.

69. Loc. cit. For the controversy concerning these and other issues see Walton Hannah, "Should a Christian be a Freemason?", LIV, no. 367, *Theology* (Jan., 1951), pp.3-10. See also the reply by J.L.C. Dart "Christianity and Freemasonry", LIV, no. 370, *Theology* (April, 1951), pp.130-36.

70. Anderson, *Constitutions* (1723), p.351.

71. See Claude E. Jones, "John Locke and Masonry", *Neuphilologische*, LXVII (1966), pp.72-81. For an account of Voltaire's association with Freemasonry see Shackleton, "The Encyclopédie and Freemasonry", *The Age of Enlightenment*, ed. Barber, et al., p.235. See Knoop and Jones, *Freemasonry and the Idea of Natural Religion*, (London, 1942).

72. James Anderson, *The New Book of Constitutions* (London, 1738), p.209.

73. See *The Age of Enlightenment: An Anthology of Eighteenth-Century Texts*, 2 vols, ed. Simon Eliot and Beverley Stern (London, 1979), II, p.249.

74. See Herbert J.C. Grierson and J.C. Smith, *A Critical History of English Poetry* (London, 1947), p.285.

75. See Maurice Lindsay, *The Burns Encyclopaedia*, p.138.

76. Belford, *Robert Burns - Freemason*, p.82.

77. Harvey, *Robert Burns as a Freemason*, p.64.

**Plate 1:** A. Slade, *A Freemason Formed out of the Materials of his Lodge* (By courtesy of the United Grand Lodge of England)

Plate 2:      William Blake, *The Ancient of Days*
(By courtesy of the Whitworth Art Gallery,
Manchester)

**Plate 3:** *A Masonic Engraving of 1769*
(By courtesy of the United Grand Lodge of
England)

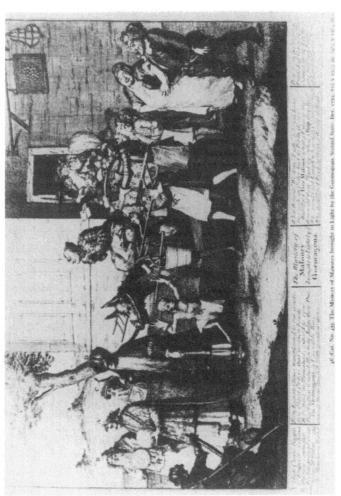

**Plate 4:** William Hogarth, *The Mystery of Masonry Brought to Light by the Gormogons* (By courtesy of the British Museum)

**Plate 5:**   *Robert Burns: Deputy Master, St James Tarbolton Kilwinning*
(By courtesy of George Draffen)

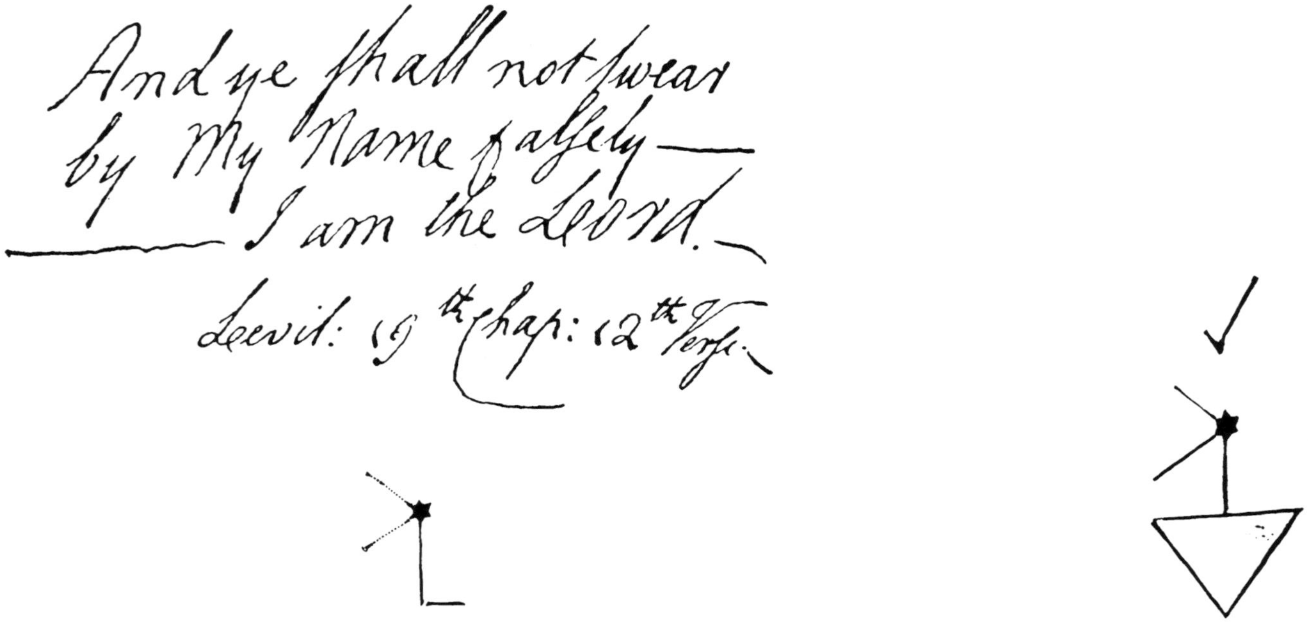

**Plate 6:** Burns's Masonic Mark in Highland Mary's Bible (By courtesy of George Draffen)

**Plate 7:**    William Hogarth, *Night,* from the series *The Four Times of Day* (By courtesy of the British Museum)

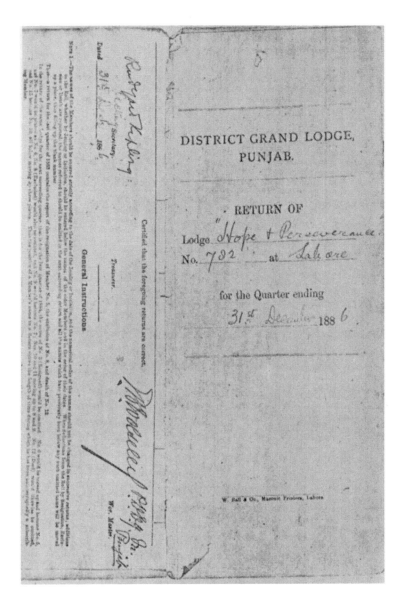

DISTRICT GRAND LODGE,
PUNJAB.

· RETURN OF

Lodge *Hope & Perseverance*
No. 782 at *Lahore*

for the Quarter ending

31st *December* 188 6

W. Bell & Co., Masonic Printers, Lahore

Rudyard Kipling:
*Acting Secretary,*
Dated 31st *March* 188 6

Certified that the foregoing returns are correct.

Treasurer.

General Instructions

Wor. Master.

**Plate 8:**     Kipling's membership certificate
(By courtesy of the Board of General Purposes
of the United Grand Lodge of England)

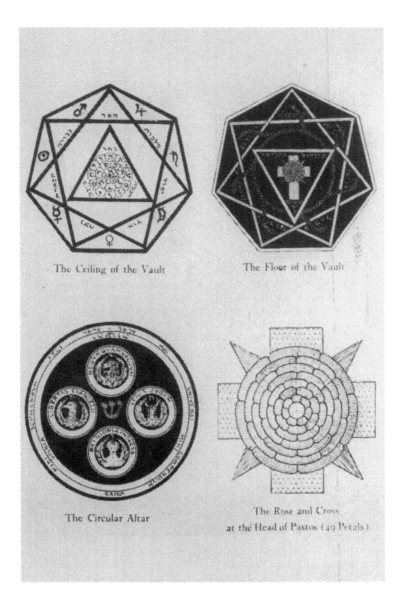

The Ceiling of the Vault

The Floor of the Vault

The Circular Altar

The Rose and Cross
at the Head of Pastos (49 Petals)

**Plate 9:**      Views of the Rosicrucian Vault
(Reproduced from Israel Regardie's *The Golden Dawn* (Minnesota, 1971) by courtesy of Llewellyn Publications, P.O. Box 43383, St Paul, MN 55164-0383)

## 4 PERCY BYSSHE SHELLEY

> You talk like a Rosicrucian, who will love nothing
> but a sylph, who does not believe in the existence
> of a sylph, and who yet quarrels with the whole
> universe for not containing a sylph.
>
> Peacock[1]

### The Bavarian Illuminati

Percy Bysshe Shelley's (1792-1822) association with secret societies
such as the Illuminati, the Assassins, and the Rosicrucians was
really an imaginative identification since he never actually
belonged to any of these organizations. The nearest Shelley had
come to joining a clandestine brotherhood was when he tried to
create his own. Mainly through literature, Shelley explored the
esoteric societies which provided a water-shed between the Gothic
imagination and the rise of Romanticism.

In the wake of the French Revolution the secret societies
were the dark spectres haunting the mass-movements of Europe.
Gothic novelists had siezed upon them as metaphors of terror. As
Walter Scott observed, no novelist was "so obtuse as not to image
forth a profligate abbot, an oppressive duke, a secret and
mysterious association of Rosycrucians [sic] and Illuminati, with
all their properties of black cowls, caverns, daggers, electric
machines, trap-doors, and dark lanterns"[2]. Shelley addressed
himself to the popular image of the secret societies as part of a
subversive movement gnawing at the fabric of Western civilisation.
He regarded them as agencies for those dark mysterious forces
which dethroned kings, dismounted generals, and toppled
governments. In 1799 the British government passed an act
banning secret and seditious societies. In 1811 Shelley published a
novel about a Rosicrucian, a member of the Brotherhood of the
Rosy Cross which had emerged during the previous century as a
Protestant consciousness-raising movement opposing the hegemony
of the Hapsburgs. In his novel, *St Irvyne or The Rosicrucian*,
Shelley explores the impact of the most radical of all earthly
revolutions, the conquest of death.

After the Continental witch-hunts of the 1790s, Shelley
found himself drawn to another secret society, the Bavarian
Illuminati, which was dedicated to anarchy and revolution. An
early version of this society was the Assassins, a Near Eastern
sect, which inspired Shelley's prose work of that title.[3] His

romantic view of this brutal secret society indicates that he had
interpreted the activities of the Assassins in the same favourable
light as had the Illuminés. The Bavarian Illuminati had been
institutionalised by Adam Weishaupt (1748-1830) at the University
of Ingoldstadt in 1776. The Illuminati regarded themselves as
guardians of the Rational Enlightenment. They aspired to
illuminate the world with the light of reason until as Weishaupt
forecasts:

> Princes and nations will disappear without violence
> from the earth, the human race will become one family
> and the world the abode of reasonable men. Morality
> alone will bring about this change imperceptibly ....
> Why should it be impossible that the human race should
> attain to its highest perfection, the capacity to
> guide itself?[4]

Since Shelley was attracted to the atheism and liberalism of this
cause, he contacted the radical Leigh Hunt about organizing a
band of "enlightened unprejudiced members" in order "to resist
the coalition of the enemies of liberty".[5] Shelley insisted that his
proposed society would be instrumental in activating political and
social reform since "it has been for want of societies of this
nature that corruption has attained the height at which we now
behold it."[6]

It is likely that Shelley's proposals had been influenced by
Robert Clifford's translation of the Abbé Barruel's *Memoirs
Illustrating the History of Jacobinism* (1797-98). Barruel was a
major contributor to the MaCarthyism of the 1790s through his
exposé of alleged Masonic, Rosicrucian and Illuminist activities.
He portrayed the secret societies as precipitators of the French
Revolution which he claimed had resulted from an anti-
monarchical and anti-ecclesiastical conspiracy. Thomas Jefferson
Hogg claimed that one of Shelley's favourite books at Oxford was
Barruel's *Memoirs* which he read and reread "swallowing with
eager credulity the fictions and exaggerations of that readily
believing, or readily inventing, author".[7] Yet Shelley condemned
the book in a letter to Elizabeth Hitchener (27 February 1812)
declaring it to be "half filled with the vilest and most
unsupported falsehood". In spite of this denunciation, Shelley went
on to recommend the *Memoirs* as "a book worth reading".[8] It is
ironic to consider that Shelley's pursuit of rational liberty should
have been inspired by Barruel's vilification of the Illuminati as a
subversive organization committed to the "annihilation of every
Empire, of all order, rank, distinction, property, and social tie".[9]

Barruel's vision of holocaust deliberately distorts Weishaupt's
ideals regarding world-wide reform which were grounded in the
principles of Rational Enlightenment. The *Memoirs* trace the
origins of the French Revolution from the Illuminati in
Ingoldstadt to the Freemasons, philosophes and Jacobins, and then
to the mobs on the street. Barruel was convinced that "*Illuminés,*

coalesced with the Sophisters who, with the Occult Masons, conspired against both Christ and Kings."[10] He also insisted that it was the adepts of anarchy, rebellion and impiety who had given birth to "the monster called JACOBIN".[11] Barruel makes extensive use of this parent-child metaphor in his account of the monster terrorising Europe. Lee Sterrenburg suggests that Mary Shelley had been influenced by Barruel's *Memoirs* while she was writing *Frankenstein* (1818) [12] particularly since the Jacobin monster was conceived at Ingoldstadt, the spiritual home of the Illuminati. In Mary Shelley's novel, Victor Frankenstein, a character based on her husband, Shelley, also produces a monster at Ingoldstadt. The disruption caused by Victor's creation has similarities with the Illuminists's strategy to destroy the social, political and religious institutions which enchain the individual. Mary Shelley's monster expressed the revolutionary fervour of the young Shelley who declared: "Indeed I think it is to the benefit of society to destroy the opinions which *can* annihilate the dearest of its ties... *Adieu.* - *Ecrasez l'infame écrasez l'impie*."[13] The above quotation from Voltaire was identified by Barruel as the motto for the Illuminati. Shelley must have used this phrase to register his determination to adopt a course of enlightened thinking by founding a secret society which would be analogous with Illuminism.

He had also been inspired by the philosophical anarchism of his father-in-law, William Godwin. Shelley was not only Godwin's heir to the Rosicrucian novel but also to his utopian vision of the "Kingless continents sinless as Eden."[14] Henry Crabb Robinson makes a distinction between the kind of anarchism preached by Godwin in his *Enquiry Concerning Political Justice* (1793) and the brand of anarchy propagated by the Illuminati. Robinson is particularly critical of the Illuminés for shrouding their objectives in secrecy: "The great difference between Godwinism and Illuminatism consists in this that Godwin proudly rejects all temporising, he shows the distant End and would have his followers strive to attain it immediately".[15] Paradoxically, the Illuminati who professed to be the arch-enemies of such obscurantists as the Jesuits had become, according to Robinson, "an Antijesuitical Jesuitism".[16] The Illuminés had not only adopted the rhetoric of their opponents but virtually the same means and end. Novelists had siezed on this internal irony by portraying the secret tribunals of the Illuminati and the authorities of the Inquisition as one order of tyranny. Consequently the Illuminati, which had originated as a "harbinger for the Enlightenment", was now represented through fiction as an instrument of repression. In this way the subversive image of the Illuminati provided a paradigm for the dialectical reversal of the Enlightenment movement which had transmogrified into its own opposite. The "Terror" of the French Revolution proved to be the most cogent example of how the "Enlightenment behaves toward things as a dictator toward men".[17]

For the middle classes, conspiracy theories sustained the

myth that political irrationality had been brought about by a conscious agency. This paranoia was exploited by Gothic novelists such as the Marquis of Grosse. In his *Horrid Mysteries* (1796), a specimen of *Schauerromantik*, a band of desperate Illuminati strive for world dominion. The English translator of the novel claims in his preface:

> Secret Societies have, at all times, and in all
> civilized countries, either held out private
> advantages, or pretended to aim at the welfare of
> whole nations, in order to increase the number of
> their members. Amongst the former, the *Rosycrucians*,
> whose order was instituted in Germany in the latter
> end of the fifteenth century, and pretended to be in
> possession of the philosophers' stone, and of many
> more valuable arcana, were, by far, the most famous;
> and among the latter, the association known under
> the name of the Secret Tribunal, acquired the
> greatest celebrity.[18]

The mythologies of the Rosicrucians and Illuminati, having acquired the dimensions of folk-lore, had carved out a permanent niche in the European popular imagination. Novelists had only to draw on those fictions already circulating in society which were being amplified by politicians and historians. Even Disraeli channels his political fears into his novel *Lothair* (1870). Elsewhere he blames the outbreak of the revolutions of 1848 and the social upheaval of the previous century on the secret societies:

> The origin of the secret societies that prevail in
> Europe is very remote. It is probable that they
> were originally confederations of conquered races
> organized    in a great measure by the abrogated
> hierarchies. In Italy they have never ceased,
> although they have at times been obliged to take
> various forms; sometimes it was a literary academy,
> sometimes a charitable brotherhood; freemasonry
> was always a convenient guise. The Inquisition
> in its great day boasted that it had extirpated
> them in Spain, but their activity in that country
> after the first French revolution rather indicates
> a suspension of vitality than an extinction of
> life. The reformation gave them a great impulse in
> Germany, and towards the middle of the eighteenth
> century, they had not only spread in every portion
> of the north of that region but had crossed the
> Rhine.
>      The two characteristics of these confederations,
> which now cover Europe like network, are war against
> property and hatred of the Semitic revelation. These
> are the legacies of their founders; a proprietary

despoiled and the servants of altars that have been overthrown. Alone, the secret societies can disturb, but they cannot control, Europe. Acting in unison with a great popular movement they may destroy society, as they did at the end of the last century.[19]

Not surprisingly, Thomas Love Peacock in his satire of the Gothic novel, *Nightmare Abbey* (1818), ridiculed the preoccupation of novelists with secret societies.

## Nightmare Abbey

In *Nightmare Abbey*, Peacock caricatures Shelley's attraction towards politically subversive secret societies through the character, Scythrop:

> He now became troubled with the *passion for reforming the world*. He built many castles in the air, and peopled them with secret tribunals, and bands of illuminati, who were always the imaginary instruments of his projected regeneration of the human species. As he intended to institute a perfect republic, he invested himself with absolute sovereignty over these mystical dispensers of liberty.[20]

Peacock satirises Shelley's fascination with "secret tribunals, and bands of illuminati" which were stock ingredients of the Gothic novel imported from Germany. Much of the poet's attraction to Gothic romance may be attributed to his reading of terror literature [21] which is parodied by Peacock in chapter three of *Nightmare Abbey*. Here Marionetta, who is based on Shelley's first wife, Harriet Westbrook, accidentally comes across Scythrop rehearsing a role as the president of some imaginary secret tribunal. After realising that he has an audience, Scythrop recovers sufficiently from his embarrassment to invite Marionetta to act out some scenes with him from one of the tales of the German Illuminati, *Horrid Mysteries*. According to Hogg, Shelley would read aloud from this novel with "rapturous enthusiasm".[22] Peacock parodies Shelley's enthusiasm for the Gothic through his description of Scythrop sleeping with *Horrid Mysteries* under his pillow while dreaming of "venerable eleutherarchs and ghastly confederates holding midnight conventions in subterranean caves."[23] Scythrop had fancifully described himself as a "transcendental eleutherarch"[24] a term which T.J. Hogg uses in his novel, *Alexy Haimatoff* (1813) for a ruler of a secret society. Scythrop had assumed this title in order to win the affections of another heroine, Stella, modelled on Shelley's second wife, Mary.

Scythrop suspects Stella to be an illuminé because she eulogises "the sublime Spartacus Weishaupt" as the "immortal founder of the sect of the Illuminati".[25] Stella eventually confesses to Scythrop that she is fleeing from persecution. Since Scythrop has given her refuge he fears that he has now harboured an illuminé in contravention of Lord Castlereagh's Alien Act (1816) which offered little protection to political refugees. Scythrop believes Stella has been a victim of the campaign against secret societies such as the Illuminati. In March 1785 the Elector of Bavaria under pressure from the Jesuits exiled all Masonic and Illuminist organisations which forced Weishaupt to escape to Gotha. Scythrop had become so agitated by this history of persecution that he feared attracting the attention of the authorities himself. Consequently he takes the precaution of having a number of cells and recesses, sliding panels and secret passages built into the tower of Nightmare Abbey where he could conceal himself should such an emergency arise. Peacock wryly comments that Scythrop had not resorted to such self-preservation for his own sake but for the greater benefit of mankind! Fortunately, Scythrop's foresight enabled him to offer Stella the protection of his "unknown apartments".[26] In his description of these, Peacock parodies the Gothic settings to be found in so many Gothic novels of the period since Scythrop's "apartments" are merely inferior imitations of the caverns and subterranean passages frequented by bands of illuminati.

Scythrop is particularly captivated by Stella because he believes that she was one of the seven people who had bought a copy of a treatise he had written. Scythrop makes this assumption when Stella recognises him as the author of *Philosophical Gas; or, a Project for a General Illumination of the Human Mind*. Even though Scythrop manages to sell only seven copies of this *opus mimum*, he consoles himself with his knowledge of numerology with which he reasons: "Seven is a mystical number, and the omen is good. Let me find the seven purchasers of my seven copies, and they shall be the seven golden candle-sticks with which I will illuminate the world."[27] Scythrop assumes that Stella must be one of his golden candlesticks as one of the seven consumers of his *Philosophical Gas*. Scythrop's treatise is a parody of one of Shelley's pamphlets for reform, the most likely being his *Proposals for an Association of those Philanthropists who convinced of the inadequacy of the moral and political state of Ireland to produce benefits which are nevertheless attainable are willing to unite to accomplish its regeneration* (1812). Here with reference to Barruel's *Memoirs*, Shelley expands on his earlier proposals to Leigh Hunt about founding a secret society. The *Proposals* for political reform were written in support of Catholic emancipation and for the repeal of the Union Act. Shelley's pamphlet was intended to launch a world-wide campaign of philanthropy which, like Scythrop's *Philosophical Gas*, was written to illuminate mankind. In order to build up the membership of his society, Shelley invited readers of his pamphlet to

communicate with him at a Dublin address. Both Shelley and
Scythrop hoped that their readers would form a vanguard which
would enlighten the world.

Scythrop who wanted to revive a "confederation of
regenerators"[28] cryptically concealed his revolutionary message in
*Philosophic Gas* where "his meanings were carefully wrapt up in
the monk's hood of transcendental technology".[29] Peacock's oblique
reference to the monastic setting of many Gothic novels alongside
an allusion to Kant's transcendentalism draws attention to
conflicting elements in Enlightenment thought. In *Nightmare Abbey*,
Mr Flosky is based on Coleridge who was a disciple of Kant.
Scythrop is recommended by Mr Flosky "to pore over ponderous
tomes of transcendental philosophy, which reconciled him to the
labour of studying them by their mystical jargon and necromantic
imagery."[30] By comparing Kant's writings to magical jargon,
Peacock satirically suggests that both are sources of mystification.
He dismisses Kantians as members of an esoteric sect who may
be compared to the initiates of a secret society since Kant
"delivers his oracles in language which none but the initiated can
comprehend."[31] According to Peacock, these cryptic sources of
wisdom express "the views of those secret associations of
illuminati, which were the terror of superstition and tyranny".[32]
By clubbing together Illuminists with Kant's transcendentalism and
the Gothic literary tradition, Peacock undermines the aspirations
of these esoteric organisations towards Rational Enlightenment.
This was in common with those Gothic novelists who represented
the secret societies of the Enlightenment as preserves of medieval
superstition. Such a bad press for the Illuminist organisations must
have gratified those who were opposed to secret societies.

It would have been interesting to have discovered whether
or not Shelley succumbed to the lure of the Gothic in his
proposed novel, *Hubert Cauvin*, where he intended to develop his
ideas for a secret society. In his early terror novel, *Zastrozzi*
(1810), Shelley comes near to portraying a degenerated image of
the Illuminati in Gothic fiction through his hero, Verezzi, who
had become "the victim of secret enemies".[33] Through *St Irvyne*
Shelley advances the Gothic novel from its preoccupation with
bands of subversive Illuminists to a rudimentary study of the
Romantic anguish of the Rosicrucian hero. A.J. Hartley detects in
*St Irvyne* an attempt to incorporate the social and political reform
advocated by the Rosicrucian tradition:

> Though Gothic convention is paramount in *St Irvyne*
> it should be noted, however, that the Rosicrucian,
> like his creator, and in conformity with the aims
> of the Rosicrucian Society, is concerned with reform,
> the book abounds in references to conscience, decries
> selfishness, and closes on a note of admonition to
> remorse and repentance.[34]

In *St Irvyne* Shelley's exploration of the metaphysics of the mortal immortal reveals how Rosicrucianism, like Illuminism, was capable of opening up new insights into the Romantic imagination.

## The Rosicrucian

Shortly after *St Irvyne* was published an excited Shelley wrote to his publisher, John Stockdale, asking "Do you find that the public are captivated by the title page of *St Irvyne?*"[35] Shelley was hoping for a favourable response to his sub-title *The Rosicrucian*, which referred to the elusive Brotherhood of the Rosy Cross. These were a species of magician-scientists whose existence had been announced by the Manifestos, *Fama Fraternatis* (1614) and *Confessio Fraternitatis* (1614). In his *Lives of the Necromancers* (1834) Godwin attempted to define the Rosicrucians:

> Nothing very distinct has been ascertained respecting a sect, calling itself Rosicrucians. It is said to have originated in the East from one of the crusaders in the fourteenth century; but it attracted at least no public notice till the beginning of the seventeenth century. Its adherents appear to have imbibed their notions from the Arabians, and claimed the possession of the philosopher's stone, the art of transmuting metals, and the *elixir vitae*.[36]

Godwin had written the first Rosicrucian novel, *St Leon* (1799) which charted the destiny of a hero who had discovered the secret of immortality. Shelley explained his use of the term "Rosicrucian" to Stockdale who was baffled by its meaning: "What I mean as "Rosicrucian" is the elixir of eternal life which Ginotti has obtained. Mr Godwin's romance of *St Leon* turns upon that superstition."[37] After reading *St Leon* Shelley had been inspired to write his own Rosicrucian novel, *St Irvyne*. But, unfortunately, he did not capitalise upon the success of his predecessor. A typical contemporary response which appeared in *The Anti-Jacobin Review and Magazine* denounced it as *"description run mad"* with "every wild expression" of the "disordered imagination of the romance-writer".[38] Later critics were just as dismissive of *St Irvyne*. Elizabeth Barrett Browning could scarcely believe Shelley to be the author of such "boarding-school idiocy".[39] William Michael Rossetti found the novel to be unintelligible to the sane reader [40] while John Cordy Jeaffreson described it as a "piece of lunacy" which had a conclusion that "surpasses all human understanding".[41] Andrew Lang went even further by claiming that *St Irvyne*" proves that Shelley at Oxford was a donkey, and also demonstrates that we can never tell how a young wild ass may turn out."[42] In view of adverse criticism Shelley felt obliged to apologise to Godwin for the defects in the novel by attributing them to a temporary state of "intellectual sickliness and lethargy".[43]

*St Irvyne* tells the story of Wolfstein, a young nobleman, who had joined a band of brigands. One of these is a man named Ginotti, a servant of the devil, who is in possession of the elixir vitae. Ginotti, however, wants to relinquish his gift of perpetual life and pass on the secret to Wolfstein. But before this transaction takes place, Wolfstein becomes romantically involved with the beautiful Megalena who has been captured by bandits. Wolfstein, aided by Ginotti, eventually escapes with her to Genoa. Shortly afterwards Megalena discovers that Wolfstein has become infatuated by the Lady Olympia. Enraged with jealousy, Magalena tries to persuade Wolfstein to murder her rival. Though he cannot bring himself to do this, Megalena is satisfied once she finds out that Olympia has conveniently committed suicide. But Megalena does not savour her victory long for she dies mysteriously in the vaults of the church of St Irvyne. Before her death Wolfstein's sister, Eloise, had already replaced her as the central female character. Eloise's adventures take place as she accompanies her dying mother on a long journey. Eventually she encounters a sinister stranger, Nempere, who sells her to an English nobleman, Mountford. At Mountford's house Eloise falls in love with his friend, Fitzeustace. Subsequently, Nempere and Mountford quarrel which leads to a duel in which the former is killed. Mountford is forced to flee to London in order to avoid the officers of justice which leaves Eloise free to settle down with Fitzeustace. Meanwhile Wolfstein arrives at St Irvyne's church where he has arranged to meet Ginotti who has promised to reveal the secret of immortality to him. But when the moment of blasphemy arrives Wolfstein finds that he is unable to renounce his creator. Consequently, Ginotti is reduced to a mouldering skeleton forced to endure all the horrors of an eternal existence in hell. Wolfstein also dies "blackened in terrible convulsions" though "over him had the power of hell no influence".[44]

Shelley's revelation in the last paragraph of the novel that Ginotti is, in fact, Nempere, considerably complicates the circumstances surrounding the Rosicrucian's death. The main problem now, of course, is that Ginotti-Nempere has died twice, once in a duel and again in the vaults of St Irvyne. Furthermore Shelley makes no attempt to disguise the fact that he has passed from chapter 4 to chapter 7 in a short-cut for which, Carl Grabo dryly remarked, "the reader is not ungrateful".[45] Shelley had barely attempted to harmonise the contradictory plot of *St Irvyne*. Stockdale, who was justifiably mystified by the confused ending to the novel, received the following explanation from the author:

> Ginotti, as you will see did *not* die by Wolfstein's hand, but by the influence of that natural magic which when the   secret was imparted to the latter, destroyed him. - Mountford, being a character of

inferior import, I do not think it necessary to
state the catastrophe of *him*, as at best it would
be uninteresting. - Eloise and Fitzeustace, are
married and happy I suppose, and Megalena dies by
the same    means as Wolfstein. - I do not myself
see any other explanation that is required.[46]

Shelley attempts to clarify his treatment of the elixir of life
saying: "I enveloped it in mystery for the greater excitement of
interest, and on a re-examination, you will perceive that
Mountford physically did kill Ginotti, which must appear from
the latter's paleness".[47]

Apart from the logistics of murder and intrigue, the main
message of the narrative emerges relatively clearly. In keeping
with the spirit of the *Fama*, Shelley condemns those whose
"wanderings of error"[48] have enticed them to procure the
blasphemous elixir vitae. *St Irvyne* ends with the warning that
endless life may only be "sought from Him who alone can give
an eternity of happiness".[49] This lesson has been gleaned from
the heresies of Ginotti who had secularised his immortality
because, as he admits to Wolfstein: "I feared, more that ever,
now, to die; and, although I had no right to form hopes or
expectations for longer life than is allotted to the rest of mortals,
yet did I think it were possible to protract existence."[50] Faced
with the prospect of death, Ginotti submits himself to the powers
of Hell which reveal to him in a vision the secret of eternal
life. As he confessed to Wolfstein: "I ascertained the method by
which *man* might exist for ever, and it was connected with my
dream."[51] Ginotti pared down the ontological problem of eternal
life into two options: "I must either dive into the recesses of
futurity, or I must not, I cannot die. Will not this nature - will
not the *matter* of which it is composed - exist to all eternity?"[52]
Ginotti's desire to perpetuate his life was derived from a desire
to retain the familiar rather than to obviate the oblivion of
non-existence. In his essay, *On a Future State* written in 1818,
Shelley draws attention to the lure of life-extension:

> This desire to be for ever as we are; the reluctance
> to a violent and unexperienced change, which is
> common to all the animated and inanimate combinations
> of the universe, is, indeed, the secret persuasion
> which has given birth to the opinions of a future
> state.[53]

Ginotti's view of death as containing "the recesses of
futurity" rather than as a negation, points to Shelley's belief in a
personal immortality. In a note to *Hellas* (1822) written towards
the end of the poet's life, he again refers to death as "that
futurity towards which we are all impelled by an inextinguishable
thirst for immortality".[54] Ginotti is not choosing between
immortality and the void but between two immortal states. Mary

Shelley's short story, "The Mortal Immortal" which was inspired by
Shelley, makes this distinction between life-extension and spiritual
immortality. The elixir vitae gives rise to a dilemma which is
expressed in the novel through a structural irony. Ginotti, who
inhabits a limbo of moral isolation, had feared death as an
estrangement from life. Instead he finds that by perpetuating his
existence he has become a stranger to himself and to society. By
distancing himself from mankind, Ginotti reinforces his
self-imposed solipsism. Instead he longs to pass on the secret and
surrender to death saying: "To one man alone, Wolfstein, may I
communicate this secret of immortal life: then must I forego *my*
claim to it, - and oh! with what pleasure shall I forego it!"[55]
Ginotti goes on to reveal: "You, Wolfstein, have I singled out
from the whole world to make the depository"[56] of the elixir.
Wolfstein's reluctance to inherit the secret of eternal life forms
part of the nightmarish struggle between himself and his
alter-ego, Ginotti, which may be described as a psychomachy, a
conflict between body and soul.[57] As Andy P. Antippas argues,
the Gothic mode lends itself to this type of combat by
representing a fragmented moral vision which manifests itself
through adversaries who contend as emblems of good and evil.
Shelley makes a direct connection between Ginotti and Nempere
by identifying them as the same person. This relates to the
*doppelgänger*, the folklore belief that the image of the projected
self was a harbinger of impending death.[58] Given Shelley's
knowledge of German literature it is possible that he adopted this
motif in order to illustrate moral conflict. The Manichean struggle
between Wolfstein and Ginotti may be viewed as a metaphor for
the divided self, even of the lost soul. But it is more likely that
Shelley was unconscious of any deep underlying meaning to these
dualities since he neglects to explore their allegorical significance.

Peacock's droll remark that "this rage for novelty is the
bane of literature"[59] may have been intended for Shelley whose
pursuit of the sensational aspects of the secret societies only
succeeded in producing inferior literature such as *St Irvyne* and
*The Assassins*. Yet Shelley's interest in Rosicrucianism and
subversive political groups such as the Illuminati, formed part of
his Romantic rebellion which contributed to his later development
as a mature poet.

## Notes

1. Thomas Love Peacock, *Nightmare Abbey* (Harmondsworth, 1976),
p.102.

2. Walter Scott, *Waverley, or, 'Tis sixty Years Since* (London, 1910),
p.64.

3. See Shelley, *The Complete Works of Percy Bysshe Shelley*, ed. Roger Ingpen and Walter Edwin Peck (London, 1965), VI, pp.155-71. Paul Dawson suggested to me that Shelley probably associated the Assassins with the Essenes.

4. *Secret Societies*, ed. Mackenzie, p.170. See also Nesta Webster, *Secret Societies and Subversive Movements* (London, 1964), pp.196-268.

5. *The Letters of Percy Bysshe Shelley*, ed. Frederick L. Jones (Oxford, 1964), I, p.54. See Richard Holmes, *Shelley the Pursuit* (London, 1974), pp.52-3. Although the Illuminati was a model, Shelley's proposed society had relatively limited aims. See Paul Dawson, *The Unacknowledged Legislator: Shelley and Politics* (London, 1980), pp.157 ff.

6. Shelley, *Letters*, ed. Jones, I, p.54.

7. Thomas Jefferson Hogg, *The Life of Shelley* (London, 1933), I, p.376.

8. Shelley, *Letters*, ed. Jones, I, p.264. See James Reieger, *The Mutiny Within: The Heresies of Percy Bysshe Shelley* (New York, 1967), pp.62-8.

9. Abbé Barruel, *Memoirs Illustrating the History of Jacobinism*, trans. Robert Clifford (London, 1797), IV, p.584. See Walter Edwin Peck, "Shelley and the Abbé Barruel", *Publications of the Modern Language Association of America*, XXXVI (1921), pp.347-53.

10. Barruel, *Memoirs Illustrating the History of Jacobinism*, I, pp.xxii-xxiii.

11. Ibid., II, p.479.

12. See *The Endurance of Frankenstein: Essays on Mary Shelley's Novel*, ed. George Levine and U.C. Knoepflmacher (London, 1979).

13. Shelley, *Letters*, ed. Jones, I, pp.27-9.

14. A.L. Morton, *The English Utopia* (London, 1978), p.154.

15. *Crabb Robinson in Germany 1800-1805: Extracts from his Correspondence*, ed. Edith T. Morley (London, 1929), p.51.

16. Loc. cit. Weishaupt modelled the organizational aspects of the Illuminati on the Jesuits who had educated him.

17. Adorno and Horkheimer, *Dialectic of Enlightenment*, p.9.

18. Marquis of Grosse, *Horrid Mysteries*, trans. P. Well, 2 vols

P.B. Shelley

(London, 1927), xxi.

. Benjamin Disraeli, *Lord George Bentinck, A Political Biography* (London, 1852), pp.553-4.

20. Peacock, *Nightmare Abbey*, p.47.

21. See Kenneth Neill Cameron, *The Young Shelley: Genesis of a Radical* (London, 1951), p.29.

22. Hogg, *The Life of Shelley*, I, p.376.

23. Peacock, *Nightmare Abbey*, p.47.

24. Ibid., p.92.

25. Ibid., p.94.

26. Ibid., p.92.

27. Ibid., p.48.

28. Loc. cit.

29. Loc cit.

30. Ibid., p.46.

31. Ibid., p.47.

32. Loc. cit.

33. Shelley, *Zastrozzi: A Romance and St Irvyne or The Rosicrucian* (New York, 1977), p.3.

34. Ibid., VI.

35. Shelley, *Letters*, ed. Jones, I, p.40.

36. Godwin, *Lives of the Necromancers* (London, 1834), pp.35-6.

37. Shelley, *Letters*, ed. Jones, I, p.21.

38. Newman Ivey White, *The Unextinguished Hearth: Shelley and His Contemporary Critics* (Durham, North Carolina, 1938), p.36.

39. Sylva Norman, *Flight of the Skylark: The Development of Shelley's Reputation* (London, 1954), p.162.

40. William Michael Rossetti, *A Memoir of Shelley* (London, 1886), p.19.

100

41. John Cordy Jeaffreson, *The Real Shelley: New Views of the Poet's Life* (London, 1885), I, p.160.

42. Edmund Blunden, *Shelley: A Life Story* (London, 1948), p.44.

43. Shelley, *Letters*, ed. Jones I, p.266.

44. Shelley, *St Irvyne*, p.219.

45. Carl Grabo, *The Magic Plant: The Growth of Shelley's Thought* (Chapel Hill, 1936), p.16.

46. Shelley, *Letters*, ed. Jones, I, p.20.

47. Ibid., I, p.21.

48. Shelley, *St Irvyne*, p.220.

49. Loc. cit.

50. Ibid., pp.199-200.

51. Ibid., p.203.

52. Ibid., p.199.

53. Shelley, *Works*, ed. Ingpen and Peck, VI, p.209.

54. Ibid., III, p.56.

55. Shelley, *St Irvyne*, p.203.

56. Ibid., p.155.

57. See Andy P. Antippas, "The Structure of Shelley's *St Irvyne*: Parallelism and the Gothic Mode of Evil", *Tulane Studies in English*, XVlll (1970), p.67.

58. See Margaret Loftus Ranald and Ralph Arthur Ranald, "Shelley's Magus Zoroaster and the Image of the Doppelgänger," *Modern Language Notes*, LXXVI (Jan., 1961), pp.7-12.

59. Peacock, *Nightmare Abbey*, p.62.

# RUDYARD KIPLING

"once a mason, always a mason"
Kipling[1]

## An Empire of Freemasons

Rudyard Kipling's (1865-1936) Masonic poems document an important phase in the history of British Freemasonry which concerns its spread to the colonies. The underground tentacles of British influence reaching out through the secret Masonic network contributed to the growth of the Empire. As an instrument of imperialism, Freemasonry had taken on a more military flavour through the phenomenon of the regimental lodge. The first permanent lodge for the armed forces was established in Gibraltar in 1728.[2] Prior to this, lodges attached to regiments were ambulatory having to travel with the army. As Pick and Knight point out, Masonry had expanded during the wars of the eighteenth century and its development continued throughout the period of British imperialism.[3] This would suggest that Masonry had become an extension of the militia as well as a symbolic stronghold of power and influence.

This process was particularly marked in India. Here in 1882 Kipling was employed as an assistant editor on the *Civil and Military Gazette*. In 1886 he started his Masonic career at Lahore where he was admitted into the "Hope and Perseverance Lodge", no. 782 E.C.[4] (see plate 8) which is referred to as *Jadoo-Gher* ("the Magic House") in his novel, *Kim* (1901).[5] Normally candidates for admission were expected to have reached their twenty first year. But as Kipling was eight months below the statutory age-limit, a special dispensation had to be obtained for him from the district Grand Master. Lodge members were eager to admit him because they needed his journalistic skills for the post of lodge secretary. Subsequently the unusual situation occurred when Kipling, as the acting secretary, recorded the minutes of his own initiation ceremonies through the first three degrees of the craft. He became the elected secretary the following year during which time he delivered two lectures to his lodge between April and July. The first, which was entitled the "Origin of the Craft First Degree", concerned the genesis of the Entered Apprentice. While preparing for this lecture, Kipling would have been reminded of his own initiation ceremony which he had recorded in the lodge minutes as follows: "THE

CANDIDATE, Mr Joseph Rudyard Kipling, was then admitted and initiated in due form into the Mysteries and Secrets of Ancient Freemasonry, the Worshipful Master giving the Degree."[6] Kipling's second lecture would have dealt with a less specialised area of Masonic history since it was called "Remarks on Popular Views of Freemasonry". Unfortunately, neither lecture has survived but Kipling borrowed the setting of the lodge lecture for his short story "A Madonna of the Trenches" where Strangwick, a shell-shocked soldier, attends the Lodge of Instruction and listens to a lecture on "The Orientation of King Solomon's Temple".

Kipling's commitment to Masonry during the time he spent in India is evident from his membership of various lodges such as the Lodge of Independence with Philanthropy no. 391, Allahabad, the Advanced Fidelity Mark Lodge and Mount Arrarat Ark Mariners' Lodge, no. 98. His association with these lodges ended in 1889 when he was forced to resign owing to his permanent return to England. Without doubt, the years in India represented the most active period of his Masonic career.

By this time Freemasonry had become well-established in India. It had been founded there in 1728 by George Pomfret only thirteen years after the formation of Grand Lodge in England. Pomfret, who opened the first Indian lodge in Bengal, was also remembered for currying favour with Grand Lodge by sending them a "chest of the best arrack"[7] along with ten guineas for charity. Initially, the destiny of Masonry in India had been harnessed to the development of the East India Company. Many lodges were set up for employees on a kind of "home from home" basis which resulted in a predominantly British membership. While lodges in India had originally insisted upon European exclusivity, gradually membership was extended to carefully selected members of the Asian majority. This gesture was in line with lodge precepts concerning cultural and racial egalitarianism. In 1844, the leading Freemason in India, Dr Burnes, who ranked as the Provincial Grand Master for Western India, founded the Rising Star Lodge, no 342, in Bombay, for the admission of indigenous citizens as well as Europeans.[8] According to the *Masonic Register for India* of 1869, this action led to the recruitment of many Indians from a cross-section of race and creed ranging from Hindu, Sikh, Muslim and Parsee.

The Masonic principles of equality and racial and religious toleration, which were practised in some lodges, greatly appealed to the young Kipling. In his poem, "The Mother-Lodge" (1896), he warmly acknowledges this multi-cultural fraternity by referring to "My Brethren black an' brown". (p.446) In the second stanza, Kipling makes an ethnic break-down of members of the lodge:

> We'd Bola Nath, Accountant,
> An' Saul the Aden Jew,
> An' Din Mohammed, draughtsman
> Of the Survey Office too;
> There was Babu Chuckerbutty,

                    An' Amir Singh the Sikh,
            An' Castro from the fittin'-sheds,
            The Roman Catholick!  (p.445)

The names listed signify the major races and creeds of India. For
example, the name Framjee Eduljee mentioned at the end of
stanza one, indicates a Parsee, while Bola Nath may be identified
as a Hindu from the United Provinces. The Muslims are
represented by Din Mohammed while the Bengalis are suggested
by the name Babu Chuckerbutty. Kipling goes beyond traditional
Eastern religions to include a Roman Catholic since the name,
Castro, is that of an Eurasian who has descended from a
Portuguese ancestor.[9] Though the term "Mother-lodge" was derived
from British Freemasonry to denote a Mason's lodge of initiation
into the craft, for Kipling's purpose it comes close to expressing
the concept of unity evoked by the image of "Mother-India".[10]
Yet, Kipling's portrayal of cultural pluralism in the brotherhood
was anachronistic. In his biographical *Something of Myself for my
Friends Known and Unknown* (1937) he describes the racial
diversity of the "Hope and Perseverance" lodge saying "Here I met
Muslims, Hindus, Sikhs, members of the Araya and Brahmo
Samaj".[11] This account explicitly conveys the impression that a
large proportion of the indigenous population was represented in
the lodge-room. In actuality, there were only four non-Europeans
recorded on the lodge register for that period while the quota
per lodge averaged around thirty members. Kipling's idealized
view of Freemasonry in India clouded the memory of his
initiation which he misreported forty years later to *The Times* in
1925:

> I was secretary for some years of Hope and Perseverance
> Lodge, no 782, Lahore, which included Brethren of at
> least four creeds. I was entered by a member of Bramo
> Samaj, a Hindu, passed by a Mohammedan, and raised
> by an Englishman. Our tyler was an Indian Jew.[12]

Apparently the lodge officials who entered, passed and raised
Kipling into the three degrees of Entered Apprentice,
Fellowcraftsman and Master Mason had all been Englishmen. None
of the four non-Europeans listed had been of sufficiently high
rank to carry out these initiation ceremonies. Presumably, these
inaccuracies had occurred as a result of Kipling's eagerness to
convince himself that Freemasonry rejected partisanship and
transcended political, social and religious discord. But
unfortunately the brethren did not always live up to their code
of moral practice.
    During the twentieth century, the craft's belief-system
continued to blanket differing religious convictions through the
Deistic concept of the Great Architect of the Universe. The
re-orientation of social values fostered religious uniformity which
ensured that there would be no dissidents within the Masonic

fold. As Kipling points out in "The Mother-Lodge":

> It often strikes me thus,
> There ain't such things as infidels,
> Excep', per'aps, it's us.
>
> (p.445)

The brethren were discouraged from discussing religion, business interests and politics during the leisure period following the official part of the lodge meeting. Yet contrary to Masonic injunctions members would frequently engage in informal discussions regarding religious differences. As Kipling reveals, such conversations drew attention to the variety of beliefs practised by Masons outside the lodge-room:

> An' man on man got talkin'
> Religion an' the rest,
> An' every man comparin'
> Of the God 'e knew the best.
>
> (p.445)

The fraternity's ideals of egalitarianism could not buttress Freemasons from internal social and religious divisions. Theoretically, the colonial lodges enabled the Indian to escape from the tyranny of the caste-system. But this was not always possible to implement for as Kipling notes in his poem:

> (We dursn't give no banquets,
> Lest a Brother's caste were broke)
>
> (p.445)

It was rarely possible for members of different religious sects and castes to eat together. A Hindu brother, for example, would not consume food prepared for him by a person from a lower caste, regardless of Masonic rank. Religious exhortations meant that Sikhs were restricted to a vegetarian diet while Muslims and Jews could only eat certain types of meat which had been prepared in accordance with their religious beliefs. Ironically, sectarianism was sometimes highlighted by the Masonic community, for, as Kipling indicates in his account of a banquet held at the "Hope and Perseverance" lodge:

> We met, of course, on the level, and the only
> difference anyone would notice was that at our
> banquets some of the Brethren, who were debarred
> by caste rules from eating food not ceremonially
> prepared, sat over empty plates.[13]

Even the symbolism of the craftsman's level could not smooth out the social divisions fostered by such partisan attitudes. These

remained irreconcilable with the egalitarian principles of
Freemasonry which are referred to as the "Ancient Landmarks" in
stanza three of "The Mother-Lodge". Although Masonry could not
break down the more intransigent cultural and religious barriers,
it did challenge the conventions surrounding other social
hierarchies as the poem's refrain reveals:

> Outside - "Sergeant! Sir! Salute!
>  Salaam!"
> Inside - "Brother," an' it doesn't do
>  no 'arm.

(p.445)

Here Kipling indicates how accepted forms of acknowledging
figures of authority were abandoned in the lodge-room. More than
this, as a tool of Westernisation, Masonry offered the Indian a
degree of refuge from the stranglehold of the caste system by
levelling out some of the differentials which were the
determinants of caste.

Viewed in this way the secret Masonic network was capable
of opening up frontiers for the empire-builders by becoming a
refined instrument of colonisation. In his book, *The Brotherhood:
The Secret World of the Freemasons*, Stephen Knight describes the
role played by the British in the spread of Freemasonry:

> But the British - the founders of Masonry -
> remained throughout the nineteenth and twentieth
> centuries the chief propagandists for the movement.
> Undaunted by the loss of the first empire and with
> it direct control over American Masonry, the British
> took Masonry with the flag as they created their
> second empire - the one on which the sun never
> set. . . .
>  Associating the native upper and middle classes
> on a peculiar, profitable and clandestine basis with
> their white rulers, some historians believe, did much
> to defuse resentment of imperial domination. Despite
> his colour, any man rather better off than the mass
> of the people - who were not sought as members -
> could, by being a Freemason, feel that he belonged
> in however humble a way to the Establishment.[14]

Kipling compares the British Empire to a Masonic lodge in his
poem, "The Song of the Dead" where he celebrates the birth of
Empire and lodge:

> When Drake went down to the Horn
> And England was crowned thereby,
>  'Twixt seas unsailed and shores unhailed
> Our Lodge - our Lodge was born
> (And England crowned thereby! (p.173)

The symbiotic relationship between Masonry and imperialism had
helped establish the craft as a world-wide organization, for as
Kipling points out towards the end of "The Mother-Lodge":

> Full oft on Guv'ment service
> This rovin' foot 'ath pressed,
> An' bore fraternal greetin's
> To the Lodges east an' west,
> Accordin' as commanded,
> From Kohat to Singapore,
> But I wish that I might see them
> In my Mother-Lodge once more!
>
> (p.446)

Kipling even expressed colonial problems in Masonic language in
a speech on "Imperial Relations" delivered to a Canadian audience
in 1907. Here he catalogued the main issues facing the imperial
bureaucracy as: Education, Immigration, Transportation, Irrigation
and Administration which, he claimed, corresponded to the five
points of fellowship relating to the five points of bodily contact
between Masons, being foot to foot, knee to knee, breast to
breast, cheek to cheek and hand to hand.[15] In the lecture
Kipling referred to "the idea of our Empire as a community of
men of allied race and identical aims, united in comradeship,
comprehension and sympathy."[16] As Bonamy Dobrée notes, "It
would almost seem that his mission" in regard to the Empire "was
to bind it together in one blood-brotherhood, a purposive Masonic
lodge, whose business it is to cleanse the world of shoddy."[17]
But sadly, Kipling's visionary ideals could not be fulfilled by the
clanking chains of the imperial machinery. Kipling's vision of the
brotherhood of man in terms of British colonialism was a fading
mirage. Instead he looked to Freemasonry, the empire "on which
the sun never set", to fulfil his dreams of a universal fraternity.

Kipling's early allegiance to the craft had been harnessed to
his approval of British influence over the sub-continent. It was
his furtherance of the interests of the Empire which aroused
George Orwell to exclaim: "Kipling *is* a jingo imperialist, he *is*
morally insensitive and aesthetically disgusting."[18] Though
Kipling rebuked the British Empire in the poem *Recessional*, his
one-time support for Britain's policies of colonisation caused
Dobrée to describe the Empire as Kipling's Catholic Church.[19]
Certainly, it is in this context of devotion that Kipling addresses
the imperial mater, Queen Victoria, in "Ave Imperatrix":

> And all are bred to do your will
> By land and sea - wherever flies
> The Flag, to fight and follow still,
> And work your Empire's destinies.
>
> (p.170)

Elsewhere, Kipling identifies the Empress of India with the legendary founder of the Freemasons as in the poem, "The Widow at Windsor". The title and opening lines refer to Queen Victoria who was known to her troops as "The Widow":

> 'Ave you 'eard o' the Widow at Windsor
> With a hairy gold crown on 'er 'ead?
>
> (p.413)

A stark reminder of Victoria's sovereignty over the colonies appears at the beginning of the second stanza:

> Walk wide o' the Widow at Windsor,
>    For 'alf o' Creation she owns:
> We 'ave bought 'er the same with the
>    sword an' the flame,
> An' we've salted it down with our bones.
>
> (p.414)

The poet argues that the property and person of the Queen should be protected which leads him to make the following injunction:

> Hands off o' the sons o' the Widow,
>    Hands off o' the goods in 'er shop.
>
> (p.414)

The image of "sons o' the Widow" is a homespun metaphor for the Empire as an extended family with Victoria as the symbol of imperial motherhood, where the sons represent her soldiers fighting for their country in foreign lands. But the epiphet "sons o' the Widow" was commonly used in lodge-circles to identify Freemasons as followers of Hiram Abif, himself, a widow's son. Undoubtedly, this usage would be instantly intelligible to any Freemason as a veiled reference to the legendary founder of the craft.

Kipling goes on to make a more specific connection between the Empress and Freemasonry in the following toast:

> Then 'ere's to the Lodge o' the Widow,
>    From the Pole to the Tropics it runs -
> To the Lodge that we tile with the rank an'
>    the file,
> An' open in form with the guns.
>
> (p.414)

Here Kipling suggests that the lodge is dedicated to Victoria and hence to the interests of the British Empire which was spreading to all parts of the world "From the Pole to the Tropics". Again Kipling makes a direct link between the tools of the

Empire-builders, the militia, and the Freemasons. It is interesting to reflect upon the aptness of these images since Masonry had originated as a kind of Medieval craft guild for the operative building trade. Kipling's vivid picture of building up the lodge with "the rank an' the file" links up a military idiom with the Masonic metaphor concerning the "temple of living stones". The pun on the word "tile" in the third line of the toast plays on the ritualised precautions taken by the brethren to ensure that no intruders or eavesdroppers are present at a meeting. The lodge official responsible for security is the tyler or guard whose emblem is the sword. In turn the lodges, themselves, were symbolic guardians of the Empire helping to preserve the secrecy which Kipling extends to Victoria as "The Secret of the Empire" (p.731) in his eulogy, "The Bells and Queen Victoria".

It is likely that the Empress would have been the patron of Kipling's lodge particularly since the monarch was traditionally the figurehead of British Freemasonry. Indeed the influx of Indian princes into the craft would suggest that the indigenous ruling class of India had assimilated the values of the Empire which were sustained throughout the colonial lodges.

## "A King and A Mason"

Monarchy had always played an ambivalent role in Masonry since technically social ranks were suspended in the lodge-room. Kipling, who was fascinated by the idea of kingship, points out in his poem, "Banquet Night":

> *But once in so often, the messenger brings*
> *Solomon's mandate: "forget these things!*
> *Brother to Beggars and Fellow to Kings,*
> *Companion of Princes - forget these things!*
> *Fellow-Craftsmen, forget these things!"*
>
> (p.751)

The exhortation here is that the brethren must forget class differences while attending Masonic functions. Often the gulf between social groups was considerable especially since members of royal families were involved in the craft. For instance, William IV, the Sailor King, who knew little about Masonry was made its Grand Patron. He confessed his ignorance to a deputation of high-ranking Freemasons saying "if my love for you equalled my ignorance of everything concerning you, it would be boundless!".[20]

Many prominent figures in Masonic history had been kings and princes. Several of these are listed in a grandiose roll-call in Anderson's *Constitutions* where numerous patriarchs and kings throughout the Old Testament, such as Moses and Solomon, are cited as leading Freemasons. Paul Fussell comments that Kipling "was amused by Anderson's attribution of Masonic knowledge and virtues to the Hebraic kings" which prompted him to write "The Man who would be King" in which two outcasts unconsciously burlesque the legendary early history of Freemasonry.[21] Kipling's story is about two Masons, Brother Peachey Carnehan and Brother Daniel Dravot, who set out to establish themselves as twin monarchs in far-off Kafiristan in Northern Afganistan. On arriving at their destination, they establish a Masonic lodge and crown themselves rulers of Kafiristan. Parallels may be seen here between the pagan cults of the Kafirs and the rites of Freemasonry. In this Masonic fable, which is also a parody of colonisation, Dravot declares himself, "Grand-Master of all Freemasonry in Kafiristan in this the Mother-Lodge o' the country, and King of Kafiristan equally with Peachey!"[22]

The concept of kingship was of central importance to Masonic mythology. King Solomon was cited as the Grand Master of all the Masons in Jerusalem and King Hiram as the Grand Master of Tyre. According to Anderson's *Constitutions*, which would have been presented to Kipling on his initiation: "The tradition is, that King Hiram had been Grand Master of all Masons; and when the temple was finished, came to survey it before its consecration, and to commune with Solomon about wisdom and art; when finding the great Architect of the Universe had inspired Solomon above all mortal men, Hiram very readily yielded the pre-eminence to Solomon *Jedidiab*, i.e. the beloved of God."[23] Biblical sources identify Hiram as one of the rulers of Solomon's vassal states who sent Hiram Abif to help with the building of the temple. This project was to realise the great dream of David which had been inherited by his son, Solomon. While every brother was encouraged to emulate Hiram Abif, it appears that Kipling was identifying with the Master of Masons, King Hiram, in his poem, "The Palace", which opens:

> When I was a King and a Mason - a Master
> proven and skilled -
> I cleared me ground for a Palace such as
> a King should build.
>
> (p.385)

In a secular context the temple represented the most splendid of palaces. The fraternity tried to recreate King Solomon's Temple in the lodge-room itself. In his autobiography, Kipling writes how he obtained advice on "decorating the bare walls of the Masonic Hall with hangings after the prescription of Solomon's Temple".[24] Temple symbolism lying at the heart of Masonic mythology expressed the divinity which had inspired the dreams of the Old Testament thinkers. The visionary aspects of Masonry are captured by Kipling in the following lines from "The Palace":

> I read in the razed foundations the heart
> of that builder's heart.
> As he had risen and pleaded, so did I
> understand
> The form of the dream he had followed in
> the face of the thing he had planned.
> (p.386)

Kipling may have been thinking of the ritual of the higher degree, Royal Arch Masonry, where through a mimed myth the brethren find a crypt in the foundations of a ruined temple. Hidden there is the "omnific name" or lost name of God which Kipling may be referring to in the last stanza as the "Word from the Darkness."

The identity of the builder mentioned above is Hiram Abif who, before the temple was completed, was brutally murdered by three apprentices. This tragic event is commemorated in the third degree of Freemasonry which enacts Hiram's symbolic death and resurrection. In Masonic terms, Kipling's messianic expression "As he had risen" is applicable to Hiram whose conquest of death is celebrated in the ceremony concerning the "raising of the master". Antecedents of this Hiramic tradition may be found in the ancient foundation sacrifice or stability rite which involved the internment of a living victim in the foundations of a projected building. Ironically, it was often the builder or apprentice who was chosen for this gruesome burial. Sometimes even the architect was sealed alive in the foundations which effectively became a tomb of his own design. Forebodings of Hiram's martyrdom are revealed in the final stanza of the poem:

> When I was a King and a Mason - in the open noon
> of my pride,
> They sent me a Word from the Darkness. They
> whispered and called me aside.
> They said - "The end is forbidden." They said -
> "Thy use is fulfilled." (p.386)

According to Masonic tradition, Hiram was struck down at high noon after three apprentices had failed to persuade him to divulge the building secrets of the Master Mason. As the candidate for the third degree of Master Mason discovers, the secrets of the craft consist of signs, tokens and words. The secret pass-word taught to the candidate is "MACHABEN or MACHBINNA" signifying the death of the builder, Hiram Abif. The retention of the Mason's Word was considered so important that Kipling even compares it to a priest recalling his litany in his poem "The Press".[25] Ambiguity between allusions to Masonry and the Bible occurs in the last stanza of "The Palace", where the "Word" sent "from the Darkness" may refer to the Mason's Word or to the Word of the Creator commanding the separation of day from night.

In the poem, the narrator comes across the ruins of a lost

palace. These are reminiscent of the remains of King Solomon's Temple which so far have eluded archeologists.[26] Kipling draws attention to the razed foundations as they are being excavated by the Mason-King:

> I decreed and dug down to my levels. Presently,
> under the silt,
> I came on the wreck of a Palace such as a King
> had built.
>
> There was no worth in the fashion - there was no
> wit in the plan -
> Hither and thither, aimless, the ruined footings
> ran -
> Masonry, brute, mishandled, but carven on every
> stone:
> *"After me cometh a Builder. Tell him, I too have
> known.* (p.385)

The royal builder in the poem does not take it upon himself to rebuild this monument to Masonry, for as he explains:

> I called my men from my trenches, my quarries, my
> wharves, and my sheers.
> All I had wrought I abandoned to the faith of the
> faithless years.
> Only I cut on the timber - only I carved on the
> stone:
> *"After me cometh a Builder. Tell him, I too have
> known!"* (p.386)

The prophetic note at the end of the poem anticipates the visionary ideal concerning the final completion of King Solomon's Temple. The mystical message "carven on every stone" of the ruin would have reminded Kipling of the Mason's Mark which was designed to identify the builder responsible for each part of a structure. From the ruins of the palace the narrator is able to ascertain that the builder had been a king.

The historic equation between monarch and Mason which is central to Masonic myth was established through the kingship of Hiram, David and his son, Solomon, of whom Kipling wrote:

> There was never a king like Solomon.
> Not since the world began.[27]

Because Freemasonry had won the patronage of kings and princes it was appropriately known among its disciples as the "royal art". As a Mason, Kipling regarded himself as a "brother to Princes"[28] and would have taken pride in the noble lineage of the fraternity particularly since a sense of tradition and rightful heritage was fundamental to the society's system of morality.

## The Labour of Lodges

The moral basis of Freemasonry has similarities with Kipling's concept of "The Law". According to Paul Fussell, this has been partly preserved within Boy Scout Law, since the founder of the movement, Baden-Powell, had been influenced by his friendship with Kipling.[29] The poet's ethical code was a blend of Hebraic morality and Anglo-Saxon idealism for, as Paul Elmor More comments:

> At its best, his sense of order and obedience rises into a pure feeling for righteousness that reminds one of the ancient Hebrew prophets. He has in him something of the stern Calvinistic temper. . . brooding over a world in which the active and mechanical virtues fulfil their mission under the law of "interdependence absolute, foreseen, ordained, decreed."[30]

For Kipling Freemasonry combined both the law of his tribe and of his craft. The language of its ritual was derived from the Old Testament while Masonic iconography exalted the moral rectitude of the craftsman symbolized through the order of a building structure. As a universal brotherhood of man, Masonry became the touchstone for Kipling's faith in a moral universe. In turn the ethics of the Fraternity converged into Kipling's notion of "The Law". This was bound up with the poet's attitude towards work. He would have approved of the importance Masons attached to the virtues of industry. "Labour" was the term given to the business part of a lodge meeting in order to remind members of the operative roots of the craft. Yet speculative Masons were only symbolic workers since they celebrated the builder's craft through ritual and symbolism. In view of this, it is surprising that Kipling regarded the Masons' idealization of work as compatible with his doctrine of action. His poem "When Earth's Last Picture is Painted" was inspired by the image of the Master Craftsman drawing building designs for his workers to copy:

> And only The Master shall praise us, and only The
> Master shall blame;
> And no one shall work for money, and no one shall
> work for fame,
> But each for the joy of the working, and each, in
> his separate star,
> Shall draw the Thing as he sees It for the God of
> Things as They are! (p.227)

The moral values of Masonry are expressed in Kipling's Masonic poem, "My New-Cut Ashlar", which first appeared as an envoy to the volume, *Life's Handicap*. The "new-cut ashlar" is a stone-mason's term referring to the freshly-hewn or squared stone to be used in a building operation. The "ashlar" was also used to denote the stone possessed by Masons as a token reminder of their operative origins. It also related to the pledge of loyalty made by the brethren to preserve the secrecy of the lodge. This was a revival of the ancient custom of swearing an oath on a stone. In *The Golden Bough*, J.G. Frazer provides various examples of vows made on sacred stones.³¹ During the eighteenth century, candidates for Masonic initiation placed their right foot on a rough ashlar in accordance with the folk-lorist belief in the virtue of fidelity which was associated with various types of stones. Kipling may have been aware of the Indian custom of initiating a Brahman boy into the mysteries of the Hindu priestly caste which involved him treading on a stone with his right foot while repeating the words "Tread on this stone; like a stone be firm".³² The Masonic vow or "Oath of the Brother-in-Blood" (p.237) was the first step in the spiritual odyssey symbolized by the ashlar.

Kipling's poem, "My New-Cut Ashlar", is an ethical statement expressing the metaphysical values of the craft. The poem could be more accurately described as a prayer since Kipling addresses the God of the Freemasons, the "Great Overseer of the Universe". This was the title used by Mark Masons who dedicated their labour to the supreme being supervising the actions of mankind. Kipling invokes Him:

> My new-cut ashlar takes the light
> Where crimson-blank the windows flare.
> Be my own work before the night,
> Great Overseer, I make my prayer. (p.511)

The poet pledges himself to the service of God who was known in Masonic circles as the Master. The leader of the lodge, called by the same name, was, therefore, a representative of the deity. The pledge below encroaches upon that shadowy territory where Freemasonry appears to overlap with religion:

> If there be good in that I wrought
> Thy Hand compelled it, Master, Thine -
> Where I have failed to meet Thy Thought
> I know, through Thee, the blame was mine.
>
> One instant's toil to Thee denied
> Stands all Eternity's offence.
> Of that I did with Thee to guide,
> To thee, through Thee, be excellence. (p.511)

Despite Freemasonry's denial that it is a religious surrogate it covets both the language and trappings of religion. Even the eschatological directives contained within the poem reveal that

Kipling's vision of the after-life had a Masonic tinge to it:

> Take not that vision from my ken -
> Oh, whatsoe'er may spoil or speed.
> Help me to need no aid from men
> That I may help such men as need! (p.512)

Kipling had internalized the Deistic creed of the Masons who abided by the "Religion in which all men agree" since he wrote in his preface to *Life's Handicap* that when men come to the gates of death all religions seem to them "wonderfully alike, and colourless".[33] In a verse which was later omitted from "My New-Cut Ashlar", Kipling communicated his fears for the after-life:

> Wherefore before the face of men.
> Great Overseer, I bring my Mark -
> Fair craft or foul. In mercy then
> Will that I die not in the dark![34]

A perception of heaven which is central to the message of the poem is bound up with the concept of the perfect ashlar. In the lodge, each Freemason's ashlar symbolized his degree of spiritual development. For example, when an individual first entered Masonry he was likened to the rough stone recently hewed from a quarry which is then polished up and perfected. Probity is signified by the smooth ashlar hence the significance of the title of Kipling's poem, "My New-Cut Ashlar". The master cultivates the moral improvement of the brethren who are figuratively "polished by the master's ring". In order to make this allegorical progression as vivid as possible, in some lodges the ashlar was literally polished or hewn. In this way the ashlar becomes a metaphor for the soul since the object of its perfection lay in the rebuilding of King Solomon's Temple. According to the Masonic allegory of life-after-death, the perfected Freemason eventually takes his place among the temple of living stones. He is winched into place by a builder's lewis:

> One stone the more swings into place
> In that dread Temple of Thy worth. (p.512)

The attainment of the perfection represented by the spiritual temple reworks the mystic return to Eden which Kipling evokes in the previous stanza:

> Who, lest all thought of Eden fade,
> Bring'st Eden to the craftsman's brain -
> Godlike to muse o'er his own Trade
> And manlike stand with God again! (p.512)

The craftsman, like the poet, is empowered through his own

creativity to act in a "Godlike" way as the mediator between heaven and earth. But for Kipling and his brother-Masons, God is the ultimate craftsman, the Master, Architect and Supreme Overseer who measured out with compass and square the most massive building operation of all time, the creation of the universe. Thus the Freemasons may be seen as a tribe of secret builders who strive to emulate the Creator. Within Masonic teaching Kipling discovered:

> The depth and dream of my desire,
> The bitter paths wherein I stray - (p.511)

It is through verse that we may begin to approach the true secret of the Freemasons even though Hannah maintains that it has been concealed from the brotherhood itself. Hannah argues that there is no particular Masonic secret, only a delusion spawned from the mythologies of the secret society. What Kipling reveals through his poetry is not a secret but a mystery which is verbally incommunicable to Mason and non-Mason alike. This relates to the Masonic way of life based on moral symbolism and allegory which the initiate, having received the ceremonial key, must discover for himself.

Ritual, as the vehicle for this journey of inner exploration, became for Kipling a way of life. In *Something of Myself* he wrote, "if one broke the ritual of dressing for the last meal one was parting with a sheet-anchor".[35] As one of his characters, Mr Burges, remarks in "In the Interests of the Brethren", "All ritual is fortifying. Ritual's a natural necessity for mankind."[36] Ritual functions to impose order upon the chaos and uncertainties of life. The Masonic fellowship helped cushion the individual from the insecurities of the world outside since the prime importance of Freemasonry lay in its consciousness as a collective body. In an address to a naval club in 1908 which appeared in *A Book of Words* Kipling would have included his lodge as one of the fraternities where, he states:

> Men of all ranks work together for aims and objects
> which are not for their own personal advantage, there
> arises among them a spirit, a tradition, and an
> unwritten law, which it is not very easy for the
> world at large to understand, or to sympathise with.[37]

Kipling's reference to the "unwritten law" may be related to the unseen bond of fellowship expressed through ritual and symbolism which unites the brotherhood of Masons.

## "In the Interests of the Brethren"

An important function of the lodge was to guide the individual through the topography of the Masonic world. This pedagogical role is prominent in a number of Kipling's short stories such as "In the Interests of the Brethren" from *Debits and Credits* (1926) which describes the meetings of a small group of London Freemasons who gather in a converted garage named the Lodge of Instruction. Other tales set around the Lodge of Instruction include "A Friend of the Family", "A Madonna of the Trenches," and "The Janeites". In "Fairy Kist" from *Limits and Renewals* (1932) Kipling describes how some members of the Lodge of Instruction of Faith and Works reformed themselves into a Masonic group called the "Eclectic *but* Comprehensive Fraternity for the Perpetuation of Gratitude towards Lesser Light."[38] The title suggests that through eclecticism the lodge aimed for universality. Such ambivalence mirrors Kipling's own attitude towards Freemasonry which oscillated between elitism and egalitarianism. His elitist tendencies may be demonstrated through his membership of numerous clubs and Masonic societies which included the Freemasons' Builders of the Silent City Lodge, Mark Masonry, the Royal Ark Mariners and the *Societas Rosicruciana in Anglia*. The last of these was an inner group restricted to Master Masons which would have satisfied Kipling's taste for circles within circles. When he joined on 8 July 1909, the ceremonial motto which appeared on his membership certificate was *Fortuna non virtute*. Since the society was dedicated to literary and antiquarian pursuits, candidates were selected on the basis of their "high moral character" and "ability to be capable of understanding the revelations of philosophy, theosophy and science, possessing a mind free from prejudice and anxious for instruction."[39] Kipling was content enough with his Rosicrucian membership to write: "For as you come and as you go, whatever Grade you be - the Rosicrucian brethren are good enough for me."[40] Kipling's love of exclusivity led him to pursue fashionable society while at Simla in India where he eventually gained entrance to the Study Five clique at United Services.[41]

His character consisted of a curious mixture of elitism and democracy since he identified with the ruling classes while, at the same time, trying to equate with the working man. Through Freemasonry Kipling made headway in reconciling this dichotomy since class and cultural differences were broken down to some extent by the Masonic hierarchies. Kipling was an advocate of the equality in rank, race and creed practised in the lodge-room. In "Banquet Night" Kipling describes the Mason as *"Brother to Beggars and Fellow to Kings, Companion of Princes"* (p.751). The poem opens with an invitation to a banquet of garlic, wine and bread issued by King Solomon to his workers:

"Once in so often," King Solomon said,
Watching his quarrymen drill the stone,
"We will club our garlic and wine and bread
And banquet together beneath my Throne.
And all the Brethren shall come to that mess
As Fellow-Craftsmen - no more and no less."

(p.750)

In the second and third stanzas the invitation is extended to Hiram Abif:

"Carry this message to Hiram Abif -
Excellent Master of forge and mine:-
I and the Brethren would like it if
He and the Brethren will come to dine."

(p.751)

Kipling seeks to demonstrate the unity between different branches of the brotherhood by linking up the conviviality of his lodge with the legends surrounding the building of Solomon's Temple. During a skilful counterpoint between past and present he draws attention to the operative traditions of the craft.

The images of the building trade and stone-masonry were retained in speculative Masonry. For example, Kipling was the founder-member of two lodges which had specific overtones of the operative craft. In 1922 as a member of the Commonwealth War Graves Commission he helped establish the Builders of the Silent City Lodge, no. 12 of the *Grand Lodge National Français*. Kipling was also one of the founders in 1925 of an English branch of this lodge, no. 4948, which he supported until his death. He belonged to two other Masonic orders, Mark Masonry and the Royal Ark Mariners. Both are mentioned in "Banquet Night" as "Masons of Mark" and the "Navy Lords from the *Royal Ark*" (p.751):

So it was ordered and so it was done,
And the hewers of wood and the Masons of Mark,
With foc'sle hands of the Sidon run
And Navy Lords from the *Royal Ark*,
Came and sat down and were merry at mess
As Fellow-Craftsmen - no more and no less.

(p.751)

Mark Masonry had evolved from the *Menatschim* or overseers who supervised the stone-masons. They were employed by Hiram Abif to reject or mark accepted stones for the temple building. The legend of the Mark Master's degree describes how an enterprising Fellowcraftsman anticipated that a key-stone would be needed to complete the building of an arch. Unfortunately the assigned stone went missing but was then recovered after a diligent search. These events are dramatically reconstructed during

an initiation ceremony which resembles a Medieval miracle play.
Eventually the ingenious Fellowcraftsman is rewarded with the
degree of Master Mason. The jewel or badge for this degree is
inscribed with the letters H.T.W.S.S.T.K.S. Kipling includes these
initials in a drawing of King Solomon in his short story, "The
Butterfly that Stamped". The letters stand for "Hiram Tyrian
Widow's Son Sent to King Solomon" which was a semi-secret
motto written on the key-stone. Another Mark-Mason's secret
concerned the pass-word which is the place-name "Joppa". It is
likely that Kipling had deliberately planted the word "Joppa" into
the final stanza of "Banquet Night" as a signal to other
Mark-Masons.

> *The Quarries are hotter than Hiram's forge,*
> *No one is safe from the dog-whips' reach.*
> *It's mostly snowing up Lebanon gorge,*
> *And it's always blowing off Joppa beach.*
>
> (p.751)

The link between Mark Masonry and the Royal Ark Mariners is
explained by Hannah in *Darkness Visible*:

> Connected with Mark Master Masonry in somewhat the
> same way that the Royal Arch is connected with the
> Craft (though the analogy is not perfect) is the
> Royal Ark Mariner Degree, which commemorates the
> salvation of the human race through Noah and the
> Ark. The ritual is distinguished only by its
> trivial silliness.[42]

Hannah is referring to the Noah's Ark symbolism coveted by the
Mariners from which they had derived their naval associations.
Kipling's description of the Mariners as "Navy Lords from the
*Royal Ark*" suggests that their operative roots must have been
inextricably involved with the wood-workers or "hewers of wood"
who were early ship-builders. The Mariner-Masons are summoned
by Solomon in stanza two:

> "Send a swift shallop to Hiram of Tyre,
> Felling and floating our beautiful trees,
> Say that the Brethren and I desire
> Talk with our Brethren who use the seas."
>
> (p.750)

An account of Hiram cutting down cedar trees appears in the
Bible though it is likely that Kipling had derived his description
from Masonic sources. In "The Merchantman" Kipling points out
that these cedars were carried by water. He then goes on to
draw a parallel between Solomon's workers and present day
sailors:

> KING SOLOMON drew merchantmen
> Because of his desire
> For peacocks, apes, and ivory,
> From Tarshish unto Tyre,
> With cedars out of Lebanon
> Which Hiram rafted down;
> But we be only sailormen
> That use in London town. (p.151)

Through the juxtaposition of past and present Kipling advanced his belief that the craft still had relevance to contemporary concerns. According to Kipling the destiny of the modern Mason was to transport the ethos of the temple-building era into the twentieth century. Through poetry he added his own voice to the dialogue which was being conducted between his Masonic brethren and the sources of ancestral wisdom belonging to the Solomonic period.

The importance of Masonry to Kipling on a personal level is apparent from his comment after his admission into the fraternity: "another world opened to me which I needed".[43] Amongst Kipling's reasons for becoming a Mason was the need for comradeship. His father had once accurately remarked, "Ruddy thirsts for a man's life and man's work."[44] Kipling preferred male companionship and he frequented bachelor gatherings such as those held at the Punjab Club. For Kipling it was the "deep-voiced men laughing together over dinner" which made "the loveliest sound in the world".[45] Since the Masonic lodges were restricted to men, Kipling was able to indulge there his preference for all-male company. He would have endorsed one of his character's enthusiastic description of Freemasonry as "veiled in allegory and illustrated in symbols - the Fatherhood of God, an' the Brotherhood of Man; an' what more in Hell *do* you want?"[46] Kipling was so devoted to Masonry that he even wrote a Masonic ritual which opens:

> Question: Halt! Who goes there?
> Candidate: A man trying to join the Main body.
> Question: Long delayed it has at last gone forward,
>   but what do you seek therein?
> Candidate: Friends who bade me follow so soon as I
>   was sure of my road.
> Question: And why do you seek them?
> Candidate: First to discuss.
> Question: And after?
> Here shall the candidate holds his peace tho' twice
>   entreated.[47]

This is a sample of the creativity inspired in Kipling by Freemasonry as a living art-form enacted in the Masons' meeting place. Kipling also managed to combine his roles of Freemason and writer as a member of the Corresponding Circle of the

*Quatuor Coronatori* Lodge, no. 2076 in 1918 and also through his honorary membership of the Author's Lodge no. 3546. As an ambassador for Freemasonry Kipling was following in the tradition of Robert Burns. He even inherited Burns's title of Masons' Poet-Laureate from 1905 to 1908 following his election as an honorary member of Burns's Canongate Kilwinning Lodge on 4 October 1899. It is fitting perhaps that Kipling had a lodge named after him which was known as "The Rudyard Kipling Lodge, no. 8169". Certainly Kipling fulfilled the promise of his Masonic career as predicted by his colleague, Brother J.J. Davies, who on hearing of the poet's departure from his Lahore lodge to Allahabad said:

Those of us who have watched his conduct since
his initiation feel sure that he has before him
a successful Masonic career, for the thoroughness
with which he conducted his duties was prompted
by a lively desire for a deeper insight into the
hidden truths of Masonry.[48]

The craft satisfied many of the poet's emotional needs. For instance, it furnished him with a sense of tradition which could be transplanted into foreign cultures. For Kipling, Masonry countered the feelings of estrangement he experienced whilst being posted overseas. He describes his feelings of alienation in *From Sea to Sea* where he records a visit to China while *en route* to India:

the faces of the Chinese frightened me more than
ever, so I ran away to the outskirts of the town
and saw a windowless house that carried the Square
and Compass in gold and teakwood above the door.
I took heart at meeting these familiar things
again, and knowing that where they were was good
fellowship and much charity, in spite of all the
secret societies in the world, Penang is to be
congratulated on one of the prettiest little
lodges in the East.[49]

While expatriated in India, Kipling discovered that the lodge reinforced his British identity and national spirit. It is appropriate that after returning to England he was elected an honorary member of the Motherland Lodge, no 3861. While in India, Kipling had valued the lodge as a channel for cross-cultural communication for when he moved from Lahore to Allahabad he insisted upon entering a lodge which was open to non-Europeans.[50] Kipling experienced his greatest need for the fraternity during his expatriation in India because the Masonic network provided him with a greater sense of security than that of the tottering British Empire. Later Kipling was to experience sharp disillusionment with his earlier vision of an imperial federation. The aftermath of the Boer War exposed the apathy of the majority of the British people towards the preservation of the Empire which was being mismanaged by its administrators. After hostilities had ceased, Kipling was disappointed to learn that a later Liberal government had returned conquered territory to the Boers. In "The Lesson" Kipling announced:

> We have had an Imperial lesson. It may make us
> an Empire yet! (p.300)

But it was too late. The Empire failed to give Kipling the sense of permanence which the ancestry of Freemasonry could provide. The historic consciousness of the craft, more than the memories of a fleeting imperial greatness, infused Kipling with an inner security which sustained him during his time overseas. Kipling's biographer, Charles Carrington, argues that "Freemasonry, with its cult of common action, its masculine self-sufficiency, its language of symbols, and its hierarchy of secret grades, provided him with a natural setting for his social ideals" and that "even a non-mason can point out scores of allusions to masonic ritual dispersed through the whole of Kipling's verse and prose, proving how deeply the cult affected his mode of thought."[51] The importance of Freemasonry to Kipling's life and work can scarcely be over-estimated for, as he wrote in "In the Interests of the Brethren", "A man's Lodge means more to him than people imagine."[52]

## Notes

1. Kipling, *Many Inventions* (London, 1904), p.163.

2. Pick and Knight, *The Pocket History of Freemasonry*, p. 243. Kipling makes a connection between the military and the Masons while discussing the American army in *From Sea to Sea and Other Sketches: Letters of Travel* (London, 1900), p.115: "That Regular Army, which is a dear little army, should be kept to itself, blooded on detachment duty, turned into the paths of science, and now and again assembled at feasts of Freemasons." Kipling also makes comparisons between Masonry and Mithraism, a religious sect which attracted the soldiers of Ancient Rome. See *Kipling's Mind and Art*, ed. Andrew Rutherford (London, 1964), p.65.

3. Pick and Knight, *The Pocket History of Freemasonry*, p.242.

4. Kipling claims that he was initiated in 1885 but the minutes of his Mother-Lodge state that the event took place on 5 April 1886. See Shamsul Islam, *Kipling's Law: A Study of his philosophy*

*of life* (London, 1975), pp.42-3.

5. See Kipling, *Kim*, (London, 1956), p.2. For a discussion of the Masonic references in *Kim* see Henry Carr "Kipling and the Craft", *Ars Quatuor Coronatorum*, 77 (1964), pp.241-2.

6. Carr, "Kipling and the Craft", p.219.

7. Pick and Knight, *The Pocket Book of Freemasonry*, p.306.

8. Ibid., p.307 ff.

9. See Ralph Durand, *A Handbook to the poetry of Rudyard Kipling* (New York, 1971), p.187.

10. See Louis L. Cornell, *Kipling in India* (London, 1966), pp.140-41.

11. Kipling, *Something of Myself for My Friends Known and Unknown* (Harmondsworth, 1977), p.43.

12. This letter was printed in *The Freemason* (London), 28 March 1925 from where it has been reproduced by Carr in "Kipling and the Craft", p.221.

13. Loc. cit.

14. Knight, *The Brotherhood*, pp.34-5.

15. Kipling, *A Book of Words: Selections from Speeches and Addresses Delivered between 1906 and 1927* (London, 1928), p.29. In *Letters of Travel*, 1892-1913 (London, 1920), p.196 Kipling describes Quebec and Victoria as Canada's two Masonic pillars of Strength and Beauty which formed part of the lodge furniture.

16. Kipling, *A Book of Words*, p.25.

17. *Kipling and the Critics*, ed. Elliot L. Gilbert (London, 1965), p.43.

18. Ibid., pp.74-5.

19. Ibid., p.43.

20. Pick and Knight, *The Pocket History of Freemasonry*, p.121.

21. Paul Fussell, "Irony, Freemasonry, and Humane Ethics in Kipling's *The Man who would be King*", *English Literary History*, XXV (1958) p.227.

22. Kipling, *Wee Willie Winkie and Other Stories* (London, 1905),

p.233. This short story is viewed as a parody of imperialism by Cornell in *Kipling in India*, pp.163-4.

23. Anderson, *Constitutions* (1723), p.28

24. Kipling, *Something of Myself*, p.43.

25. See *Rudyard Kipling's Verse*, p.534.

26. See Horne, *King Solomon's Temple in the Masonic Tradition*, p.65.

27. Kipling, *Just So Stories For Little Children* (London, 1955), p.229.

28. Kipling, *Puck of Pook's Hill* (London, 1906), p.291.

29. See Fussell, "Irony, Freemasonry, and Humane Ethics", p.229.

30. Paul Elmor More, *Shelburne Essays*, 11 vols (London, 1905), II, p.111.

31. James George Frazer, *The Golden Bough: A Study in Magic and Religion* (London, 1978), p.43.

32. Loc. cit.

33. Kipling, *Life's Handicap: Being Stories of Mine Own People* (London, 1952), p.viii.

34. Basil M. Bazley in "Freemasonry in Kipling's Works", *The Kipling Journal*, XVII (April, 1950), p.10.

35. Kipling, *Something of Myself*, p.51.

36. Kipling, *Debits and Credits* (London, 1949), p.61.

37. Kipling, *A Book of Words*, pp.55-6.

38. Kipling, *Limits and Renewals* (London, 1949), p.153. In his short story, "The Inexperienced Ghost" from *Twelve Stories and a Dream*, H.G. Wells mentions a lodge of Instruction: "the lodge of the Four Kings, which devotes itself so ably to the study and elucidation of all the mysteries of Masonry past and present", *The Complete Short Stories of H.G. Wells* (London, 1974), p.909.

39. Carr, "Kipling and the Craft", p.231. One fictional character who did not meet the rigorous moral standards demanded by Rosicrucian membership was the villainous Count Fosco, who describes himself as the "Perpetual Arch-Master of the Rosicrucian Masons of Mesopotamia," in Wilkie Collins, *The Woman in White*

(Boston, 1969), p.475.

40. Albert Frost, "R.K.'s Masonic Allusions", *The Kipling Journal*, XIII (Oct., 1942), p.17.

41. See Robert E. Moss, *Rudyard Kipling and the Fiction of Adolescence* (London, 1982), pp.12-13. See also Hilton Brown, *Rudyard Kipling: A New Appreciation* (New York, 1974), pp.97-8.

42. Hannah, *Darkness Visible*, p.198.

43. Kipling, *Something of Myself*, p.43.

44. Carr, "Kipling and the Craft", p.216.

45. Kipling, *Something of Myself*, p.16.

46. Kipling, *Debits and Credits*, p.67.

47. Lord Birkenhead, *Rudyard Kipling*, (London, 1978), pp.209-10. Thomas Pinney who is editing Kipling's correspondence informed me in a letter of 30 December 1984 that, during the 1920s, Kipling wrote an elaborate ritual for the society of Canadian engineers to be used in their ceremonies of initiation.

48. Carr, "Kipling and the Craft", p.224.

49. Kipling, *From Sea to Sea*, p.249.

50. See Angus Wilson, *The Strange Ride of Rudyard Kipling: His Life and Works* (London, 1977), p.314.

51. Charles Carrington, *Rudyard Kipling: His Life and Work* (Harmondsworth, 1970), p.543.

52. Kipling, *Debits and Credits*, p.69.

# WILLIAM BUTLER YEATS

Now all the truth is out
Be secret and take defeat...
Be secret and exult,
Because of all things known
That is most difficult.

Yeats[1]

## Poet and Magician

The attraction of the poet to the world of secret societies is best illustrated by William Butler Yeats (1865-1939). Having been associated with a hermetic society and the Theosophical movement, he is best remembered for his membership of the magical Order of the Golden Dawn which incorporated his interests in the Cabala and Rosicrucianism. During the early years of his writing career Yeats regarded his roles as poet and magician as inseparable. In *Reveries Over Childhood and Youth* (1915) Yeats recollects that as a boy he "began to play at being a sage, a magician or a poet".[2] Since the involvement with esoteric sects and occult traditions permeated his life and work, it is difficult to separate the man from the mask or divest the poet from his garments of myth and symbolism. But as Yeats himself insisted, "the antagonism must be made the antagonism between the poet and the magician".[3]

The threshold between poetry and magic will be explained in terms of the influence the secret societies exerted on Yeats. These supplied him with a source of inspiration which helped shape his poetic outlook. Virginia Moore in *The Unicorn* argues that Yeats's involvement with the Golden Dawn throughout his life and work could never be regarded as a side issue since "a man does not belong to a society nearly thirty years, submitting to rigorous disciplines and striving to pass all grades up through the highest, as a pastime, or out of curiosity, or indeed for any lesser reason than conviction."[4] Yeats, himself, believed that an understanding of the action of a poet illuminates his written word and that "above all it is necessary that the lyric poet's life should be known, that we should understand that his poetry is no rootless flower but the speech of a man."[5]

Through the secret societies Yeats sought a symbolic language for his life and art which eventually led to the creation of his own mythology articulated in his prose work, *A Vision* (1925). Yeats, however, claimed that poetry could record the voice of myth since he believed that the speech of poets is an eternal and immutable version of everyday language. In "What is Popular Poetry?" (1901) he wrote:

> I learned from the people themselves, before I
> learned it from any book, that they cannot separate
> the idea of an art or a craft from the idea of a
> cult with ancient technicalities and mysteries. They
> can hardly separate mere learning from witchcraft,
> and are fond of words and verses that keep half
> their secret to themselves.[6]

Yeats maintained that unless literature was immersed in ancient belief-systems it would have no spiritual roots or meaning beyond the mere chronicling of circumstances. For Yeats, poetic language had the potential to unlock the secrets of magical initiation and mystical experience. Moreover, he claimed that a work of art could be used as a mandala or symbol for meditation as a means of advancement upon a path of mystical awareness. Yeats narrowed the gap between art and ritual by making them interact and even interchange. For instance, Yeats saw in the talismanic quality of a poem the power to invoke what he described as the "disembodied powers" of ceremonial magic. In *The Shadowy Waters* (1906) Yeats shows that poetic creation could become a sacramental act which may be compared to an ancient offering to the gods:

> *I have made this poem for you, that men may*
> *read it*
> *Before they read of Forgael and Dectora,*
> *As men in the old times, before the harps began,*
> *Poured out wine for the high invisible ones.*
>
> *(p.406)*

Through poetry, Yeats combined the arts of rhetoric with the skills of the spiritually adept. Within a tradition of mystic literature the iconoclastic nature of the poem emerges to reveal that it is an artefact composed of the symbols of magic and religion. Consequently the poet may be licensed to use the symbols employed by the magician. For as Yeats insisted "I cannot now think symbols less than the greatest of all powers whether they are used consciously by the masters of magic, or half unconsciously by their successors, the poet, the musician and the artist."[7] The poet, like the magician, is an enchanter who is able to cast a spell over other minds with the power of his own. The liturgical powers of both art and magic have the potential to summon the gods. In order to realise such moments of revelation Yeats believed that the poet-magician had a sacred duty to convey to the reader a vision of universal consciousness which he regarded as the ultimate reality. In an early draft of *Ego Dominus Tuus* (1915) Yeats warns against the self-deception of those whose impulses strive for but cannot grasp this totality:

127

> the rhetorician would deceive his neighbours
> the sentimentalist himself; while art
> is but a vision of reality.
> What can the artist and magician know
> who have been awakened from the common dream
> But dissipation and despair?[8]

Yeats regarded magic and poetry as vehicles of a mystical illumination which would yield a cosmic truth derived from a common source. His occult pursuits guided him towards revitalising an ancient myth based upon the quest for absolute knowledge, the recovery of total consciousness for fallen mankind. According to Golden Dawn teaching "The Fall as a state of consciousness is analogous to that condition described by various mystics as the dark Night of the Soul".[9] Presumably the analogy refers to the precarious spiritual state which precedes divine revelation. During a ritual Yeats was shown two altar diagrams depicting the Garden of Eden before and after the Fall. The memory of this may have inspired the following lines from *The King's Threshold*:

> "I can remember now,
> It's out of a poem I made long ago
> About the Garden in the East of the World,
> And how spirits in the images of birds
> Crowd in the branches of old Adam's crab-tree.[10]

The magical doctrines of the Golden Dawn encouraged Yeats to reject the empiricism of scientific truth in favour of the poetic or mystical truth which stemmed from personal revelation. In "The Song of the Happy Shepherd" from *Crossways* Yeats declares:

> ...there is no truth
> Saving in thine own heart. Seek,then ,
> No learning from the starry men,
> Who follow with the optic glass
> The whirling ways of stars that pass -
> Seek, then, for this is also sooth,
> No word of theirs-the cold star-bane
> Has cloven and rent their hearts in twain,
> And dead is all their human truth. (pp.7-8)

Yeats's search for divine truth directed him towards the ancient theologies in the hope of recovering the legendary lost wisdom of the ancients, the *prisca sapientia*.

It was predictable that he would be attracted to the secret societies because of their claim to have preserved the continuity of the occult tradition within their arcana of ritual and symbolism. The mystical teaching of such societies provided an alternative to the religious scepticism of modern mankind.

Membership enabled the individual to rebuild the figurative heap of broken images and icons upon the spiritually barren landscape of the twentieth century. In this way the clandestine organisations competed with the churches to replenish the religious aridity of western civilisation. Thus a spate of these societies emerged, many of which were modern inventions. Steeping themselves in an illusion of antiquity they simulated a sense of tradition out of which they generated their own mythologies. Esoteric hybrids such as the Order of the Golden Dawn draped themselves in the borrowed raiment of eastern religions and European mysticism.

Eclecticism appealed to Yeats who, in 1885, with his friend Charles Johnston founded the Dublin Hermetic society which incorporated spiritualism, the mysteries of Odic force, and Esoteric Buddhism. Inspiration for this group had been derived from the Theosophical Society which aimed to be a synthesis of all the great world religions. The attraction of such pantheology was that it provided a blanket solution for all the complexities of modern-day life. From 1887 until 1890 Yeats was associated with the Theosophical movement whose founder, Madam Helena Petrovna Blavatsky, he described as "a sort of female Dr. Johnson".[11] Blavatsky had been greatly influenced by the occult novels of Edward Bulwer-Lytton. Her interest in Egyptian occultism had been stimulated by Bulwer's account of the cult of Isis in *The Last Days of Pompeii* (1834). By 1877 Blavatsky had published *Isis Unveiled*, a monumental work celebrating the ancient Egyptians as the ancestors of all occult wisdom. Though this book contained over two thousand plagiarisms Bulwer had provided Blavatsky with her main source. In *Isis Unveiled* Blavatsky acknowledged Bulwer's importance by saying that "no author in the world of literature ever gave a more truthful or poetic description of these beings (the elemental spirits) than Sir E. Bulwer-Lytton, the author of *Zanoni*."[12] In his Rosicrucian novel, *Zanoni* (1842) Bulwer introduces the sinister "Dwellers of the Threshold". Blavatsky's colleague, a Mr Felt, had promised to publicly materialise these supernatural entities by using techniques derived from the mystic measurements of the pyramids. Blavatsky, who was also known as H.P.B., had agreed to send a theosophist to Egypt in order to fetch an African wizard who would assist in the invocation. H.P.B.'s fascination with invisible beings was more apparent after 1879 when she claimed to be receiving guidance from hidden masters or Mahatmas who lived beyond the Himalayas. Yeats referred to these ·spirit mentors as "trance personalities".[13] Apparently they were responsible for guiding H.P.B. away from Egyptian lore to Hindu mysticism.

In *Isis Unveiled* she set out to provide a rationale for her eclectic system by stressing the family resemblances between the old religions, claiming that they were based upon a common secret doctrine. For Yeats, Blavatsky embodied "all the folk-lore of the world".[14] She developed her theories further in *The Secret Doctrine* (1888) where she attempted to trace the spiritual evolution of the human race. Here she combined Eastern and

Western ideas through a blend of Hermeticism and Hinduism which she declared to be the two oldest systems of thought. One of Blavatsky's disciples, A.P. Sinnett, summarised her doctrines in *The Occult World* (1881). He went on to write a book based upon Buddhist Scriptures and the *Upanishads* called *Esoteric Buddhism* (1883) which was read by Yeats.

The poet was later to find himself overwhelmed by the importance placed on Asian mysticism by the Theosophists. One of Blavatsky's agents from India was Mobini Chatterji whose doctrines were derived from the ancient Hindu philosophy, *Samkara*. This proved to be too abstract for Yeats who expressed growing concern that the Theosophical society was becoming too speculative and detached from reality. Yeats confided to his friend John O'Leary that "they were turning a good philosophy into a bad religion."[15] Practical magic and experimentation had been forbidden by H.P.B. but she did concede to the demands of a presssure group to form an Inner Circle devoted to the theory though not to the practice of the Cabala. Yeats, however, was instrumental in plunging this group into occult research. He instigated an experiment to try and raise the ghost of a flower from its ashes using the details of a magical ritual described by Ebenezer Sibly in his *Celestial Science of Astrology* (1784) which contains an account of various forms of necromancy. Yeats's defiance of Blavatsky's edicts represented a protest against the theoretical bias of the organization. His views advocating the principle of experimentation were eventually formulated in the following credo:

> I BELIEVE IN THE PRACTICE and philosophy of what
> we have agreed to call magic, in what I must call
> the evocation of spirits, thought I do not know
> what they are, in the power of creating magical
> illusions, in the visions of truth in the depths
> of the mind when the eyes are closed; and I believe
> in three doctrines, which have, as I think, been
> handed down from early times, and been the found-
> ations of nearly all magical practices. These
> doctrines are:-
>    (1) That the borders of our mind are evershifting,
> and that many minds can flow into one another, as
> it were, and create or reveal a single mind, a
> single energy.
>    (2) That the borders of our memories are as
>    shifting, and that our memories are a part of one
> great memory, the memory of Nature herself.
>    (3) That this great mind and great memory can be
> evoked by symbols.[16]

Because of his insistence upon experimental verification Yeats was asked to resign from the Theosophical society. His desire to promote the practical importance of the Cabala was shared by Samuel Liddell Macgregor Mathers, author of *The Kabbalah Unveiled* (1887). H.P.B. had invited Mathers to join the Theosophical organization but he had declined since he was busy forming his own society for practical Cabalism. Part of this preparation involved researching into ancient magical texts at the British Museum where he met Yeats who had now left the Theosophical Society. Mathers invited the poet to join his newly-formed occult group. This invitation was to mark the beginning of Yeats's long association with the Order of the Golden Dawn.

## The Hermetic Order of the Golden Dawn

Yeats was initiated at the Isis-Urania Temple, no. 3, at 17, Fitzroy Street in London, on Friday March 7 1890 at 6.30 p.m. His ceremonial attire consisted of red shoes and a black gown bound at the waist with three pieces of rope. A high-ranking member, known as a Hierophant, who was dressed in scarlet robes and held a scepter announced "I give permission to admit William Butler Yeats, who now loses his name and will henceforth be known among us as D.E.D.I. *"Demon Est Deus Inversus"*. Yeats must have borrowed the Cabalistic tag *"Demon Est Deus Inversus"* ("the Devil is God inverted") from Blavatsky's *Secret Doctrine* where it is used as an epigraph.[17]

Yeats swore never to divulge the rituals and magical practices of the Golden Dawn:

I [William Butler Yeats] in the Presence of the
LORD of the Universe...do, of my own freewill,
hereby and hereon, most solemnly promise to keep
secret this Order, its Name, the Names of its
Members and the proceedings that take place at
its meetings, from every person in the world who
has not been initiated into it....Furthermore,
if I break this, my Magical Obligation, I submit
myself, by my own consent, to a Stream of Power,
set in motion by the Divine Guardians of this
Order, Who live in the Light of their Perfect
Justice and before Whom my Soul now stands.[18]

If Yeats broke this pledge then he realised that his body would be "broken" and his blood "poured out",[19] a threat symbolized by a vial of bright red liquid. This ritual penalty did not refer to loss of life but to the destruction of the higher ego. After passing through the threshold grade of Neophyte, Yeats then proceeded to work his way through the "outer" Order which consisted of the degrees of Zelator, Theoricus, Practicus, and Philosophus. From there he moved on to his admission into the "inner" Order known as the *Ordo Rosae Rubeae et Aureae Crucis*, the Order of the Rose of Ruby and the Cross of Gold consisting of the grades, *Adeptus Minor, Adeptus Major* and the *Adeptus Exemptus* which he attained in 1916. The remaining three degrees belonged to the *Unbekannten Oberen* or Secret Chiefs. These were supernatural beings who acted as the Order's spirit guides. The meanings, numbers and Cabalistic significance of the degrees are tabulated in the following chart:[20]

| CABALISTIC ORDER | SIGNIFICANCE | TITLE AND GRADE | |
|---|---|---|---|
| Kether | Spirit | Ipsissimus | 10=1 |
| Chokmah | Wisdom | Magus | 9=2 |
| Binah | Understanding | Magister Templi | 8=3 |
| Chesed | Mercy | Adeptus Exemptus | 7=4 |
| Geburah | Might | Adeptus Major | 6=5 |
| Tiphareth | Harmony | Adeptus Minor | 5=6 |
| Netzach | Victory (fire) | Philosophus | 4=7 |
| Hod | Splendor (water) | Practicus | 3=8 |
| Yesod | Foundation (air) | Theoricus | 2=9 |
| Malkuth | Kingdom (earth) | Zelator | 1=10 |

The first figure in the order-grade equation was often placed in a heavenly circle while the last digit was set in an earthly square. This was to indicate that the degrees were graded on two contrasting scales, the divine and the sublunary. The corresponding Hebrew letters relate to the Cabala on which the Golden Dawn teaching was based. Cabalism is a system of Jewish mystical thought whose doctrines are expressed through the image of the Tree of Life. The ten spheres of the Tree are the Sefiroth, aspects or emanations of God, which are listed in the first column above. The Sephirotic Tree inspired one of Yeats's favourite poems, "The Two Trees" (1893) which begins:

> Beloved, gaze in thine own heart,
> The holy tree is growing there;
> From joy the holy branches start,
> And all the trembling flowers they bear.
> The changing colours of its fruit
> Have dowered the stars with merry light;
> The surety of its hidden root
> Has planted quiet in the night. (p.48)

The title of the poem may have been derived from the Right and Left Pillars of the Sephiroth on the Tree of Life revealed to the poet during his magical instruction in the outer Order of the Golden Dawn.
  Both men and women were admitted into the Order where they were known as *fratres* and *sorores*. By 1900 there were

approximately a hundred members. The Golden Dawn succeeded in recruiting such eminent figures as Brodie-Innes, the Astronomer Royal of Scotland, the socialist Herbert Burrows, and Annie Horniman, the theatre manager. Writers included A.E. Waite, George William Russell the poet and painter known as "A.E.", Arthur Machen who wrote tales of mysticism and the macabre, and Charles Williams a poet and novelist of supernatural thrillers. Arthur Conan Doyle who created Sherlock Holmes considered joining the Order after an encounter with two members, Dr Henry Pullen Burry and Dr R.W. Felkin, which he described in an essay on "Early Psychic Experiences" published in *Pearson's Magazine* for March 1924. Since Conan Doyle was an investigator into psychic phenomena, it is appropriate that his suitability for admission should have been determined by an "astral visitation" by a member of the Golden Dawn. Finding that "their line of philosophy or development is beyond me",[21] Conan Doyle decided not to pursue his application to join. Aubrey Beardsley also contemplated joining the society. Though Yeats never managed to persuade him, Beardsley's fascination with magic is apparent from his drawing, *Of a Neophyte, and of How the Black Art was Revealed*. Novelists alleged to have been recruited into the Golden Dawn contributed to the mythology already surrounding the Order. According to Louis Pauwel and Jacques Bergier's *Le Matin des Magiciens* (1960) membership had included Bram Stoker, the author of *Dracula*, and Sax Rohmer, a student of sorcery and the inventor of the "Dr Fu Manchu" mystery stories. Fact and fantasy also converged when they confused Aleister Crowley, the alleged black magician, with Yeats by describing the latter as presiding over rituals clad in a kilt with a golden ceremonial dagger and wearing a black mask. Yet such allegations did not seem so extraordinary in the light of Yeats's wide-ranging occult activities. He was also a member of the Mystical Society of the Three Kings named after the three Magi who visited the Christ-child. Members included John M. Watkins and Algernon Blackwood, the novelist who was also a member of the Golden Dawn.

The Order had been founded by William R. Woodman, William Wynn Westcott, and the Reverend A.F.A. Woodford who were all prominent Freemasons. The Triumvirate also belonged to the Masonic *Societas Rosicruciana in Anglia* whose Grand Patron was Edward Bulwer-Lytton. Mathers, another Freemason, joined Woodman and Westcott to form the Isis-Urania branch of the Golden Dawn. In *Data of the History of the Rosicrucians* (1916) Westcott records:

> In 1887 by permission of S.D.A. [*Sapiens Dominabitur Astris* - Fraulein Sprengel] a continental Rosicrucian Adept, the Isis-Urania Temple of Hermetic Students of the G.D. [Golden Dawn] was formed to give instruction in the mediaeval occult sciences. Fratres M.E.V. [*Magna Est Veritas Et Praelavebit* - Woodman] with S.A. [*Sapere Aude* - Westcott] and S.R.M.D. ['*S Rioghail Mo*

*Dhream* - Mathers] became the chiefs, and the latter
wrote the rituals in modern English from old Rosicrucian
mss. (the property of S.A.) supplemented by his own
literary researches.[22]

The head of the Order was Westcott who had to resign in
1897 because the rumours of necromancy surrounding the Golden
Dawn meant that his membership was considered to be
incompatible with his public position as coroner. Mathers took
over the leadership but alienated many of the fratres and sorores
by elevating himself to the position of Supreme Magus, a grade
considered to be beyond the reach of any mortal being. The
Golden Dawn was largely Mathers's own creation. He had
constructed a coherent magical system out of a synthesis of the
Cabala, ritual magic, the Tarot, Masonic symbolism, and
Rosicrucianism. His wife, Moina Bergson, the sister of the
philosopher Henri Bergson, had claimed that the teachings of the
Order were based upon some Rosicrucian documents provided by
an unnamed person described as "the reputed instructor in magic
of Bulwer Lytton"[23] who was thought to be Kenneth Mackenzie.
But Westcott disputed this claim by insisting that he, himself, had
unearthed the cipher manuscripts from the library of the *Societas
Rosicruciana* where they had been deposited by Robert Wentworth
Little. Westcott then alleged that he had passed the manuscripts
on to Mathers to decipher the outer rituals many of which were
written out in bat's blood. One of the messages which he
transcribed urged that contact be made with Anna Sprengel who
was empowered to authorise the London Rosicrucians to establish
the Order of the Golden Dawn.

The mysterious Sprengel who communicated by letter to
Westcott was said to be involved with the Rosicrucian Rite of
Continental Masonry. The Golden Dawn, which often met at Mark
Masons' Hall, was intricately involved with Freemasonry partly
because membership between the two societies frequently
overlapped. The three founder members of the Golden Dawn were
Magi of the *Societas Rosicruciana* which meant that they had
passed through all nine degrees. Accordingly they adopted the
names of these grades for the Golden Dawn. Yeats was later to
express concern that his colleagues, who regarded themselves as
Rosicrucians, were drifting into Freemasonry. The
Hermetic-Cabalistic teachings of the Golden Dawn owed much to
Rosicrucianism. Mrs Mathers, however, claimed that the rituals
were based upon a Rosicrucian Rite of Continental Freemasonry.
In his *Autobiography*, Yeats challenged this view:

> I add, however, that I am confident from internal
> evidence that the rituals as I knew them, were in
> substance ancient though never so in language unless
> some ancient text was incorporated. There was a little
> that I thought obvious and melodramatic, and it was
> precisely in this little I am told that they resembled

Masonic rituals, but much that I thought beautiful and profound.[24]

Yeats, who has been described as "the canny unacknowledged mason,"[25] played down these Masonic connections. This was because he was trying to recruit into the Golden Dawn, Maud Gonne, who was bitterly opposed to Freemasonry describing it as "a bulwark of the British Empire".[26] As an Irish patriot, Gonne was distrustful of the society which she regarded as a stronghold of Britain's politics and power. Yeats would have been sympathetic towards this point of view since circa 1886 he became a member of the Irish Republican Brotherhood before joining a breakaway organization, the Irish National Alliance. Nevertheless Gonne was persuaded by the poet to overcome her scruples and join the fellowship of the Golden Dawn. In her autobiography, Gonne conveys the cynicism she felt towards its members by observing that they were the "very essence of British middle-class dullness. They looked so incongruous in their cloaks and badges at initiation ceremonies; their mysterious titles, "Guardians of the Gates of the East and of the West", "Commanders of the Temple".[27] Her suspicions regarding the affiliations of the Order were aroused when she realised that initiations took place in Mark Masons' Hall on Euston Road, London. Determined to establish an even more conclusive link between the two societies, Gonne tried out current Golden Dawn passwords on the Freemason, Claude Lane. His response confirmed that she was using Masonic pass-words including one for a higher degree of Freemasonry. Gonne resigned in indignation leaving Yeats to ponder that Mathers, the official scribe of the sacred texts, must have innocuously introduced Masonic pass-words into the arcana of the Golden Dawn. It did not escape his notice that Mathers's mind "like the minds of so many students of these hidden things, was always running on Masonry and discovering it in strange places."[28]

The state of Mathers's mind which demonstrated "much learning but little scholarship, much imagination and imperfect taste"[29] was to cause Yeats and others some concern. It soon became apparent that he was getting intoxicated by his own magical powers. Mathers's increasing ineptitude impeded his ability to distinguish between the imaginative and material worlds. By this time his followers began to suspect that his spiritual authority, which rested on his communication with superior intelligences, the Secret Chiefs, was really the "fabrication of his own diseased mind."[30] Indeed Mathers had gambled with his sanity by undergoing perilous journeys into his own psyche. With his wife he conjured up evocations to sway world-events for the purpose of forestalling the future horrors of the Apocalypse. Yeats had observed that sometimes these magical operations were so harrowing that they would even cause Mathers to spit blood.

After Mathers's death in 1918, Yeats evoked his ghost in the poetical necromancy of "All Souls' Night" (1920):

I call MacGregor Mathers from his grave,
For in my first hard spring-time we were friends,
Although of late estranged.
I thought him half a lunatic, half knave,
And told him so, but friendship never ends;
And what if mind seem changed,
And it seem changed with the mind,
When thought rise up unbid
On generous things that he did
And I grow half contented to be blind!

He had much industry at setting out,
Much boisterous courage, before loneliness
Had driven him crazed;
For meditations upon unknown thought
Make human intercourse grow less and less;
They are neither paid nor praised.
But he'd object to the host,
The glass because my glass;
A ghost-lover he was
And may have grown more arrogant being
    a ghost. .

(p.229)

Richard Ellmann describes this as a ritualized poem since it incorporates the appropriate invocation ceremony for November 2.[31] Yeats also summons the spirits of two other Golden Dawn members, William Horton and Florence Farr Emery. After praising Mathers's pioneering skill in helping to set up the Order, Yeats condemns him for retreating into the spirit world where now he resided permanently. Yeats goes on to warn that "No living man can drink from the whole wine" for it was MacGregor's undiluted vision which led him "To where the damned have howled away their hearts,/ And where the blessed dance" (p.230). In contrast Yeats was determined that he himself would not perish in the labyrinth of mystic consciousness before making "Such thought - such thought have I that hold it tight/Till meditation master all its parts" (p.230).

By introducing Yeats to Cabalistic vision techniques, Mathers provided him with powerful images which had a profound impact on his poetry:

> It was through him [Mathers] mainly that I began certain
> studies and experiences, that were to convince me that
> images well up before the mind's eye from a deeper source
> than conscious or subconscious memory.[32]

At their home, Mr and Mrs Mathers taught Yeats how to meditate upon a Tarot card so that he could release himself into a stream of pure consciousness. Through such yantric methods

Yeats was able to enter into visionary states which he recorded in his verse. As an adept Yeats was able to activate moments of mystical revelation in more prosaic settings:

> My fiftieth year had come and gone,
> I sat, a solitary man,
> In a crowded London shop,
> An open book and empty cup
> On the marble table-top.
>
> While on the shop and street I gazed
> My body of a sudden blazed;
> And twenty minutes more or less
> It seemed, so great my happiness,
> That I was blessed and could bless.
>
> (p.251)

Yeats also believed that he was able to perceive the Rosicrucian spirit world which consisted of the elementals of the four elements; Sylphs (air), Gnomes (earth), Nymphs or undines (water) and Salamanders (fire):[33]

> *For the elemental creatures go*
> *About my table to and fro,*
> *That hurry from unmeasured mind*
> *To rant and rage in flood and wind;*
> *Yet he who treads in measured ways*
> *May surely barter gaze for gaze.*
>
> (p.50)

Mathers interpreted one of Yeats's waking dreams as a visitation of "a being of the order of Salamanders".[34] This was when Yeats had witnessed a "black Titan raising himself up by his two hands from the middle of a heap of ancient ruins"[35] situated in a desert. Yeats probably adapted this imagery for the nightmarish *The Second Coming* (1919) which had been inspired by Mathers's vivid pre-cognition of the destructiveness of World War I:

> The Second Coming! Hardly are those words out
> When a vast image out of *Spiritus Mundi*
> Troubles my sight: somewhere in sands of the desert
> A shape with lion body and the head of a man,
> A gaze blank and pitiless as the sun,
> Is moving its slow thighs, while all about it
> Reel shadows of the indignant desert birds.
> The darkness drops again; but now I know
> That twenty centuries of stony sleep
> Were vexed to nightmare by a rocking cradle
> And what rough beast, its hour come round at last,
> Slouches towards Bethlehem to be born?
>
> (p.187)

The beast is the metamorphosis of the black titan. Yeats may have derived its demonic identity from that of a fellow-member of the Golden Dawn, Aleister Crowley, the notorious "Beast 666". As a grotesque parody of the birth of Christianity, "The Second Coming" draws on Crowley's conviction that he had fulfilled the prophecy of the Beast in the "Book of Revelation." Some verbal hints suggest that Yeats may have been thinking of this blasphemy toward the end of "The Magi":

> Now as at all times I can see in the mind's eye,
> In their stiff, painted clothes, the pale
> unsatisfied ones
> Appear and disappear in the blue depth of the sky
> With all their ancient faces like rain-beaten stones,
> And all their helms of silver hovering side by side,
> And all their eyes still fixed, hoping to find
> once more,
> Being by Calvary's turbulence unsatisfied,
> The uncontrollable mystery on the bestial floor.
>                                         (p.126)

Crowley believed himself to be the Messiah of a new religion. This was a new anti-Christ cult known as "Thelema" which enshrined the magical formula "Do what thou wilt". Disciples used this injunction to open a ritual sacrifice during which a frog was crucified:

> The slave-God is in the power of the Lord of
> Freedom. Thine hour is come; as I blot thee out
> from this     earth, so surely shall the eclipse pass;
> and light, Life, Love and Liberty be once more the
> Law of Earth. Give thou place to me, O Jesus; thine
> aeon is passed; the Age of Horus is arisen by the
> Magick of the Master the Great Beast.[36]

Crowley as the self-styled "Baphomet" or "Great Beast" believed his destiny was to usurp the Christian God. In view of this, his announcement to Mathers that he had promoted himself to the leadership of the Golden Dawn could not have been entirely unexpected. Crowley hoped to dispose of any objection by insisting that through spirit communication the Secret Chiefs had authorised his appointment. Consequently he adopted the name MacGregor and even used his rival's Golden Dawn motto on his stationary.
     Crowley started to imagine that his rapid progress through the degrees of the Order and the privileged rapport he enjoyed with the Secret Chiefs had aroused the envy of his fellow-members since "we have to consider the evil work of others in the Order, such as E.F.E.J., who, envious of his progress and favour with the Chiefs, were attempting to destroy him."[37]

E.F.E.J. was a disguised reference to Yeats which may be
deciphered by moving up the initials of the poet's ceremonial
motto, D.E.D.I. to the next letters of the alphabet. Crowley
intensely disliked Yeats whom he described as "a lank dishevelled
demonologist who might have taken more pains with his personal
appearance without incurring the reproach of dandyism."[38] While
priding himself as a poet, Crowley wrongly assumed that Yeats
was jealous of his poetic talents. Yeats's luke-warm response to
Crowley's play *Jephthah* (1899) had convinced the author that he
was "not only a poetaster but a dabbler in magic, and black
jealousy of a younger man and a far finer poet [Crowley]
gnawed at his petty heart."[39]

Yeats and the other adepts who refused to elevate Crowley
to a higher degree were displeased with Mathers for admitting his
protege into the Order. Mathers's support of Crowley was one of
the factors which led to his expulsion in April 1900. Mathers
took refuge in Paris where he illegally initiated Crowley into the
exalted grade of Adeptus Minor. In order to quell the disputes in
London over his leadership Mathers, unwisely, sent Crowley in
disguise as his emissary for the purpose of reinstating them both
back into the society. Having reached his destination, Crowley in
the role of the "Laird of Boleskine" melodramatically broke into
the Order rooms wearing full Highland dress, a black mask, and
armed with a golden dagger only to find Yeats and the police
waiting to evict him. Later that day the Second Order Committee
decreed that "no person shall be deemed to belong to the London
branch who has not been initiated by that body in London."[40]
The intention behind this resolution was to repudiate Mathers's
unauthorised initiation of Crowley into a higher degree in Paris.
Meanwhile a quarrel between Mathers and Crowley was escalating
into a magical combat. Mathers "employed" a vampire to destroy
Crowley who retaliated by smiting her "with her own current of
evil".[41] Crowley subsequently formed his own magical association
in accordance with his libertine creed which was characterized by
perverse sexual rites. Known as the A. A. (*Argenteum Astrum*, "The
Silver Star"), the society constituted the Inner Order of the Great
White Brotherhood. The Outer Order was the Golden Dawn which
Crowley eventually abandoned proving that he had not after all
lived up to his magical title, *Perdurabo* ("I will endure to the
end").

Following the catastrophic Crowley episode Yeats condemned
those who abused their magical powers by engaging in evil
sorcery. In his essay "Is the Order of R.R. & A.C. to remain a
Magical Order?" (1901) he recommended a more rigorous vetting
system to safeguard against the admission of potentially
undesirable members. Yeats was also opposed to proposals that the
Golden Dawn should be reorganization into a system of
sub-groups. He insisted that the Golden Dawn could not be
sub-divided since unlike a society for experiment and research it
was a Magical Order which had "an Actual Being, an organic
life".[42]

> If we preserve the unity of the Order, if we make
> that unity efficient among us, the Order will
> become a single very powerful talisman, creating
> in us, and in the world about us, such moods and
> circumstances as may best serve the magical life,
> and best awaken the magical wisdom.[43]

Preparations were made for a legal constitution which would be voted in by the adepti. In 1902 proposals were drafted for the complete reorganization of the Golden Dawn which was renamed *Morgenröthe*. A year later the society split into two factions led by Dr. R.W. Felkin and A.E. Waite respectively. Unable to achieve a reconciliation, Felkin and the majority seceded and formed the Amoun Temple known as the *Stella Matutina* ("The Morning Star").

Yeats, who had the title "Imperator" belonged to the Amoun Temple which was situated in Earls Court, London. This was run by Christina Mary Stoddart who, in 1919, complained that the Stella Matutina was "rent by dissensions, jealousies, underground whisperings and open strife and rebellion."[44] Stoddart was not convinced of the authenticity of the Order's source of inner teaching and its origins which, according to Yeats, were "almost as obscure as that of some ancient religion."[45] Stoddart insisted on an investigation and argued:

> You must realise that unless we know the SOURCE
> of our INNER Teaching and the foundations of our
> Order, also may I add unless we get further teachings
> from a recognised source we are merely the blind
> leading the blind - and into what snares and pitfalls
> ... If we are merely a school of experimental
> Occultism then we must make all members recognise
> the risks and the responsibilities they are taking
> upon themselves when they join us.[46]

Stoddart's research led her to the conclusion that "the history of the Order consists of a long series of mystifications, the one following and overlapping the other".[47] Among these she included the Cipher MS and the Anna Sprengel correspondence with Westcott. Internal textual evidence suggests that Westcott had forged the documents himself and had invented Sprengel. Convinced that the Golden Dawn had been founded upon an elaborate hoax, Stoddart closed the temple at 56 Redcliffe Gardens in March 1923 declaring "it is a great relief to have got rid of that awful incubus-house and Order".[48] Yeats, weary from all the internal squabbles, admitted in 1922 that he had become disillusioned with the Stella Matutina saying:

> My connection with "The Hermetic Students' ended amid
> quarrels caused by men, otherwise worthy, who claimed

a Rosicrucian sanction for their own fantasies, and I
add, to prevent needless correspondence, that I am not
now a member of a Cabalistic society.[49]

**Father Rosycross**

Yeats stated that he had resigned from the Golden Dawn because
of those members "who claimed a Rosicrucian sanction for their
own phantasies". Under the leadership of Felkin, the Order had
become increasingly immersed in Rosicrucianism. Felkin sought
contact with the Secret Chiefs who were now known as the Sun
Masters. By 1914 he was convinced that Christian Rosencreutz, the
legendary founder of the Brotherhood of the Rosy Cross, would
manifest himself in the Second Coming. Inspired by this idea,
Felkin planned a spiritual pilgrimage to the "Old Vault", the tomb
of Christian Rosencreutz. In a memorandum written in June 1918
Felkin recollected:

> I was told TWELVE, were to be picked out of the
> Temples to help C.R.C. [Christian Rosencreutz]
> when he again manifestedin 1926-33 or 35. The
> whole of that was to have been told me face to
> face in 1914 when we went to Germany. We had
> tickets there which took us to a place S.S.E.
> of Austria, where we were to have been met and
> been taken to the Old Vault, and also to have
> met several hidden Chiefs.[50]

Felkin was so wrapped up in his Rosicrucian dreams that he
did not even allow the outbreak of war between Germany and
France to deter him from his mission. Nevertheless communication
between himself and the society in London was disrupted as
explained by a circular letter sent out to members by his
daughter. This pointed out that Felkin would be "unable to
communicate with us until after the war is over".[51] Eventually
with the help of some Hanoverian Freemasons, he was able to
leave Germany in safety and return to London.
    During this period Felkin formulated a 6°=5° Rosicrucian
ritual. On 16 October 1914 Yeats participated in this ceremony
which included the recreation of the tomb of Christian
Rosencreutz described as "the mystic Cavern in the Sacred
Mountain of Initiation."[52] Mathers had devised a replica of the
fifteenth-century vault in which Rosencreutz was buried in the
Abigenus Mountain at the age of 106. Initiation into the second
Order was conducted in the vault. Since Crowley had been
refused admission into the Inner Order he retaliated by
attempting to steal the vault during the protracted drama
mentioned earlier which had involved Yeats.[53] The vault was a

141

sanctum for contemplation and the postulant was encouraged to meditate upon the symbolism of its seven sides including the roof and floor (see Plate 9). It was also revered as a chamber of initiation which would enable the initiate to pass into the Portal of the Vault of the Rose of Ruby and the Cross of Gold. Instructions for the use of the vault warned against the misuse of its magical properties:

> All who are eligible should use the Vault when it
> is in its place. When working it is well to be
> clothed in the White Robe and yellow sash, yellow
> slippers and yellow and white Nemyss on your head.
> Rose Cross should be upon the breast. Remember that
> within the Vault you never use a banishing Ritual.
> The chamber is highly charged by the Ceremonies
> which have been held there and the atmosphere thus
> created should not be disturbed.[54]

At one stage during the ritual Yeats actually lay in the coffin or pastos contained in the vault where he heard "the ringing of thirty-six bells" which accompanied the following chant:

> At the Thirteenth Bell he is faint; at the
> Fourteenth he is very cold; at the Sixteenth he
> again emerges into a further higher plane; at
> the Seventeenth he is like a transparent rainbow.
> The Colours of the Planets play upon him. Then
> they merge into brilliant Light and for the rest
> of the Bells he shone with it. The Rising from
> the Tomb and the Sprinkling appear to involve a
> very great and serious effort on the part of both
> Postulant and Officers....[55]

According to Virginia Moore, since 1909 Yeats had experimented with meditation techniques while lying in a coffin.[56] From the vantage point of a symbolic burial Yeats could evoke his various incarnations and confront his anti-self:

> By the help of an image
> I call to my own opposite, summon all
> That I have handled least, least looked upon....
> I call to the mysterious one who yet
> Shall walk the wet sands by the edge of the stream
> And look most like me, being indeed my double,
> And prove of all imaginable things
> The most unlike, being my anti-self.
> (pp.160-62)

The conflict between self and anti-self may be viewed in terms of the psychosis existing between body and soul. In "To a Shade" (1913) Yeats describes a ghost returning to his home town to visit

his own monument. The visitor is advised to renounce the world
of the living and return to the security of his grave:

> Go, unquiet wanderer,
> And gather the Glasnevin coverlet
> About your head till the dust stops your ear,
> The time for you to taste of that salt breath
> And listen at the corners has not come;
> You had enough of sorrow before death -
> Away, away! You are safer in the tomb.
>
> (p.110)

The tomb of Christian Rosencreutz was a microcosm of the
universe. In the first Rosicrucian manifesto, the *Fama Fraternitatis*
(1614), the seven-sided vault is described as containing a round
altar covered with a brass plate upon which was inscribed: *"Hoc
universi compendium unius mihi sepulchrum feci"* (This compendium
of the universe I made in my lifetime to be my tomb"). [57]
Yeats would have been acquainted with the details of the
Rosicrucian tradition since they were taught to him on his
initiation into the grade of Adeptus Minor. During this ceremony
the history of Christian Rosencreutz is recounted as follows:

> In 1378 was born the Chief and Originator of
> our Fraternity in Europe. He was of noble German
> family, but poor, and in the fifth year of his
> age was placed in a cloister where he learned
> both Greek and Latin. While yet a youth he
> accompanied a certain brother P.A.L. on a pil-
> grimage to the Holy Land but the latter, dying
> at Cyprus, he himself went to Damascus. There
> was then in Arabia a Temple of the Order which
> was called in the Hebrew tongue "Damkar"... that
> is "The Blood of the Lamb." There he was duly
> initiated, and took the Mystic title Christian
> Rosenkreutz, or Christian of the Rosy Cross....[58]

From here Rosencreutz went on to found the Brotherhood of the
Rosy Cross which devoted itself to the study of the writings of
their founder as well as the transcription of a magical language.
After the mysterious death of Rosencreutz, his tomb was
eventually discovered by his disciples. He had left instructions
requesting that the door of the vault was not to be opened for
120 years. In *The Rosicrucian Enlightenment*, Yates suggests that the
opening of the vault signalled the dawn of a general reformation.
[59] It was this concept of a cosmic renewal which was central to
the doctrines of the Golden Dawn. In order to hasten this
apocalyptic event, Felkin sent his representative, Neville Meakin,
to retrace Rosencreutz's journey in the Middle East. But the
moment of prophecy had not yet arrived. As Yeats reveals in his
poem "The Mountain Tomb" Rosencreutz, the founding father, lay

undisturbed:

> Pour wine and dance if manhood still have pride,
> Bring roses if the rose be yet in bloom;
> The cataract smokes upon the mountain side,
> Our Father Rosicross is in his tomb.
>
> Pull down the blinds, bring fiddle and clarionet
> That there be no foot silent in the room
> Nor mouth from kissing, nor from wine unwet;
> Our Father Rosicross is in his tomb.
>
> In vain, in vain; the cataract still cries;
> The everlasting taper lights the gloom;
> All wisdom shut into his onyx eyes,
> Our Father Rosicross sleeps in his tomb.

(pp.121-2)

During his initiation ceremony for the degree of Adeptus Minor Yeats would have witnessed the chief adept or Hierophant lying in a coffin to symbolize the preserved body of Rosencreutz. Those in attendance were told that their leader had been "Buried with that Light in a mystical death, rising again in a mystical resurrection, cleansed and purified through Him our Master, O Brother of the Cross and the Rose".[60] In an essay on "The Body of Father Christian Rosencrux" (1895) Yeats uses the Rosencreutz legend to allegorize the history of the creative imagination which he sees as incarcerated within the sepulchre of criticism, the revenge of the intellect upon art. For Yeats the body of Rosencreutz is a beacon to the imagination illuminated by the "inextinguishable magical lamps"[61] of the tomb. These refer to the perpetual-burning light placed in the vault which Yeats describes as the "ever-lasting taper" in "The Mountain Tomb". The idea of a tomb as a receptacle of knowledge enables it to become a shrine for seekers after "wisdom and romance".[62] According to Yeats, it is these pilgrims who saw the universality of Rosicrucianism as a refuge for the imagination which freed mankind from the external standard of reality imposed upon the individual by the material world. He urges that if we trust our own being then we will learn that "the great Passions are angels of God".[63] According to this parable, art could embody eternal glory since it was capable of transcending the socialistic and humanitarian particulars of our times. In the light of this, "Art is a revelation, and not a criticism".[64] It is significant that in depicting the universality of art, Yeats should choose to relay his message through the legend of Christian Rosencreutz whose tomb contained "the symbols of all things in heaven and earth".[65] By reiterating the message of the Rosicrucian manifestos, Yeats advocates that the artist should surrender to the life of the imagination by becoming a pilgrim to the tomb of Christian Rosencreutz:

> The wind bloweth where it listeth, and thou
> hearest the sound thereof, but canst not tell
> whence it cometh and whither it goeth; so is
> every one that is born of the Spirit.[66]

Yeats borrowed this passage from Golden Dawn teaching on "The Microcosm-man!" which perceived the physical body of the individual as "The Magical Mirror of the Universe".[67]

Yeats wrote "The Body of Father Christian Rosencrux" shortly after his initiation into the degree of Adeptus Minor in 1895. He recognised that the Rosicrucian tradition was capable of inspiring works of art since after reading Westcott's Masonic lecture on Rosencreutz he decided that "somebody should write a romance about Father Rosycross in which the magical doctrine should be ... less a romance ... than a testament."[68] After a visionary dream Yeats articulated the "faith of the Rosy Cross" saying "Father Rosy Cross was the first who saw that beauty is in holiness" for "He set the rose upon the cross and this by uniting religion and beauty, the spirit and nature - and the union of spirit and nature is magic."[69] The fusion between art and magic, the actual and the ideal, is realised through the iconography of the rosy cross. In the ceremony for the grade of Adeptus Minor the aspirant is told:

> Know, then, O Aspirant, that the Mysteries of
> the Rose and the Cross have existed from time
> immemorial, and that the Rites were practised,
> and the Wisdom taught, in Egypt, Eleusis,
> Samothrace, Persia, Chaldea and India, and in
> far more ancient lands.[70]

During the "Consecration Ceremony of the Vault of the Adepti" the Adeptus Minor is expected to explain the symbolic significance of the Rose and Cross. The adept would surely believe that the full import of this symbolism cannot be construed within the ordinary consciousness since it is meaningful only in the context of mystical experience. In this way symbols are discovered which may never be translated. But art can often bridge this gap by acting as the finite vehicle which reveals the infinite. Another Golden Dawn poet, Aleister Crowley, tries to convey the mystical illumination inherent in this symbolism in his poem "The Rose and the Cross":

> The glowing medley moved the tune unsung
> Of perfect love: thence grew the Mystic Rose.
> Its myriad petals of divided light;
> Its leaves of the most radiant emerald;
> Its heart of fire like rubies. At the sight
> I lifted up my heart to God and called:
> How shall I pluck this dream of my desire?

And lo! there shaped itself the Cross of Fire![71]

This poem has similarities with Yeats's bifurcation of the rose
and cross in "A Song of the Rosy-Cross":

> He who measures gain and loss,
>      When he gave to thee the Rose,
> Gave to me alone the Cross;
>      Where the blood-red blossom blows
> In a wood of dew and moss,
>      There thy wandering pathway goes,
> Mine where waters brood and toss;
>      Yet one joy have I, hid close,
> He who measures gain and loss,
>      When he gave to thee the Rose,
> Gave to me alone the Cross.
>
> (pp.535-6)

Special emphasis has been given here to the cross presumably
because of its associations with Calvary. In contrast to this, Yeats
celebrates the tradition of the Rosy Cross by relying mainly on
the image of the rose in the cycle of poems, *The Rose* (1893) and
the stories from *The Secret Rose* (1897). In the opening poem to
*The Rose* collection called "To the Rose upon the Rood of Time",
Yeats addresses the rose on the cross. In this context, the rose
denotes the dying Christ on the blood-stained cross. This
Crucifixion imagery re-appears in "The Secret Rose":

> Far-off, most secret, and inviolate Rose,
> Enfold me in my hour of hours; where those
> Who sought thee in the Holy Sepulchre,
> Or in the wine-vat, dwell beyond the stir
> And tumult of defeated dreams; and deep
> Among pale eyelids, heavy with the sleep
> Men have named beauty. Thy great leaves enfold
> The ancient beards, the helms of ruby and gold
> Of the crowned Magi; and the king whose eyes
> Saw the Pierced Hands and Rood of elder rise
> In Druid vapour and make the torches dim;
>
> (p.69)

The poem is followed by a short story, "The Crucifixion of the
Outcast" set in a Gaelic Golgotha. The outcast is Cumhal who is
crucified for his songs which curse the hypocrisy of the local
abbot. Together the poem and the fable create the synthesis of
the rose on the cross. In "To the Rose upon the Rood of Time"
Yeats reveals the rose to be a key to the Celtic wisdom of "old
Eire" which will enable seekers after wisdom to "learn to chaunt
a tongue men do not know" (p.31):

*Red Rose, proud Rose, sad Rose of all my days!*

> *Come near me, while I sing the ancient ways:*
> *Cuchulain battling with the bitter tide;*
> *The Druid, grey, wood-nurtured, quiet-eyed,*
> *Who cast round Fergus dreams, and ruin untold;...*
> *Come near; I would, before my time to go,*
> *Sing of old Eire and the ancient ways:*
> *Red Rose, proud Rose, sad Rose of all my days.*
>
> (p.31)

Yeats's secular use of the image emerges through his concept of the "Rose of all Roses, Rose of all the world!" (p.37) which is explored in the poem "The Rose of Battle". This contrasts with the preceding poem, "The Rose of Peace", which looks towards a "rosy peace" being the "peace of Heaven with Hell" (p.37). The perfection of this Rosicrucian symbolism is conveyed through Yeats's epiphets, "the Immortal Rose" (p.72), "the Incorruptible Rose" (p.69), and "inviolate Rose" (p.69). He evokes the rose-cross imagery in *The Shadowy Waters*:

> The red rose where the two shafts of the cross,
> Body and soul, waking and sleep, death, life,
> Whatever meaning ancient allegorists
> Have settled on, are mixed into one joy.
> For what's the rose but that? miraculous cries,
> Old stories about mystic marriages,
> Impossible truths? [72]

In the medieval tale, "Out of the Rose" Yeats focuses on the divinity of the rose symbolism through a partial allegory of the Golden Dawn. The main character of the fable is an aged knight wearing rusty armour who is the last remaining member of a mystic fellowship. This secret chivalric order had been founded by a knight from the Holy Lands which suggests that Yeats was drawing on the legendary connection between the Crusaders and the Brotherhood of the Rosy Cross. The founder had been sent a vision of a "great Rose of Fire, and a Voice out of the Rose had told him how men would turn from the light of their own hearts, and bow down before outer order and outer fixity." [73] The reference to an "outer order" would alert Golden Dawn members to recall that the title of their "inner Order" was "Roseae Rubae". The hero of the tale wears a Rose of Rubies on his helmet which he claims is "the symbol of my life and of my hope"[74] since he is pledged to die in the service of the Rose. The knight who is close to death addresses the sun as the Rose of Faith saying "O Divine Rose of Intellectual Flame, let the gates of thy peace be opened to me at last!".[75] In doing so he equates the Kingdom of God with the "Heart of the Rose".[76] This is the "eternal" or "celestial" rose which is witnessed by Dante once he had transcended the limits of time and space. In the *Paradiso*, after Dante bathes his eyes in the river of light which is also the river of time, he is ready to contemplate the infinite in the form of the Celestial Rose, the circle of eternity "for here eternal law doth so enact/ All thou beholdest."[77] At the extreme edge of the rose Dante sees the Virgin Mary, the Queen of Heaven who is surrounded by angels.

In the story "Rosa Alchemica", the narrator in a waking dream is told of Dante's Beatrice and the Mother of God who is holding a rose "whose every petal is a god". [78] Michael Robartes, the fiery visionary, invites him to commune with many gods by becoming a member of the Order of the Alchemical Rose which embraces the paganism of the Rose-Cross tradition. The narrator is puzzled by the necessity for this polytheism and enquires "why should I go to Eleusis and not to Calvary?"[79] The answer is that only in this way can the creative writer become receptive to "all those countless divinities who have taken upon themselves spiritual bodies in the minds of the modern poets and romance writers."[80] Yeats regarded himself as one of the last of the Romantic artists whose sacred duty was to awaken in himself the "power of the old divinities".[81] For him, the imagination was the crucible for the Romantic transformation of the artist which paralleled the alchemical transmutation of base metal into gold. The etymology of "ros" from "Rosicrucian" is not only derived from the word "rose" but also from the Latin word for "dew" (*"ros"*) which was considered by alchemists to be a vital solvent for the process of transmogrification. Alchemy constituted part of the secret tradition associated with the "ros" or "rose" which had figured in the ancient mystery religions. Included among these were the Eleusinian Mysteries as well as the cult of Dionysus whose main festival was a celebration of the rose known as the *Rosalia*. The alchemists' *Opus Magnum* was also believed to produce the elixir of life, a legendary attribute of the Rosicrucians which Crowley explores in his poem, "The Rosicrucian":

> I pass, in my eternal youth,
> And watch the centuries wax and wane:
> Untouched by Time's corroding tooth,
> Silent, immortal, unprofane![82]

The narrator in Yeats's "Rosa Alchemica" visits an alchemical library containing the works of adepts such as Morienus "who hid his immortal body under a shirt of hair-cloth" and Flamel who "achieved the elixir many hundreds of years ago".[83] In the next story, "The Tables of the Law", the narrator discovers that the Order of the Alchemical Rose is not intended for mere mortals. In this respect it resembles the third Order of the Golden Dawn which technically could only admit the eternal Secret Chiefs.

In "Adoration of the Magi" the narrator recognises that the multiplicity of gods are really different aspects of one superior immortal being. He realises this after being visited by the Magi, three old men, who have been sent by the spirit of the dead Michael Robartes. The narrator suspects these mysterious night visitors to be immortal demons who are trying to lead him astray. But he concludes "Whatever they were, I have turned into a pathway which will lead me from them and from the Order of the Alchemical Rose".[84] This change of direction is significant since it reflected Yeats's own rejection of the Rosicrucianism inherent in the Golden Dawn and then finally of the Order itself.

## The End of all Mythologies

Yeats's disenchantment with the Golden Order had grown from his recognition that it was incapable of reconciling his twin vocations of artist and adept.[85] To remedy this, he attempted to found an order of Celtic mysteries to fulfil his dream of an Irish Eleusis which would become a mouthpiece for his patriotism. The reworking of an ancient Celtic mystery cult would have provided Yeats with the perfect vehicle for his mysticism and growing nationalism which he expressed in "Under Ben Bulben"

> Many times man lives and dies
> Between his two eternities
> That of race and that of soul
> And ancient Ireland knew it all.
> (p.325)

Yeats intended to harness radical Christian truths to those of a more ancient world. As part of the groundwork for the society he even employed the methods of telepathic ritual learnt from Mathers which involved pressing symbols to his forehead in order to conjure up talismanic images. At one stage, Yeats came near to being overwhelmed by the maze of imagery he had evoked. In *The Tower* (1928) he wrote:

> A man in his own secret meditation
> Is lost amid the labyrinth that he has made
> In art or politics.
> (p.209)

Yeats believed that his Celtic revival would contribute to the Irish literary Renaissance which would eventually give rise to a philosophy of Ireland. To this end he formulated his mystical rites as "a ritual system of evocation and meditation-to reunite the perception of the spirit, of the divine, with natural beauty", saying:

> I wished by my writings and those of the school I
> hoped to found to have a secret symbolical relation
> to these mysteries, for in that way, I thought,
> there will be a great richness, a greater claim upon

the love of the soul, doctrine without exhortation
and rhetoric.[86]

The final comment suggests that Yeats recognised that initiates
were usually subjected to a degree of coercion through the
seductive language of ritual. This would indicate that he
questioned the tribal mandate of the secret society so often
consummated by rhetoric and ceremonial exhortation. In his
semi-autobiographical novel, *The Speckled Bird*, Yeats charts the
failure of this Celtic project. Perhaps as part of an unconscious
desire not to renounce his adeptship for art, Yeats never
completed the novel, the artistic counterpart to his spiritual
aspirations.

The plot of the novel parallels Yeats's own life in that it
chronicles the hero's unsuccessful attempts to establish a mystical
brotherhood. The protagonist, Michael Hearne, is a Yeatsian figure
who, in failing to deny the materialism of art, is deprived of his
status as a magician by a character called Maclagan, who is
actually based on Mathers. In a letter to Hearne, Maclagan's
description of how he had tried to found a new occult order
resembles Mathers's efforts in setting up the Golden Dawn:

> I spoke of the Temple of the Holy Spirit and of
> the great magical tradition of Europe which centres
> itself about the Father Rosy Cross. A little later
> I tried, as you know, to gather that tradition into
> a new order....When I met you I accepted your idea
> of an order centering in the Grail castle, thinking
> it better than nothing, but as we worked on I more
> and more realized that a wide gulf divided us. You
> thought all of forms - I of the inner substance.
> When I was thinking about the gathering into the
> order of ancient tradition, you were thinking of
> making it the foundation for patterns. I have come
> to recognise that you are not a magician, but some
> kind of an artist, and that the *summum bonum* itself,
> the potable gold of our masters, were less to you
> than some charm of colour, or some charm of words.[87]

Yeats attempts to rationalise Maclagan's antagonism towards the
artist in his annotations to the text. He explains that Maclagan
rejects Michael's artistic ideas because he misconstrues them. Yeats
intends Maclagan's letter to demonstrate that "Rosicrucian magic
means the assertion of the greatness of man in its extreme
form"[88] which may even extend to the rejection of art.

The poet described lovers of the arts as the priesthood of
an almost forgotten religion. Intent upon creating his own
mythology Yeats marshalled the symbols of poetry and magic
towards a synthesis which materialised in *A Vision*. This work had
started with Mrs Yeats's automatic writing dictated to her by
spirits who claimed "we have come to give you metaphors for

poetry".[89] The result was a configuration of human experience
built up on a comparative system of magic, mysticism and myth.
Yeats represented this totality through a diagram of the Great
Wheel divided into twenty eight segments marking the days of
the lunar month. One revolution of the Lunar Wheel corresponded
to a single Great Year or approximately two thousand ordinary
solar years. The cyclic imagery of the gyre and the phases of the
moon express a unity of being which dissolves the distinctions
between the material and spiritual universe. On announcing the
completion of *A Vision* in a letter to Olivia Shakespeare (9
February 1931) Yeats declared "I have constructed a myth, but
then one can believe in a myth - one only assents to
philosophy".[90] By demanding belief not assent for his work Yeats
was adopting a doctrinaire attitude towards visionary literature.
He went even further than this to claim:

> I had made a new religion, almost an infallible
> Church of poetic tradition, of a fardel of
> stories, and of personages, and of emotions,
> inseparable from their first expression, passed
> on from generation to generation by poets and
> painters with some help from philosophers and
> theologians.[91]

Yeats had now progressed beyond the fictions generated by
the secret societies to create a mythology out of his own life in
such works as *Autobiographies* and *A Vision*. By investing in his
own creativity, Yeats opened up greater scope for his
self-determinism. For example, in "A Coat" he symbolically divests
himself of his garments of myth:

> I made my song a coat
> Covered with embroideries
> Out of old mythologies
> From heel to throat;
> But the fools caught it,
> Wore it in the world's eyes
> As though they'd wrought it.
> Song, let them take it,
> For there's more enterprise
> In walking naked.
>                     (p.127)

Jung described the initiate of a secret society as one who is
trapped in "undifferentiated collectivity".[92] He argued that the
maturing individual must advance beyond this intermediary stage
of development by entering regions "where there are no chartered
ways and no shelter spreads a protecting roof over his head."[93]
To this extent Yeats, by "walking naked", was prepared to
embrace a doctrine of individualism which rejected the constraints
of clandestine brotherhoods. By refusing to surrender to the

collective, Yeats freed himself from the tyranny of other voices, and stripped himself of alien mythologies to formulate his own in *A Vision*. Notwithstanding his estrangement from the world of secret societies he never lost sight of the mystic goal which had initially attracted him to the occult underworld. Yeats's desire for adeptship remained intact throughout his life though now it would never be sublimated to the demands of art or to the dictates of a secret society. He realised that the Golden Dawn in uniting his role as artist and adept was creating a false concomitant.

Yeats found that he was able to preserve the opposition between art and magic, the material and the non-material by means of an appeal to Kant's system of antinomies. In a rebuttal of the Hegelian synthesis of opposites he wrote "I am Blake's disciple, not Hegel's: "contraries are positive. A negation is not contrary."[94] In this sense he would have agreed with Blake that "without contraries there is no progression."[95] Yeats's rejection of the notion that distinctions could be dissolved through a unified vision of the world is indicated in his poem "Nineteen Hundred and Nineteen" where he writes:

> Now days are dragon-ridden, the nightmare
> Rides upon sleep: a drunken soldiery
> Can leave the mother, murdered at her door,
> To crawl in her own blood, and go scot-free;
> The night can sweat with terror as before
> We pieced our thoughts into philosophy,
> And planned to bring the world under a rule,
> Who are but weasels fighting in a hole.
>
> (p.207)

Through the teaching of the Golden Dawn, Yeats eventually recognised that he could only achieve adeptship alone rather than through the communality of a secret society. And so he progressed unaccompanied down the path of mystic truth believing with his friend, George Russell:

> Everything in nature has intellectual significance,
> and relation as utterance to the Thought out of
> which the universe was born, and we, whose minds
> were made in its image, who are the microcosm of
> the macrocosm, have in ourselves the key to unlock
> the meaning of that utterance.[96]

As Curtis Bradford cynically remarked, Yeats's occultism is "the price we had to pay for his poetry".[97] We would be forced to agree with Bradford's conclusion that Yeats's poetry and esoteric studies were inseparable. Certainly he borrowed images for his verse from the Golden Dawn such as the twin pillars from the grade of Neophyte, the four elements from "The Ritual of the Cross," the dolphin from the Great *Hermetic Arcanum*, the

"Hodos Chameliontos" ("the path of the Chameleon") from the title
of a Golden Dawn text, the tower from the Tarot pack, and the
winding stair from Masonic symbolism. Through the secret
societies Yeats cultivated his interests in magic and mysticism,
symbolism and evocation, sorcery and poetry. He believed that the
rhythms of verse could help prolong the moment of contemplation
which would give way to mystic trance.

Yeats arrived at the Jungian view-point that the need to
belong to a secret society was only a transitional stage in his
own spiritual development towards adeptship. He admitted to
having been initiated into the Golden Dawn at an impressionable
age during which time he was "shaped and isolated".[98] While
discussing whether or not the Golden Dawn should remain a
magical Order, Yeats draws attention to the limitations of a
secret society for the individual in terms of the spiritual
progression of the supreme adept who eventually must transcend
the restrictions of the group:

> He will remember, while he is with them, the old
> magical image of the Pelican feeding its young
> with its own blood; and when, his sacrifice over,
> he goes his way to supreme Adeptship, he will go
> absolutely alone, for men attain to the supreme
> wisdom in a loneliness that is like the loneliness
> of death.[99]

Yeats came to the conclusion that supreme wisdom may only be
achieved through the struggles of the solitary individual since no
secret society or group "not even a "group" "very carefully
organized," has ever broken through that ancient gate."[100]

## Notes

1. *W.B. Yeats: The poems A New Edition* ed. Richard J. Finneran
(London, 1984), p.109. Page references following quotations will be
taken from this edition.

2. Yeats, *Autobiographies* (London, 1966) p.64.

3. Yeats, *The Speckled Bird,* ed. William O'Donnell (Dublin,
1974), II, p.90.

4. Virginia Moore, *The Unicorn: William Butler Yeats's Search for
Reality* (New York, 1954), p.27. See also Graham Hough, *The
Mystery Religions of W.B. Yeats* (Sussex, 1984).

5. Quoted from an unpublished speech delivered by Yeats
reprinted in Richard Ellmann, *Yeats: The Man and the Masks*

(London, 1961), p.5.

6.   Yeats, *Essays and Introductions* (London, 1961), p.10.

7.   Ibid., p.49.

8.   Mary Catherine Flannery, *Yeats and Magic: The Earlier Works* (Gerrards Cross, 1977), p.133.

9.   Regardie, *The Golden Dawn*, I, pp.59-60.

10.  Yeats, *The King's Threshold* (London, 1937), p.105.

11.  Yeats, *Autobiographies*, p.175.

12.  H. P. Blavatsky, *Isis Unveiled: A Master Key to the Mysteries of Ancient and Modern Science and Theology* (London, 1877), p.285.

13.  Yeats, *Autobiographies*, p.186.

14.  Ibid., p.175.

15.  *The Letters of W.B. Yeats*, ed. Allan Wade (London, 1954), p.160.

16.  Yeats, *Essays and Introductions*, p.28.

17.  See H.P. Blavatsky, *The Secret Doctrine: The Synthesis of Science, Religion and Philosophy* (London, 1888), I, p.411.

18.  Regardie, *The Golden Dawn*, II, pp.22-4.

19.  Ibid., II, p.38.

20.  Moore, *The Unicorn*, p.134. Mathers identified the twenty two letters of the Hebrew alphabet with the Great *Arcana* of the Tarot pack. See Kathleen Raine, *Yeats, the Tarot and the Golden Dawn* (Dublin, 1976).

21.  Arthur Conan Doyle, "Early Psychic Experiences", *Pearson's Magazine*, LVII-16, no. 339 (March, 1924), p.210.

22.  Regardie, *The Golden Dawn*, I, p.17.

23.  Yeats, *Autobiographies*, p.575.

24.  Ibid., p.476.

25.  Tom Paulin, *The Observer*, Sunday 10 June 1984.

26.  Maud Gonne Macbride, *A Servant of the Queen: Reminiscences*

(London, 1938), p.345.

27. Ibid., p.258.

28. Yeats, *Essays and Introductions*, p.34.

29. Yeats, *Autobiography*, p.187.

30. Harbans Rai Bachans, *W.B. Yeats and Occultism* (Delhi, 1965) p.83.

31. See Richard Ellmann, *The Identity of Yeats* (London, 1983), p.174.

32. Yeats, *Autobiography*, p.183.

33. See also the poem "The Poet pleads with the elemental Powers", (p.72).

34. Yeats, *Autobiography*, p.186.

35. Loc. cit.

36. John Symonds, "Aleister Crowley", *Man, Myth and Magic*, XX (1970), p.562.

37. Ellic Howe, *The Magicians of the Golden Dawn: A Documentary History of A Magical Order*, 1887-1923 (London, 1972), p.195.

38. Crowley, *Moonchild: A Prologue* (London, 1929). This novel had been inspired by the Golden Dawn.

39. Howe, *The Magicians of the Golden Dawn*, p.195. In *Moonchild* Yeats, who is called Gates, is described as having "a pretty amateur talent for painting in watercolours: some people thought it stronger than his verses," ibid., p.161.

40. Howe, *The Magicians of the Golden Dawn*, p.226.

41. John Symonds, *The Great Beast: The Life and Magick of Aleister Crowley* (St. Albans, 1973), p.72.

42. Yeats, *Is the Order of R.R. and A.C. to remain a Magical Order?* (London, 1901), p.11. This document is reproduced by George Mills Harper in *Yeats's Golden Dawn* (London, 1974), pp.259-68.

43. Yeats, "*Is the Order of R.R. and A.C. to remain a Magical Order?* p.28.

44. Howe, *The Magicians of the Golden Dawn*, p.277.

45. Yeats, *Autobiography*, p.575.

46. Howe, *The Magicians of the Golden Dawn*, p.279.

47. Ibid., p.282.

48. Ibid., p.283.

49. Yeats, *Autobiography*, p.576.

50. Howe, *The Magicians of the Golden Dawn*, p.271.

51. Ibid., p.273.

52. Regardie, *The Golden Dawn*, II, p.287.

53. See Symonds, *The Great Beast*, pp.49-51.

54. Regardie, *The Golden Dawn*, II, p.287.

55. Howe, *The Magicians of the Golden Dawn*, p.273.

56. See Moore, *The Unicorn*, p.209.

57. The *Fama Fraternitatis* is reproduced by Frances A. Yates in *The Rosicrucian Enlightenment* (St Albans, 1975), p.291.

58. Regardie, *The Golden Dawn*, II, pp.216-17.

59. See Yates, *The Rosicrucian Enlightenment*, pp.74-5.

60. Regardie, *The Golden Dawn*, II, p.227.

61. Yeats, *Essays and Introductions*, p.196.

62. Loc. cit..

63. Ibid., p.197.

64. Loc. cit.

65. Ibid., p.196.

66. Ibid., p.197.

67. Regardie, *The Golden Dawn*, I, p.203.

68. Moore, *The Unicorn*, p.168.

69. Loc. cit.

70. Regardie, *The Golden Dawn*, II, p.216.

71. *The Collected Works of Aleister Crowley* (London, 1905), I, p.202.

72. *The Variorum Edition of the Plays of W.B. Yeats*, ed. Russell K. Alspach (London, 1966), p.323.

73. *The Secret Rose, Stories by W. B. Yeats: A Variorum Edition*, ed. Phillip L. Marcus, Warwick Gould, and Michael J. Sidnell (London, 1981), pp.22-3.

74. Ibid., p.22. Ellmann in *Yeats, The Man and the Masks*, p.97 suggests that Yeats, in his adulation of the rose was following the example set by Stanislas de Guaita the founder of the Kabbalistic Order of the Rosy Cross in 1888 who wrote in *Rosa Mystica*:

> The Rose that I invite you to pluck - sympathetic
> friend who turn these pages - does not flower
> on the shores of far-away countries; and we
> shall take, if you please, neither the express
> train nor the transatlantic steamer. Are you
> susceptible to a deep emotion of the intellect?
> and do your favourite thoughts so haunt you as to
> give you at times the illusion of being real?...
> You are then a magician, and the mystic Rose will
> go of her own accord, however little you desire it,
> to bloom in your garden.

75. Yeats, *The Secret Rose*, p.17.

76. Ibid., p.23.

77. Dante, *The Divine Comedy: Paradise*, trans. Dorothy L. Sayers and Barbara Reynolds (Harmondsworth, 1962), p.335.

78. Yeats, *The Secret Rose*, p.134.

79. Ibid., p.132.

80. Ibid., p.133.

81. Loc. cit.

82. Crowley, *Collected Works*, I, p.209.

83. Yeats, *The Secret Rose*, p.140.

84. Ibid., p.171.

85. For a study of this conflict sce William H. O'Donnell, "Yeats as Adept and Artist, *The Speckled Bird, The Secret Rose* and *The Wind Among the Reeds*" in *Yeats and the Occult*, ed. George Mills Harper (London, 1976) pp.55-79.

86. Yeats, *Memoirs: Autobiography - First Draft Journal*, ed. Denis Donoghue (London, 1972), pp.123-4.

87. Yeats, *The Speckled Bird*, ed. O'Donnell, II, p.55.

88. Ibid., p.93.

89. Yeats, *A Vision* (London, 1978), p.8.

90. *The Letters of W.B. Yeats*, ed. Wade, p.781.

91. Yeats, *Autobiographies*, pp.115-16.

92. Jung, *Memories, Dreams, and Reflections*, p.316.

93. Ibid., p.316. This is quoted from Goethe's *Faust* Part 2.

94. *The Variorum Edition of the Poems of W.B. Yeats*, ed. Peter Altt and Russell K. Alspach (New York, 1957), p.835.

95. Blake, *The Complete Works*, ed. W.H. Stevenson (London, 1971), p.105.

96. A.E., *The Candle of Vision* (London, 1931), pp.114-5.

97. Curtis B. Bradford, "George Yeats: Poet's Wife" *Sewanee Review*, 77 (Summer, 1969), p.403.

98. Yeats, *Autobiographies* p.183.

99. Yeats, *Is the Order of R.R. and A.C. to remain a Magical Order?*, p.27.

100. Loc. cit.

# BIBLIOGRAPHY

Abbott, C.D. "Christopher Smart's Madness," *Publications of the Modern Language Association*, XLV (Dec., 1939), pp.1014-22

Adorno, T. and Horkheimer, M. *Dialectic of Enlightenment*, trans. J. Cumming (Allen Lane, London, 1973)

A.E. *The Candle of Vision* (Macmillan, London, 1931)

Ainsworth, E.G. and Noyes, C.E. *Christopher Smart: A Biographical and Critical Study* (University of Missouri, Columbia, 1943)

Alspach, Russell K., ed. *The Variorum Edition of the Plays of W.B. Yeats* (Macmillan, London, 1966)

Altt, P. and Alspach, R.K. ed. *The Variorum Edition of the Poems of W.B. Yeats* (Macmillan, New York, 1957)

Anderson, J. *The New Book of Constitutions of the [...] Free and Accepted Masons [...]* (T. Payne, London, 1738)

Anon. *A Defence of Freemasonry* (W. Flexney, London,1765)

- "Act concerning the Mason-Oath," *Scots Magazine*, XIX (Aug., 1757), pp.432-3

*A Master-Key to Freemasonry: by which all the Secrets of the Society are Laid Open; and their Pretended Mysteries Exposed to the Public* (J. Burd, London, 1760)

*Burns as Others saw him* (The Saltire Society, Edinburgh, 1959)

*Hiram: or, the Grand Master-Key to the door of both Antient and Modern Freemasonry. By a member of the Royal Arch*, 2nd ed. (W. Griffin, London, 1766)

*Jachin and Boas: Or an Authentic Key to the Door of Free-Masonry - both Ancient and Modern* (E. Newberry, London, 1797)

*Monthly Review*, XXVIII (April, 1763) pp.320-21

*Solomon in all his Glory: or The Master-Mason being a True Guide to the inmost recesses of Free-Masonry* (Robinson and Roberts, London, 1768)

*The Free-Mason's Melody, Being a General Collection of Masonic Songs* (R. Hellawell, Bury, 1818)

*The Justice and the Footman* (J. Wright, London, 1744)

*The Three Distinct Knocks or The Door of the Most Antient Free-Masonry opening to all Men, neither Naked nor Cloath'd, Barefoot nor shod* (Thomas Wilkinson, London, 1785)

Antippas, A.P. "The Structure of Shelley's *St Irvyne*: Parallelism and the Gothic Mode of Evil", *Tulane Studies in English*, XVIII (1970), pp.59-71

Bachans, H.R. *W.B. Yeats and Occultism* (Motilal Banarsidass,

*Bibliography*

Delhi, India, 1965)

Balderston, K.C. ed., *Thraliana: The Diary of Mrs Hester Lynch Thrale* (later Mrs. Piozzi) 1776-1809, 2nd ed. 2 vols (Clarendon Press, Oxford, 1951)

Barber, W.H., Brumfitt, J.M., Leigh, R.A., Shackleton, R. and Taylor, S.S.B. ed., *The Age of Enlightenment* (Oliver and Boyd, London, 1967)

Barruel, Abbé trans. Clifford R., *Memoirs Illustrating the History of Jacobinism*, 2nd edition, 4 vols (T. Burton, London, 1797)

Bazley, B.M. "Freemasonry in Kipling's Works," *The Kipling Journal*, XVII (April, 1950) pp.7-11

Belford, F.J. "Robert Burns - Freemason" *Year Book of the Grand Lodge of Antient, Free and Accepted Masons of Scotland* (Edinburgh, 1955) pp.82-97

Beswick, S. *The Swedenborg Rite and the Great Masonic Leaders of the Eighteenth Century* (Masonic Publishing Co., New York, 1870)

Birkenhead, Lord *Rudyard Kipling* (Weidenfeld and Nicolson, London, 1978)

Blanchard, C.A. *Modern Secret Societies* (Britons Publishing Co, London, 1903)

Blavatsky, H.P. *Isis Unveiled: A Master-key to the Mysteries of Ancient and Modern Science and Theology*, 2 vols (Bernard Quaritch, London, 1877)
*The Secret Doctrine: The Synthesis of Science, Religion and Philosophy*, 2 vols (Theosophical Publishing Co., London, 1888)

Blunden, E. *Shelley: A Life Story* (Collins, London, 1948)

Bok, S. *Secrets: Concealment and Revelation* (Oxford University Press, London, 1984)

Bond W.H. ed. Christopher Smart, *Jubilate Agno* (Rupert Hart-Davis, London, 1954)

Bradford, C.B. "George Yeats: Poet's Wife," *Sewanee Review*, 77 (Summer, 1969), pp.388-404

Brain, W., Russell "Christopher Smart: The Flea that Became an Eagle", *Medical Bookman and Historian*, II, no. 7 (July, 1948) pp.295-300

Brittain, R.E. ed. *Poems by Christopher Smart* (Princeton University Press, New Jersey, 1950)

Brown, H. *Rudyard Kipling: A New Appreciation* (Hashell House Publishers, New York, 1974)

Browne, J. *An Estimate of the Manners and Principles of the Times*, (L. Davis and Reymers, London, 1757)

Browning, R. *The Works of Robert Browning*, 10 vols (Ernest Benn, London, 1912)

Bullamore, G.W. "The Beehive and Freemasonry" *Ars Quatuor Coronatorum*, XXXVI (1923) pp.219-33

Butt, J. ed. *The Poems of Alexander Pope* (Methuen, London, 1963)

Butterworth, L.M.A. *Robert Burns and the eighteenth-century revival in Scottish Vernacular Poetry* (Aberdeen University Press, Aberdeen, 1969)

Callan, N. ed. *The Collected Poems of Christopher Smart*, 2 vols (Routledge and Kegan Paul, London, 1949)

Cameron, K.N. *The Young Shelley: Genesis of a Radical* (Victor Gollancz, London, 1951)

Carr, H. "Kipling and the Craft", *Ars Quatuor Coronatorum*, 77 (1964) pp.213-53

Carr, J.D. *The Demoniacs* (Hamish Hamilton, London, 1962)

Carr, J.L. "Gorgons, Gormogons, Medusists and Masons", *Modern Language Review*, LVIII (Jan., 1963) pp.73-8

Carrington, C. *Rudyard Kipling: His Life and Work* (Penguin, Harmondsworth, 1970)

Chailley, J. *The Magic Flute, Masonic Opera: An Interpretation of the Libretto and the Music*, trans. Herbert Weinstock (Gollancz, London, 1972)

Chambers, R. ed. *The Life and Work of Robert Burns*, revised William Wallace, 4 vols (W. and R. Chambers, London, 1896)

Cleland, J. *The Way to Things by Words, and to Words by Things* [...] *On the Real Secret of the Freemasons* (1766), facsimile reprint (Scholar Press, Yorkshire, 1968)

Collins, W. *The Woman in White* (Houghton Mifflin Co, Boston, 1969)

Cornell, L.L. *Kipling in India* (Macmillan, London, 1966)

Crabbe, G. *The Borough: A Poem*, 2 vols (J. Hatchard, London, 1810)

Crawford, T. "Political and Protest Songs in Eighteenth - Century Scotland II: Songs of the Left," *Scottish Studies*, XIV (1970), pp.105-31.

Cross, W. *The Life and Times of Laurence Sterne*, 3rd edition (Oxford University Press, London, 1939)

Crowley, A. *Collected Works*, 2 vols (Foyers, Society for the Propogation of Religious Truth, London, 1905)

- *Moonchild: A Prologue* (The Mandrake Press, London, 1929)

Daiches, D. *Robert Burns* (A. Deutsh, London, 1966)

Dante, *The Divine Comedy: Paradise*, trans. Dorothy L. Sayers and Barbara Reynolds (Penguin, Harmondsworth, 1962)

Daraul, A. *Secret Societies Yesterday and Today* (Frederick Muller, London, 1961)

Dart, J.L.C. "Christianity and Freemasonry" LIV, no. 370, *Theology* (April, 1951) pp.130-36

Dawson, P. *The Unacknowledged Legislator* (Oxford University Press, London, 1980)

De Quincy, T. *Works* ed. David Masson reprint, 16 vols (A. and C. Black, Edinburgh, 1880)

Defoe, D. *The Perjur'd Free Mason Detected: and yet the Honour and Antiquity of the Society of Free Masons Preserv'd and Defended* (T. Warner, London, 1730)

Dennis, C.M. "A Structural Conceit in Smart's *Song to David*",

*Review of English Studies*, XXIX, no. 115 (1978)
pp.257-66

Devlin, C. *Poor Kit Smart* (Rupert Hart-Davis, London, 1961)

Disraeli, B. *Lord George Bentinck: A Political Biography*,
revised edition (Colburn and Co, London, 1852)

Donoghue D. ed. *Yeats, Memoirs: Autobiography - First Draft*
(Macmillan, London, 1972)

Dougall, C.S. *The Burns Country* (A. and C. Black, London,
1904)

Douglas, H. *Robert Burns:- A Life* (Robert Hale, London, 1976)

Doyle, A. C. "Early Psychic Experiences," *Pearson's Magazine*,
LVII-16, no. 339 (March, 1924) pp.203-10

Duncan Eaves T.C. and Kimpel, B.D. *Samuel Richardson: A
Biography* (Clarendon Press, Oxford, 1971)

Durrand, R. *A Handbook to the Poetry of Rudyard Kipling* (Kraus
Reprint Co, New York, 1971)

Eliot S. and Stern B. ed. *The Age of Enlightenment: An
Anthology of Eighteenth-Century Texts*, 2 vols (Ward
Lock Educational in association with Open
University Press, London, 1979)

Elliot, L. G. ed. *Kipling and the Critics* (Peter Owen, London,
1965)

Ellmann, R. *The Identity of Yeats*, reprint (Faber and Faber,
London, 1983)

- *Yeats: The Man and the Masks* (Faber and Faber,
London, 1961)

Fellows, J. *The Mysteries of Freemasonry* (Reeves and Turner,
London, 1877)

Ferguson, J. De Lancey, *Letters of Robert Burns*, 2 vols
(Clarendon Press, Oxford, 1931)

- *Robert Burns: Pride and Passion* (Oxford University
Press, New York, 1939)

Finneran, R.J. ed. *W.B. Yeats: The Poems: A New Edition*
(Macmillan, London, 1984)

Fitzhugh, R.T. *Robert Burns: The Man and the Poet* (W.H. Allen,
London, 1971)

Flannery, M.C. *Yeats and Magic: The Earlier Works* (Colin
Smythe, Gerrards Cross, 1977).

Foucault, M. *Madness and Civilization: A History of Insanity
in the Age of Reason* (Tavistock Publishers, London,
1967)

Frazer, J.G. *The Golden Bough: A Study in Magic and   Religion*
(Macmillan, London, 1978)

Frost, A. "R.K.'s Masonic Allusions", *The Kipling Journal*,
XIII (Oct., 1942) pp.16-18

Fussell, P. "Irony, Freemasonry, and Humane Ethics in
Kipling's *The Man who would be King*", *English
Literary History*, XXV (1958) pp.216-33

Gibson, J. *Robert Burns and Masonry* (Privately Printed,
Liverpool, 1873)

Glick, C. ed. *A Treasury of Masonic Thought* (R. Hale, London,

1961)
Godwin, W. *Lives of the Necromancers or An Account of the Most Eminent Persons in Successive Ages, who have claimed for themselves, or to whom has been imputed by others, the Exercise of Magical Power* (F.J. Mason, London, 1834)

Grabo, C. *The Magic Plant: The Growth of Shelley's Thought* (University of North Carolina, Chapel Hill, 1936)

Grantham, J.A. "An Introduction to Mark Masonry" *Transactions of Manchester Association for Masonic Research,* XXIII (Nov., 1933) pp.124-96

Grierson, H.J.C. and Smith, J.C. *A Critical History of English Poetry* (Chatto and Windus, London, 1947)

Griffiths, D. "The Poetry of Christopher Smart" (University of Leeds,unpublished Ph.D., 1951)

Grosse, Marquis C.F.A. *Horrid Mysteries,* trans. P. Will, 2 vols (Robert Holden, London, 1927)

Hall-Stevenson, J. *Crazy Tales* (Thomas Ewing, Dublin, 1772)

Hannah, W. *Darkness Visible: A Revelation and Interpretation of Freemasonry* (Augustine, London, 1952)

- "Should a Christian be a Freemason?", *Theology,* LIV, no. 367 (January, 1951), pp.3-10

Harper, G.M. ed. *Yeats and the Occult* (Macmillan, London, 1976)

- *Yeats's Golden Dawn* (Macmillan, London, 1974)

Harvey, W. *Robert Burns as a Freemason,* (T.M. Sparks, Dundee, 1921)

Hauser, W. "An Analysis of the Structure, Influences, and Diction of Christopher Smart's *A Song to David*" (University of Pittsburgh, Ph.D. 1963)

Havens, R.D. "The Structure of Smart's *Song to David, Review of English Studies,* XIV, no. 54 (April, 1938), pp.178-82

Hecht, H. *Robert Burns: The Man and his Work* (William Hodge, London, 1936)

Henley, W.E. and Seccombe, T. ed. *The Works of Tobias Smollet,* 12 vols, (Constable, London, 1899-1901)

Hill G.B. ed, *Boswell's "Life of Johnson",* revised L.F. Powell, 6 vols, (Oxford University Press, Oxford, 1934-50)

Hobsbawm, E.J. *Primitive Rebels: Studies in Archaic Forms of Social Movement in the 19th and 20th Centuries* (Manchester University Press, Manchester, 1959)

Hogg, T.J. *The Life of Shelley* (J.M. Dent, London, 1933)

Holmes, R. *Shelley the Pursuit* (Weidenfeld and Nicolson, London, 1974)

Horne, A. *King Solomon's Temple in the Masonic Tradition* (The Aquarian Press, Wellingborough, 1972)

Hough, Graham, *The Mystery Religion of W.B. Yeats* (Harvester Press, Sussex, 1984)

Howe, E. *The Magicians of the Golden Dawn: A Documentary History of a Magical Order 1887-1923* (Routledge and Kegan Paul, London, 1972)

Ingpen, R. and Peck, W.E. ed. *The Complete Works of Percy Bysshe Shelley*, 10 vols (Ernest Benn, London, 1965)

Islam, S. *Kipling's "Law": A Study of his Philosophy of Life* (Macmillan, London, 1975)

Jacob, M.C. *The Radical Enlightenment: Pantheists, Freemasons and Republicans* (George Allen & Unwin, London, 1981)

Jamieson, A. *Burns, Burns and Religion* (W. Heffer and Sons, Cambridge, 1931)

Jarrett, D. *The Ingenious Mr Hogarth* (M. Joseph, London, 1976)

Jeaffreson, J.C. *The Real Shelley: New Views of the Poet's Life*, 2 vols (Hurst and Blackett, London, 1885)

Jones, B.E. *Freemasons' Book of the Royal Arch* (Harrap, London, 1957)

- *The Freemasons' Guide and Compendium* (Harrap, London, 1956)

Jones, C.E. "John Locke and Masonry", *Neuphilologische*, LXVII (1966) pp.72-81

Jones, F.L. ed. *The Letters of Percy Bysshe Shelley*, 2 vols (Clarendon Press, Oxford, 1964)

Jones, L.C. *The Clubs of the Georgian Rakes* (Columbia University Press, New York, 1942)

Jung, C.G. *Memories, Dreams, Reflections*, recorded and edited by Aniela Jaffé, trans. Richard & Clara Winston (Collins & Routledge & Kegan Paul, London, 1963)

Kinsley, J. ed. *The Poems and Songs of Robert Burns*, 3 vols (Clarendon Press, Oxford, 1968)

Kipling, R. *A Book of Words: Selections from Speeches and Addresses Delivered between 1906 and 1927* (Macmillan, London, 1928)

*Debits and Credits* (Macmillan, London, 1949)

*From Sea to Sea and Other Sketches: Letters of Travel* (Macmillan, London, 1900)

*Just So Stories for Little Children* (Macmillan, London, 1955)

*Kim* (Macmillan, London, 1956)

*Letters of Travel (1892-1913)* (Macmillan, London, 1920)

*Life's Handicap: Being Stories of Mine Own People* (Macmillan, London 1952)

- *Limits and Renewals* (Macmillan, London, 1949)

- *Many Inventions* (Macmillan, London, 1904)

- *Puck of Pook's Hill* (Macmillan, London, 1906)

- *Rudyard Kipling's Verse: Definitive Edition* (Hodder & Stoughton, London, 1945)

- *Something of Myself for my Friends Known and Unknown* (Penguin, Harmondsworth, 1977)

- *Wee Willie Winkie and Other Stories* (Macmillan,

London, 1905)

Knight, S. *The Brotherhood: The Secret World of the Freemasons* (Granada, London, 1984)

Knoop, D., Jones, G.P. and Hamer, D. ed. *Early Masonic Pamphlets* (Manchester University Press, Manchester, 1945)
*Early Masonic Catechisms* (Manchester University Press, Manchester, 1943)
*Freemasonry and the Idea of Natural Religion* (Butler and Tanner, London, 1942)
*The Medieval Mason* (Manchester University Press, Manchester, 1933)
- *The Scottish Mason and the Mason Word* (Manchester University Press, Manchester, 1939)

Kuhn, A.J. "Christopher Smart: The Poet As Patriot of the Lord," *English Literary History*, XXX (June, 1963), pp.121-36

Legman, G. *The Horn Book: Studies in Erotic Folklore and Bibliography* (Jonathan Cape, London, 1970)

Levine, G. and Knoepflmacher, U.C. ed. *The Endurance of Frankenstein: Essays on Mary Shelley's Novel* (University of California Press, London, 1979)

Lindsay, M. *The Burns Encyclopaedia*, revised (Robert Hale, London, 1980)

Lockhart, J.G. *Life of Robert Burns*, reissued (Dent, London, 1976)

Lovegrove, H. "Three Masonic Novels" *Ars Quatuor Coronatorum*, XXXII (1919) pp.79-95

Low, D.A. ed. *Robert Burns: The Critical Heritage* (Routledge and Kegan Paul, London, 1974)

Lyon, D.M. *History of the Lodge of Edinburgh* (Mary's Chapel) no. I: *Embracing an Account of the Rise and Progress of Freemasonry in Scotland* (The Gresham Publishing Co., London, 1900)

Macalpine, I. and Hunter, R. *George III and the Mad-Business* (Allen Lane, The Penguin Press, London, 1969)

Macbride, M. G. *A Servant of the Queen: Reminiscences* (Gollancz, London, 1938)

MacDonald, M. *Mystical Bedlam: Madness, Anxiety, and Healing in Seventeenth-Century England* (Cambridge University Press, London, 1981)

Mackenzie, N. ed. *Secret Societies* (Aldus Books, London, 1967)

Mackey, A.G. *An Encyclopaedia of Freemasonry*, 2 vols (Masonic Publishing Company, New York, 1912)

Marcus, P. L., Gould, W. and Sidnell, M.J. ed. *The Secret Rose, Stories by W.B. Yeats: A Variorum Edition* (Cornell University Press, London, 1981)

Marshall, J. *A Winter with Robert Burns* (Edinburgh, Peter Brown, 1846)

Moore, J.R. *A Checklist of the Writings of Daniel Defoe* (Indiana University Press, Bloomington, 1960)

Moore, V. *The Unicorn: William Butler Yeats' Search for Reality* (Macmillan, New York, 1954)

More, P.E. *Shelburne Essays*, 11 vols (G.P. Putnam's and Sons, London, 1905)

Morgan, G.B. ed. *The Works of William Law* (G. Moreton, Brokenhurst, 1892-93)

Morley, E.J. ed. *Crabb Robinson in Germany 1800-1805: Extracts from his Correspondence* (Oxford University Press, London, 1929)

Morton, A.L. *The English Utopia* (Lawrence and Wishart, London, 1978)

Moss, R.E. *Rudyard Kipling and the Fiction of Adolescence* (Macmillan Press, London, 1982)

Murry, J.M. *Discoveries* (Jonathan Cape, London, 1930)

Noorthouck, J. ed. James Anderson, *Constitutions of the Ancient Fraternity of Free and Accepted Masons* (1723) (J. Rozea, London, 1748)

Norman, S. *Flight of the Skylark: The Development of Shelley's Reputation* (Max Reinhardt, London, 1954)

Paget, T. and Whibley, L. ed. *Correspondence of Thomas Gray*, 3 vols (Clarendon Press, Oxford, 1935)

Paton, C.I. *Freemasonry: Its Symbolism, Religious Nature and Law of Perfection* (Reeves and Turner, London, 1873)

Paulin, T. *The Observer*, Sunday, 10 June, 1984

Paulson, R. *Hogarth: His Life, Art and Times*, 2 vols (Yale University Press, London, 1971)

Peacock, H.C. and Mackenzie, A. *Robert Burns Poet-Laureate of Lodge Canongate Kilwinning: Facts substantiating his Election and Inauguration on 1st March 1787* (published by authority of the Lodge, Printed by Christie & Son, Edinburgh, 1894)

Peacock, T.L. *Nightmare Abbey* (Penguin, Harmondsworth, 1976)

Peck, W.E. "Shelley and the Abbé Barruel", *Publications of the Modern Language Association of America*, XXXVI (1921) pp.347-53

Pick, F. and Knight, G. Norman, *The Pocket History of Freemasonry* 6th edition (F. Muller, London, 1977)

Piozzi, H.L. (Mrs Thrale) *British Synonymy; or, An Attempt at Regulating the Choice of Words in Familiar Conversation*, 2 vols (G.G. and J.Robinson, London, 1794)

Pope, A. and W. Warburton, ed. *The Works of Alexander Pope*, 9 vols (J. and P. Knapton, London, 1751)

Preston, W. *Illustrations of Masonry*, 2nd edition (J. Wilkie, London, 1775)

Prichard, S. *Masonry Dissected* (J. Wilford, London, 1730)

Raine, K. *Yeats, the Tarot and the Golden Dawn* (revised Dolmen Press, Dublin, 1976)

Ranald, M. Loftus and Ranald, R.A "Shelley's Magus Zoroaster and the Image of the Doppelgänger," *Modern Language Notes*, LXXVI (Jan., 1961) pp.7-12

Regardie, I. *The Golden Dawn: An Account of the Teachings,*
*Rites and Ceremonies of the Order of the Golden*
*Dawn,* revised, 2 vols. (Llewellyn Publications,
Minnesota, 1971)

Rieger, J. *The Mutiny Within: The Heresies of Percy Bysshe*
*Shelley,* (George Braziller, New York, 1967)

Roberts, J.M. *The Mythology of the Secret Societies* (Secker
and Warburg, London, 1972)

Rogers, K.M. "The Pillars of the Lord: Some Sources of *A Song*
*to David,*" *Philological Quarterly,* XL (Oct., 1961),
pp.525-34

Rosen, G. *Madness in Society: Chapters in the Historical*
*Sociology of Mental Illness* (Routledge & Kegan Paul,
London, 1968)

Rossetti, W.M. *A Memoir of Shelley* (Shelley Society, London,
1886)

Rutherford, A. ed. *Kipling's Mind and Art* (Oliver and Boyd,
London, 1964)

Saltmarsh, J. Review of Douglas Knoop and G.P. Jones, *An*
*Introduction to Freemasonry* in *Economic History*
*Review,* VIII (Nov., 1937), pp.102-104

Sartre, J. P. *Critique of Dialectical Reason,* ed. Jonathan
Rée, trans. Alan Sheridan-Smith (New Left Reviews,
London, 1976)

Scott, W. *Waverley, or 'Tis Sixty years Since,* reprint (J.M.
Dent, London, 1910)

Shelley, P.B. *Zastrozzi: A Romance and St. Irvyne or The*
*Rosicrucian,* (Arno Press, New York, 1977)

Shepard O. and P. Spencer Wood, *English Prose and Poetry*
*1600-1800* (Houghton Mifflin Co., Boston, 1934)

Sherbo, A. "Christopher Smart, Free and Accepted Mason"
*Journal of English and Germanic Philology,* LIV
(Oct., 1955) pp.664-9
"Christopher Smart's Knowledge of Occult Literature"
*Journal of the History of Ideas,* XVIII (April, 1957)
pp.233-41
*Christopher Smart: Scholar of the University*
(Michigan State University Press, Michigan, 1967)
"The probable time of composition of Christopher
Smart's *A Song to David, Psalms,* and *Hymns and*
*Spiritual Songs,*" *Journal of English and Germanic*
*Philolgy,* LV (Jan., 1956), pp.41-57

Simmel, G. "The Sociology of Secrecy and Secret Societies,"
*The American Journal of Sociology,* XI, no. 4 (Jan.,
1904), pp.441-98

Stead, W.F. ed. Christopher Smart, *Rejoice in the Lamb: A Song*
*from Bedlam* (Jonathan Cape, London, 1939)

Stevenson, W.H. *Blake: The Complete Works* (Longman, London,
1971)

Stevenson, Y.H. *Burns and Highland Mary* (T.M. Gommell, Ayr,
1979)

Swift, J. *Prose Works,* ed. Herbert Davies, 14 vols (Blackwell, Oxford, 1939-68)

Symonds, J. "Aleister Crowley," *Man, Myth and Magic,* 20 (1970), pp.558-63

- *The Great Beast: The Life and Magic of Aleister Crowley* (Granada, St. Albans, 1973)

Taswell, - *The Deviliad: A Heroic Poem* (W. Bickerton, London, 1744)

Taylor, S. F. *The Alchemists,* reprint (Paladin, London, 1976)

Thompson, E.P. *The Making of the English Working Class,* revised (Penguin, Harmondsworth, 1968)

Thorp, J.T. ed. *Rite Ancien de Bouillon: An Old English Ritual* (1740) Masonic Reprints, IX (Johnson, Wykes and Paine, Leicester, 1926)

Wade, A. ed. *The Letters of W.B. Yeats* (Rupert Hart-Davis, London, 1954)

Waite, A.E. *A New Encyclopaedia of Freemasonry,* 2 vols (William Rider & Son, London, 1925)

Walpole, H. *The Letters of Horace Walpole,* 9 vols (Richard Bentley & Son, London, 1886)

Webster, A. *Burns and the Kirk: A Review of what the Poet did for the Religious and Social Regeneration of the Scottish People* (James Thin, Edinburgh, 1888)

Webster, N.H. *Secret Societies and Subersive Movements* (Britons Publishing Co, London, 1964)

Wells, H.G. *Complete Short Stories* (Ernest Benn, London, 1974)

Whalen, W.J. *Handbook of Secret Organizations* (Bruce Publishing Company, Milwaukee, 1966)

White, Newman, Ivey, *The Unextinguished Hearth: Shelley and His Contemporary Critics* (Duke University Press, Durham, North Carolina, 1938)

Williamson, K. "Christopher Smart's *Hymns and Spiritual Songs,*" *Philological Quarterly,* XXXVIII (Oct. 1959) pp.413-24

*The Poetical Works of Christopher Smart: Jubilate Agno,* I (Clarendon Press, Oxford, 1980)

- and Walsh, M. *Religious Poetry 1763-71,* 2 (Clarendon Press, Oxford, 1983)

Wilson, A. *The Strange Ride of Rudyard Kipling: His Life and Works* (Secker and Warburg, London, 1977)

Wood, F.T. ed. *The Poems of Henry Carey* (E. Partridge, London, 1730)

Wright, D. *Robert Burns and Freemasonry* (Alexander Gardner, Paisley, 1921)

- *Robert Burns and his Masonic Circle* (Cecil Palmer, London, 1929)

Yates, F.A. *The Rosicrucian Enlightenment* (Paladin, St Albans, 1975)

Yeats, W.B. *Autobiographies,* reprint (Macmillan, London, 1966)

- *A Vision* (Macmillan, London, 1978)

- *Essays and Introductions* (Macmillan, London, 1961)

*Is the Order of R.R. and A.C. to remain a Magical Order?* (Privately Printed, London, 1901)
*The King's Threshold* (Macmillan, London, 1937)
*The Speckled Bird* ed. O'Donnell W.H. 2 vols (The Cuala Press, Dublin, 1974)

# INDEX

Abif see Hiram Abif
AE 158, 159
Abbot, C.D. 45, 159
Adamson, H. 56
Adeptus Exemptus 132
Adeptus Major 132
Adeptus Minor 132, 139,
    143-5
Adorno, T. 13, 46, 99, 159
adulthood 1
Aiken, R. 63
Ainslie, R. 57
Ainsworth, E.G. 28, 32,
    41, 49, 51, 159
alchemists 38
alchemy 38, 77
Allahabad 103, 120
Alien Act 93
Alloway 66
All-seeing Eye 30, 37, 38
Allt, P. 158, 159
alpha 30, 32-4, 41
Alspach, Russell K. 157-8,
    159
Anarchy 6, 8, 90
Ancient Order of Druids
    see Druids
Anderson, J. 17, 23, 27,
    32, 47, 79, 86-7, 110,
    124, 159
Antients, The 17, 18, 23,
    59
Antigallicans 9
Antippas, A.P. 98, 101, 159
Apprentice 6
apron 40, 64-7
arch 23, 34
    see also Royal Arch
architects 6, 19, 29, 65,
    74, 111, 116
architecture, 19, 28, 29,
    32
ark 21
Armour, J. 68
ashes 2

ashlar 114
    Rough Ashlar 42
    Smooth Ashlar 26, 42
Ashmole, Elias 6
Assassins, The 2, 5, 88-9
    98-9
asylum 12, 15, 17
    see also mad-houses
Augustans, The 12, 17
Augustus, Emperor 79

Baal 20
Bachans, H.R. 155, 159
Bachelors Club 68
Bacon, F. 32
Baden-Powell, Lord 113
Balderstone, K.C. 46, 159
Ballantine, J. 55, 81
Baphomet 138
Barber, W.H. et al. 48,
    160
Barruel, Abbé 6, 89-90,
    93, 99, 160
Battie, W. 11
Bavaria, Elector of 93
Bavarian Illuminati 2, 5,
    6, 9, 80-92, 94
Bazley, B.M. 124, 160
Beardsley, A. 133
Bedlam 14,18
    see also Bethlam
    Hospital
bee 22, 23, 42
Belford, F.J. 82-4, 87,
    160
Benedict XIV 19
Bergier, J. 133
Bergson, H. 134
Bergson, M. 134
Beswick, S. 47, 160
Bethlem Hospital 11
Bethnal Green 11
Bible 18, 19, 21, 22, 26,
    36, 38, 50, 66, 109,
    113

Birkenhead, Lord 125, 160
birth 1
Blackwood, A. 133
Blake, W. 31, 158
Blanchard, C.A. 7, 160
Blavatsky, H.P. 129-31,
    154, 160
Blue Rite 57
    see also Scottish Rite
Blunden, E. 101, 160
Bok, S. 7
Boas 39
Boehme, J. 15
Bombay 103
Bond, W.H. 21, 47, 160
Book of Common Prayer 21
Book of Revelation 21, 41,
    138
Boswell, J. 4, 46
Boy-Scout 113
Bradford, C.B. 152, 158,
    160
Brahman 114
Brain, W. Russell 14, 46
    160
breast 34
British Empire 102-8,
    121-2, 135
British Museum 1, 131
Brittain, R.E. 20, 48
broached thurnel 26
Brodie-Innes 133
brother 3, 29
Brotherhood 19, 22, 44, 64,
    104, 113, 139, 160
Brother-in-Blood 1, 114
Brown, H. 125, 160
Browne, J. 15, 46, 160
Browning, E. Barrett 95
Browning, R. 27, 49, 160
builder 6, 19, 24, 25,
    27-30, 66. 111-13
building 6, 110, 118
building trade 5
Bulwer-Lytton, E. 129
    133-4
bull, papal 19, 20, 57
Bullamore, G.W. 48, 160
Burnes, Dr 103
Burns, G. 54

Burns, R. 4-6, 52-79
    "A Masonic Song" 77
    "Address to the Devil"
    77
    "Death and Doctor
    Hornbook" 58
    "Epistle to John
    Ranken" 52
    "Epistle to J. Lapraik"
    67
    "Holy Willie's Prayer"
    63
    "Lines to John Ranken"
    52
    "Scotch Drink" 68
    "Second Epistle to
    Davie" 68
    "Tam Samson's Elegy" 58
    "The Author's Earnest
    Cry and Prayer" 68
    "The Brigs of Ayr" 54
    "The Farewell" 53, 73,
    85
    "The Kirk of Scotland's
    Garland" 63
    "The Master's Apron" 64
    "The Sons of Old
    Killie" 73, 75
Burns Street 52
Burns, W. 77
Burrows, H. 133
Burry, H.P. 133
Butt, J. 47, 160
Butterworth, L.M.R. 81,
    160
Byron, Lord 6

Cabala 4, 130-2, 136, 141
    157
cable-rope or cable-tow 33
Callan, N. 161
Calendar, Masonic 32, 59
Cameron, K.N. 100, 161
candles 36
Canongate Kilwinning Lodge
    54, 55, 72, 121
Carbonari 6
Carey, H. 4, 8
Carr, H. 123, 124-5, 161

Carr, J.D. 8, 161
Carr, J.L. 8; 161
Carrington, C. 122, 125, 161
Castrators, The 2
Castlereagh, Lord 93
Catholicism 19, 20, 104
Cawardine, T. 12
Celtic 149-50
ceremony 2, 6, 23
Chailley, J. 51, 161
Chambers, R. 54, 81, 161
chapitre 39
charcoal-burners 6
Charlatans 1
Charteris, F. 55
Chatterji, M. 130
Chatterton, T. 12
childhood 1
Christ, J. 24, 25, 29, 31, 37, 41, 90, 146
Christianity, 5, 6, 11, 13, 17, 19, 21, 22, 25, 26, 27, 31, 35, 38, 75, 138
Churchill, C. 4, 161
church 6, 8, 24, 25, 26
circle 41
Clare, J. 12
Cleland, J. 9, 161
Clement XII 19, 57
Clifford, R. 99
clouds 33
clubs 6, 9, 14
Coleridge 94
Collins, W. 124, 161
compass 30, 31, 36, 41, 70
*Confessio Fraternitatis* 95
Constitutions 17, 21, 23, 27, 109
  *see also* Anderson, J.
Continental Freemasonry 6, 134
Cornell, Louis L. 123-4, 161
corporation 6
cornucopia 16
Cowper, W. 6, 12
Crabbe, G. 87, 161
craft 6, 11, 19, 29, 52, 60, 79, 113, 118

craft guilds 6
Crawford, T. 82, 161
Creation 32, 33-5, 40, 42
Creech, W. 63, 81
Cross, W.L. 8, 161
Crowley, A. 133, 138-9, 141, 145, 148, 155, 157, 161
Crucifixion 35
Cruickshank, W. 72
Cumberland, Duke of 61
Cumming, J. 46
Cunningham, A. 81
crusaders 147
cyclothymia 14

Daiches, D. 81, 161
Dalrymple, J. 62
Dante 147-8, 157, 161
Daraul, A. 81, 161
darkness 27, 33, 35
Dart, J.L.C. 86, 161
David, King, 16, 25, 27, 42, 110, 112
  *see also* Smart, *A Song to David*
Dawson, P. 99, 161
*De Lunatica Inquirendo* 11
De Quincey, T. 25, 26, 49, 84, 161
De Veil 71, 84
death 1, 8, 26, 41, 42, 97, 115, 142, 144
*Defence of Freemasonry, A* 45
Defoe, D. 8, 60, 61, 161
Deism 17, 79, 115
Demoniacs, The 4, 8
Dennis, C.M. 51, 161-2
Desauguliers, J.T. 32
Devlin, C. 49, 162
Disraeli, B. 91, 100, 162
Dobrée, D. 107
Dolswinton, P.M. 81
dome 31, 41
Donne, J. 18
Donoghue, D. 158, 162
Doppelgänger 98, 101
Dorchester labourers 2
Dougall, C.S. 81, 162

Douglas, H. 84, 162
*Dowlands Ms* 19
Doyle, A.C. 133, 154, 162
drinking habits 11, 14, 26,
    29, 67-73
Druids, Ancient Order of 5,
    9, 147
*Dumfries Ms* 35
Duncan Eaves, T.C. 9, 162
Dunkerley, T. 23, 24
Durrand, R. 123, 162

East India Company 103
Eden 5, 115, 128
Eglinton, Earl of 62
Egyptian 4, 129
Elcho, Lord 62
elements 137
elementals 137
Eliot, S. 87, 162
elixir vitae 95, 97-8
Elliot, L.G. 162
Ellmann, R. 136, 153, 155,
    157, 162
England 9, 15
Enlightenment, The 6, 65,
    79, 89, 90, 94
entered apprentice 26, 33,
    52, 57, 70, 102, 104
Essenes, The 99
eta 30, 33, 36
Euclydes 28
execution 2, 111
Eyemouth 57
Ezra 48

Fall of Man, The 5, 21, 44,
    77, 128
*Fama Fraternitatis* 95, 97,
    156
Farr, F.F. 136
Felkin, R.W. 140-1
Fellowcraftsman 6, 33, 34,
    35, 52, 57, 65, 104,
    118-9
Fellows, J. 20, 48, 162
Felt, Mr 129
Ferguson, J. De Lancey 81,
    83, 86, 162
fidelity 114

Finneran, R.J. 153, 162
Fitzhugh, R.T. 83, 162
Flannery, M.C. 154, 162
folk-lore 7
Foucault, M. 45, 162
fraternity 2, 6, 9, 32,
    62, 68, 110, 113
Frazer, J.G. 114, 124, 162
Frederick, Prince of Wales
    61
*Free-Mason's Melody, The*
    49-50, 51
Freemasonry 3, 5, 6, 10-27
Freethinkers 13, 17
French Revolution 6, 88-9,
    90
Frost, A. 125, 162
Fussell, P. 110, 113,
    123-4, 162

gamma 30, 33-4
Garden of Eden *see* Eden
gaol 4
    *see also* prison
gauge 70
*Generous Freemason, The* 30
Genesis 37, 40
Geometry 43
George II 23, 61
George III 62
Gibson, J. 81, 162
Gilbert, E.L. 123
Gin Act 71
Glencairn, Lord 62
Glick, C. 9, 162
Globe Tavern 65
gnomes 137
Gnosticism 78
God 1, 3, 16, 20, 21, 24,
    25, 31, 36, 38, 40, 43
    *see also* Great
    Architect of the
    Universe
Godwin, W. 90, 95-6, 100,
    163
Goethe 158
Golden Dawn *see* Hermetic
    Order of the Golden
    Dawn
Goldsmith, O. 6

Gonne, M. 135
Gormogons 5, 8, 9, 59, 82-3
Gotha 93
Gothic 6, 88, 91-4, 98
Grabo, C. 96, 101, 163
Grand Lodge of England 6,
  9, 17, 21, 59, 60
Grand Lodge of Scotland 52
Grand Master 22, 23
Grand Pontiff 41
Grantham, J.A. 48, 163
Gray, J. 72
Gray, T. 12, 14, 27, 46
Great Architect of the
  Universe, The 20, 31,
  33, 37, 75, 79
Great Chain of Being 33
Greek letters 29
  *see also* alpha, gamma,
  eta, theta, iota, sigma,
  omega
Gregorians, The 4, 8
Grierson, H.J.C. 79, 87,
  163
Griffiths, D. 35, 50, 163
Grosse, Marquis 9, 91, 99,
  163
guild 6, 11

Haggai 23, 48
Hall, M. 54
Hall-Stevenson, J. 8, 163
Ham 22
Hamilton, G. 62
handshake 6, 70
Hannah, W. 47, 48, 50, 51,
  86, 116, 125
Hanover 8
Hapsburgs, The 88
harp 39, 42, 51
Harper, G.M. 155, 163
Hartley, A.J. 94
Harvey, W. 70-1, 81-3, 84,
  87, 163
Hauser, W. 40, 50, 51, 163
Havens, R.D. 51, 163
Hayley, W. 12
heart 3
heaven 115-6
Hebrew 19, 113

Hecht, H. 53, 81, 84, 163
Hegel, G.W.F.152
hell-fire clubs 4
Henley, W.E. 9, 163
Hermetic 126, 129-30, 134
Hermetic Order of the
  Golden Dawn 4, 5, 7,
  126, 128, 129, 131-41,
  147, 149-50, 153
hieroglyphics 4, 22, 74-5
hierophant 144
Hill, G.B. 46, 163
Hindu 103-5, 114, 130
Hiram Abif 19, 20, 26, 29,
  39, 65, 72, 77, 110-12,
  118-9
Hiram of Tyre 72, 110
Hitchener, E. 89
Hobsbawn, E.J. 8, 163
Hogarth, W. 60, 61, 71, 82
Hogg, T.J. 56, 89, 92, 99,
  163
Holmes, R. 99, 163
Holmes, S. 133
Holy Lands 147
Horkeimer, M. 13, 46, 99
Horniman, A. 133
horn 16
Horne, A. 47, 49, 51, 124,
  163
Horton, W. 136
Hough, G. 153, 163
Howe, E. 155-6, 164
Humphrey, J. 58, 81
Hunt, L. 89, 93
Hunter, C. 27
Hunter, R. 45, 165

Illuminati *see* Bavarian
  Illuminati
imperialism 5, 102, 107-8,
  124
*In Eminente* 19
India 103, 106, 114, 121,
  130
*Inigo Jones Ms* 19
Ingoldstadt 89-90
Ingpen, R. 99, 101, 164
initiation 2, 6

insanity 62
  *see also* madness
iota 30, 39
Irish Republican
  Brotherhood 135
Irvine 57, 70, 81
Islam 122, 164
Israel 30
Italy 9

Jachin 39
Jacob, M.C. 82, 164
Jacob's Ladder 30, 36
Jacobin, 89-90
Jaffē, A. 7, 164
Jamaica 74-5
Jamieson, A.B. 86, 164
Jarrett, D. 84, 164
Jeaffreson, J. Cordy 95,
  101, 164
Jehova 20
Jesuits 93
Jew 104-5
John the Baptist 59
Johnson, Dr 12, 14, 129
Jones, B.E. 22, 38, 48,
  49, 51, 66, 83, 84, 164
Jones, C.E. 86, 164
Jones, L.C. 9, 164
Jones, F.L. 99, 101, 164
Jones, G.P. 9
Joppa 119
Joshua 23
Journeyman 6
Jubela 21
Jubelo 21
Jubelum 21
Judaism 4, 6
*Judges* 42
Jung, C.G. 7, 8, 151, 153,
  158, 164

Kant, E. 94
Khyber 1
Kilmarnock 62-3, 77
*Kim* 102
Kimpel, Ben D. 9
Kingship 11, 45, 65, 88,
  90, 109-12, 117

King Solomon's Temple 19,
  23, 24, 30, 31, 35, 36,
  39, 41, 65-6, 102-3,
  110, 112, 115, 118,
  *see also* Solomon, King
  *see also* temple
Kinsley, J. 80, 164
Kipling Rudyard, 102-25,
  164-5
  *A Book of Words* 116,
  123-4, 164
  *A Friend of the Family*
  117
  "A Madonna of the
  Trenches" 102
  "Banquet Night" 109,
  117-8
  *Debits and Credits* 117,
  124-5, 164
  "Fairy Kirst" 117
  *From Sea to Sea* 121-2,
  125
  "In the Interests of
  the Brethren" 116-17,
  122
  *Just So Stories* 124
  *Letters of Travel* 123
  *Life's Handicap* 124,
  164
  *Limits and Renewals*
  117, 124, 164
  *Many Inventions* 122
  "My New-cut Ashlar"
  113-6
  *Puck of Pook's Hill*
  124, 164
  "Recessional" 107
  *Something of Myself*
  104, 116, 123-5, 164
  "The Bells and Queen
  Victoria" 109
  "The Butterfly that
  Stamped" 119
  "The Man who would be
  King" 109-10
  "The Merchantman" 119
  "The Mother-Lodge" 103,
  105-6
  "The Palace" 110-12

"The Press" 111
"The Secret of the Empire" 109
"Wee Willie Winkie" 123, 164
"When Earth's Last Picture is Painted" 113
kirk 74-5, 78
Knight, G. Norman 8, 47, 49, 83, 166
Knight, S. 61, 83, 102, 106, 123, 165
Knights Templar 63-4
Knoepflmacher, U.C. 99, 165
Knoop, D. et al. 9, 49, 82, 86, 165
knowledge 4
  forbidden knowledge 5
Kuhn, A.J. 46, 165

Lahore 102
lamb 21
lamb-skin 21, 65
Lane, L. 135
Lang, A. 95
latitudinarianism 17
Law, The 113
Law, William 15
Legman, G. 70, 84, 165
level 105
Levine, G. 99, 165
Leviticus 66
lewis 115
light 27, 33, 44, 79
lightning 26, 49
Lindsay, M. 81, 87, 165
line see plumb-line
linen 37
lion 42
Lisbon 15
Lochley 52
Locke, J. 79
Lockhart, J.G. 86, 165
lodge see Freemasonry
logos 33
London 15, 131, 139
loom 36
Lovegrove, H. 84, 165
Lovelace 9
Loudon Kilwinning Lodge 80

Low, D.A. 83, 165
Lowth, R. 47
Luciferianism 44
luddites 2
Lyon, D.M. 55, 56, 82, 165

Macalpine, I. 45, 165
Macbride, M.G. 154, 165
MacDonald, M. 45, 165
Mackenzie, A. 82
Mackenzie, Dr 59, 71
Mackenzie, H. 6, 58, 63, 71, 81
Mackenzie, N. 82, 99, 165
Mackey, A.G. 51, 165
madness, 10-18, 27
  mad-house 11, 13, 15, 45
Mahatmas 129
magic 5
Magic Flute, The 43
mallet 69-70
Mark Masonry 24, 103, 112, 114, 117-19, 134-5
Marshall, J. 165
Mason see Freemason
Mason, W. 27
Mason's Tavern 51, 54
Masonry see Freemasonry
Masson, D. 49
master mason 6, 19, 23, 24, 25, 26, 33, 36, 40, 52, 57, 65-6, 68, 104, 111
Master key to Freemasonry, A 51
Mathers 131-6, 138-9, 141, 150
Mrs Mathers 134, 136
Matthew's Gospel 35, 41, 66
Mauchline 63
Meakin, N. 143
medieval 5, 11, 13
Medmenham Abbey 4
mercury 38
meridian see initiation
messiah 20, 24, 79
Metaphysical Poets 18
millenarianism 13, 16

miracle play 6
Mithraism 122
M'Lauchlan 54
Moderns, The 17, 18, 23, 59
Montague, Duke of 61
Montgomerie, J. 75
Montgomery, A. 71
moon 36, 37, 38
Moore, J.R. 165
Moore, R. 83
Moore, V. 126, 142, 153-4,
   156, 166
Moorfields 15
morality 3, 6, 29, 31, 34,
   41, 63, 65, 75, 98, 113,
   116
More, P.E. 113, 124, 166
Morgan, G.B. 46, 166
Morley, E. 99, 166
Morton, A.L. 99
Moses 109
Moss, R.E. 125, 166
mouth 3
Mozart 43
murder 2
Murry, J.M. 12, 45, 166
Muslim 103-5
mysteries 2, 4, 5
mystery religions 4
Mystical Society of the
   Three Kings, The 133
mysticism 4, 5, 6, 7, 13,
   16, 17, 77
mythologies 1, 13, 19, 91,
   110, 149-53
   building myths 11, 66
   Creation myth 31, 32

Namyth 81
Nasmith, A. 63
Naubert, C. 9
neophyte 4, 34, 44, 131
New Church 16
Newton, I. 32
Newtonianism 17, 32
Nicol, W. 81
Nimrod 22
Noah 21, 22
Noah's Ark 119
Noorthouck, J. 47

Norman, S. 100
Norman Conquest 5
Noyes, C.E. 28, 32, 41, 49
numerology 4
   Pythagorean numerology
   43
nymph 137

oath 1, 2, 13, 17, 19, 78,
   113-4
   oath-taking 1, 2
occultism 19
O'Donnell, W. 153, 158
O'leary, J. 130
*Old Charges* 39
Old Commercial Inn 75
omega 30, 40-1
Omniscient Eye 75
Operative Freemasonry 6,
   11, 21, 24, 66, 85, 113
Order of the Golden Dawn
   see Hermetic Order of
   the Golden Dawn
Osiris 20

pagan 20,77
Paget, T. 46, 166
papacy 19
parade, Masonic 59
Parker, W. 76, 81
Paris 39
Parousia 16
Parsee 103-4
pass-words 4, 111
Paton, C.I. 46, 166
patronage 6
Paulin, T. 154, 166
Paulson, R. 83, 166
Pauwel, C. 133
Peacock, H.C. 82, 166
Peacock, T.L. 88, 92, 98,
   100-1, 166
Peck, W.E. 99, 101, 164,
   166
Penang 121
perjury 2, 8
persecutions 2
philosophes 89
philosophus 131

Pick, F. 8, 47, 49, 83, 102, 122-3, 166
pillar 36, 39, 40
pillars 36
  two pillars 39
  Seven Pillars 33
Piozzi, H.L. 15, 46
Pitsligo, Lord 62
plumb-line 30, 31, 39, 70
Poet-Laureate 5, 52-9, 72
point-within-the-circle 37, 38, 77
Pomfret, G. 103
Pope, A. 6, 8, 47
Potter, Mr 11, 27
Powell, L.F. 46, 163
Practicus 131
precautions 2
Pre-Raphelite Brotherhood 4, 27
Presbyterians 17, 78
Preston, W. 50, 51, 166
Prichard, S. 35, 50, 61, 166
priesthood 27
prison 14
*Providas Romanorum* 19
Punjab Club 120

Rabelasian 4
Raine, K. 154, 166
Ramsay, M. 56, 57
Ranald, M. Loftus and Ranald, R.A. 101, 166
Rankin, John 52
Reason 79, 89
  Reason, The Age of 12-13, 15
rebirth 41
Regardie, I. 8, 154, 156-7, 167
regeneration 42
Reiger, J. 99, 167
*Revelation see Book of Revelation*
Richardson, S. 9, 167
ritual 2, 3, 4, 5, 6, 7, 13, 23, 24, 33, 116, 134
  terror ritual 2
Roberts, J.M. 7, 167

*Roberts Constitutions* 28
Robinson, H. Crabb 90
Robinson, J. 6
Rogers, K.M. 50, 167
Rohmer, S. 133, 167
Roman Catholic *see* Catholicism
romance 7
Romanticism 5, 7, 88, 98
Rosalia 148
Rosen, G. 46, 167
Rosencreutz, C. 141, 143
  *see also* Rosicrucianism
Rosicrucianism 38, 88, 89, 91, 95, 98, 117, 124, 129, 134, 137, 140-50
Rossetti, D.G. 27
Rossetti, W.M. 95, 100, 167
Royal Arch 17, 21, 23, 24, 33, 41, 57, 62, 111
Royal Ark Mariners 117-9
rule 8, 31, 32, 40
Russell, G.W. 133, 152
Rutherford, A. 122, 167
Ryedale 73

St Andrew's Lodge 55, 70, 80
St David's Lodge 52, 53
St James's Lodge 52-3, 62-3, 67
St John 54, 60, 63, 80
St Luke's Asylum 16
  *see also* St Luke's Hospital
St Luke's Hospital 11
salamanders 137
Saltmarsh, J. 1, 7, 167
Samber, R. 26, 27
Samson, 42
Sartre, J.P. 2, 7, 167
Savage, R. 12
Saxon 6
Sayer, A. 61
Scientific Revolution 32
Scott, W. 6, 63, 88, 98, 167
Scottish Rite 57
Seccombe, T. 9, 163

secret chiefs 132, 135,
141
secrets 3, 18, 103
secret signs 4, 6, 37,
65, 76-7
secrecy 1, 3, 5, 102, 114
Sefiroth 132
self-interest 62
Shackleton, R. 48, 86
Sharpe, C. 65
Shelley, Mary 90, 92, 98
Shelley, P.B. 5, 6,
80-101, 167
*Hellas* 97
*On a Future State* 97
*Proposals for an
Association* 93
*St Irvyne* 88, 95-101
*Zastrozzi* 100
Shepard, O. 30, 38, 50,
51, 167
Sherbo, A. 21, 24, 28, 45,
48, 49, 167
Sheridan-Smith, A. 8
Shinaar 22
Sibley, E. 130
sigma 30, 40
signs 4, 6, 23
Sikh 103, 105
Simla 117
Simmel, G. 7
Sinnett, A.P. 130
*Skoptsi* 2
Smart, C. 4, 5, 6, 10-51
*A Song to David* 10, 11
27
*Immortality* 25
*Jubilate Agno* 10, 12,
13, 17, 23, 27, 28
*Prayer* 15
*Song* 10-11
*Taste* 42
*The Headstone in the
Corner* 25
Smith, J.C. 87
*Societas Rosicruciana in
Anglia* 117, 134
Solomon, King 29, 109-10,
112, 117-9

*see also* King Solomon's
Temple
Solomon in All his Glory 51
spade 36
Speculative Freemasonry 6,
11, 66, 113, 118
spire 26
Sprengel, A. 134, 140
square 8, 30, 36
star 36, 38, 44
Star and Garter, The 55
Stead, W.F. 12, 20, 45, 167
Stern, B. 87
Sterne, Laurence 4, 8
Sterrenburg, Lee 90
Stevenson, J.H. 3, 8
Stevenson, W.H. 167
Stevenson, Y.H. 84, 167
Stewart, D. 81
Stirling Castle 56
Stockdale, J. 95-6
Stoddart, C.M. 140
Stoker, B. 133
stone 10, 24, 25, 114-5
corner-stone 10, 24,
25, 26
foundation-stone 23, 24
living stones 26, 66
monumental stone 8
sacred stones 24
stone-mason 6, 31, 114, 118
Stuarts, The 56, 57
Study Five 117
sulphur 38
sun 33, 36, 37, 38
Supreme Magus 134
Swedenborg, Emmanuel 16
Swedenborgians 16, 47
Swift, J. 6, 22, 48, 71,
84, 168
sword 34, 44
sylphs 88, 137
symbolism 2, 3, 4, 6, 24,
25, 27, 31, 34, 41, 65,
113, 114, 127, 134,
147, 153
Symonds, J. 155-6, 168

Talmud, The 50
Tarot, The 134, 136
Taswell 84, 168
Taylor, S.F. 86, 168
temple 25, 28, 29, 72, 131, 140
Tetragrammaton 24
Thelema 138
Theoricus 131
Theosophical 126, 129-30, 131
theta 30, 37-8
Thompson, E.P. 7, 83, 168
Thornhill, J. 60
Thorp, J.T. 48, 168
Thrale, Mrs *see* Hester Lynch Piozzi
three 6, 43
throat 3
thunder 26, 49
Tolpuddle Martyrs 2
tongue 3
tools, working 31, 69-70
  *see also* compass, loom, plumb-line, rule, spade, square
Tracing board 33, 37, 41
trade 6
Trade Unions 2
transportation 2
treachery 2, 6, 88, 92, 98
Tree of Knowledge 5
Tree of Life 132
trestle table 33
  *see also* tracing board
triangle 38
tribal taboos 1
Trollope, A. 4
trowel 36-7
trumpet 44
Tschink, Cajetan 9
tyler 71

Ulster 71
undine *see* nymph
Union Act 93

value-systems 2, 3
vatican 20, 57
Vauxhall Gardens 60

veil 35
Venice 20
Victoria, Queen 107-8
virtues *see* morality
Voltaire 79, 90

Wade, A. 154, 158, 168
Waite, A.E. 47, 140, 168
Wallace, William 81
Walpole, H. 60, 83, 168
Walsh, M. 45 49
Warberton, W. 8
Warrington 6
wasp 23
Watkins, John M. 133
Watson, S. 55, 66
Webster, A. 86, 168
Webster, N.H. 99, 168
Weishaupt, A. 89, 93, 99
Well, P. 99
Wells, H.G. 124, 168
Wesley, C. and J. 15
Westbrook, H. 92
Westcott, W.W. 133-4, 140, 145
Whalen, W.J. 7, 168
Wharton, P. 9
Whibley, L. 46
White, Newman I. 100, 168
Whitefoord, J. 81
Wilde, Oscar 4
Wilkes, J. 4
William IV 109
Williamson, K. 19, 45, 47, 49, 168
Wilson, A. 125, 168
Wilson, J. 63, 81
Winston, R. and C. 7
Wood, A. 52, 81, 168
Wood, F.T. 8, 168
Wood, P.S. 30, 38, 50-1
Woodford, A.F.A. 133
Woodman, W.R. 133
words *see* pass-words
World War I 137
Wright, D. 81-2, 85-6, 168

Yates, F.A. 1, 156, 168
Yeats, W.B. 5, 126-158, 168-9

"A Coat" 151
"A Song of the Rosy
Cross" 146
*A Vision* 126, 150-1, 158
"Adoration of the Magi"
148
"All Soul's Night" 135
*Autobiographies* 134,
151, 153-6, 158
*Essays and Introductions*
154-6
"Is the Order of R.R.
and A.C. to remain a
Magical Order?" 139,
155, 158
"Nineteen Hundred and
Nineteen" 152
*Rosa Alchemica* 148
"The Body of Father
Christian Rosencrux" 144
"The Crucifixion of the
Outcast" 146
*The King's Threshold*
128, 154
*The Magi* 138
*The Mountain Tomb* 143-4
*The Rose* 146
*The Secret Rose* 146
*The Second Coming* 137-8
*The Shadowy Waters* 127,
147
*The Speckled Bird* 150,
153
*The Tables of the Law*
149
*The Tower* 149
"To a Shade" 142
"To the Rose upon the
Rood of Time" 146
"Under Ben Bulben" 149
"What is Popular
Poetry?" 127

Zelator 131
Zerubbabel 23
    *see also* Zorobabel
Zorobabel 23